JESAN M. SORRELLS

12 RULES —FOR— LEADERS

THE FOUNDATION OF INTENTIONAL LEADERSHIP

WITH BRADLEY MATICAN

HSCT PUBLISHING, LLC

HSCT Publishing, Registered Offices

6387 Camp Bowie Blvd., Suite B #405, Fort Worth, TX 76116

First published in the United States of America by HSCT Publishing.

This edition is the first printing.

Hardcover ISBN: 978-0-9974088-2-9

Paperback ISBN: 978-0-9974088-4-3

E-Book ISBN: 978-0-9974088-5-0

Printed in the United States of America

Set in Adobe Garamond Pro text

Interior Design by Carlotta Kane

Disclaimer: If there are any discrepancies between the information provided in this book's content, and your organization's practices, please defer to your organization's best practices.

For permission requests, write to the author, addressed "Attention: Permissions Coordinator," at the email address below: HSCT Publishing, LLC | info@hsconsultingandtraining.com.

Ordering Information: Quantity sales. Special discounts are available on quantity (i.e., bulk) purchases by corporations, associations, and others.

For details, contact the publisher at the email address above.

Cover Designer & Interior Designer: Carlotta Kane. All Rights Reserved.

Back Cover Photo: Courtesy of Stephen J. Ponesse. All Rights Reserved.

Copy Editor/Proofreader: Sheila Milden.

Except where otherwise noted, all images used in this text are copyrighted to their respective owners.

Without limiting the rights under copyright, no part of this publication may be reproduced, distributed, or transmitted in any form or by any means, including photocopying, recording, or other electronic or mechanical methods, without the prior written permission of both the copyright owner, and the publisher of this book, except in the case of brief quotations embodied in critical reviews and certain other noncommercial, uses permitted by copyright law.

All of the quotes, resources, and materials used in this book are copyrighted to their owners as well. The scanning, uploading, and distribution of this book via the Internet or via any means without the permission of the publisher is illegal and punishable by law. Please purchase only authorized electronic editions and do not participate in or encourage electronic piracy of copyrightable materials. Your support of the author's rights (and the rights of others) is appreciated.

While the author has made every effort to provide accurate titles, telephone numbers, and Internet addresses at the time of publication, neither the publisher or the author assumes any responsibility for errors, or for changes that occur after publication. Further, the publisher does not have any control over and does not assume any responsibility for author, or third-party Web sites or their content.

All Other Materials Copyright © 2022 HSCT Publishing, LLC.
All Rights Reserved.

DEDICATION

This book is a "thank you" to all who have had to put up with my leadership learning curve at home, at work, at church, and in the community over the last twenty years.

I am still learning.

I am staying on the path.

Jesan, congratulations on finishing this remarkable book. The years of training, education, and teaching students, professionals and executives that you have done for the last eight years is really evident and inspiring to read about. Not only is it relevant, but this book is a cumulation of knowledge equity that is hard to find these days. Furthermore, It is amazing how our ideas from 5 years of mentorship and collaboration resulted in a book that should influence the actions that leaders can take, the way they think, and how they lead in our current chaotic world. Every leader, from a newly developed, to a senior level, to the very top of an organization, should read this book. Not only is it relevant, but the thoughts, examples, and the facts are shocking, motivating, and most importantly, drive the feeling of going into action, rather than staying complacent. Especially coming out of the pandemic, we have had an organizational shift and there are leaders who have not learned what to do in the aftermath. The first thing they need to do is read this book. I am looking forward to working on more impactful books like this that will change the leadership dynamic.

Bradley Matican

FOREWORD

"Every problem in every organization can be solved through the intentional application of effective leadership principles."
Jesan Sorrells

Leadership, the active, intentional act of moving individuals and teams down an invisible path toward accomplishing a goal that may or may not matter emotionally to all of them, is on the ropes.

And maybe it has always been "on the ropes."

However, it seems that from the days of Marcus Aurelius—who wrote the world's first business motivational self-help leadership book—to the present day when all manner of authors opine about different leadership approaches, leadership advice—or instruction—seems to be suffering from several self-inflicted, and other-inflicted, wounds, some of which include:

Too many books (over 60,000 results for "leadership" on Amazon as of a search during the writing of this book) with too many ideas based on what the author chooses to believe about research, insights, and attitudes they have personally witnessed and then want to apply to others...

Too many videos on YouTube, Vimeo, and other services designed to inspire and motivate based on the "great man" or "great woman" myth that cannot possibly be replicated by anyone other than the "great man" or "great woman," they originally came from, and maybe even they would not be capable of replicating results if challenged...

Too many leadership "theories" are based more on idealism about how "the world" (i.e., of work, home, community, etc.) should be and anecdotal evidence rather than delivering on the hard truths about what does or does not work in the world outside the anecdotal and the ideal…

Too many consultants, facilitators, trainers, and leadership development organizations committed to hawking their next "cure" for a manager's, supervisor's, or executive's leadership "problems"…

Too many software companies "flooding the zone" with apps, platforms, lines of code, or series of webinars that promise everything and deliver nothing to the end user who just wants their specific leadership problem solved…

All of these "solutions" cause individuals, teams, organizations, and even cultures, to flounder. Even worse, these factors propagate mediocre leadership in good times; and in bad times promote and protect toxic leadership that leads to systemic organizational failures.

And the average person, leader, or follower, it doesn't matter, scratches their metaphorical head, and wonders why nothing significant in their families, their teams, their communities ever changes for the better; why our global and national body politics fail; and why any individual, much less any team, can seem to accomplish a goal, move down a path, or even get to a victory without massive emotional and psychological struggle.

After almost a decade of training, coaching, advising, mentoring, talking with, and even challenging senior and mid-level leaders across multiple enterprises, we believe there are five core principles every leader—even the leader of their home—should work to "dial in" on intentionally, and then back up with knowledge and skills gained from understanding 12 basic rules to be an effective leader.

- **Be intentional** with mindsets, thoughts, and behaviors to role model leadership effectively.
- **Be engaged** with the world—internally and externally—to be effective as a leader.
- **Be able and willing** to confront dysfunctional and destructive communication behaviors quickly and unequivocal-

ly in the team.
- **Be empathetic** with both the left and the right brain by listening before speaking.
- **Be ready to fail**—sometimes spectacularly—when leading.

These five principles merge to form our foundational assertion that intentional leadership—through understanding and applying the 12 rules of intentional leadership—is the way for leaders to pioneer people, teams, and organizations to the future we all want to experience.

A future with a hope and promise for all.

The motto of intentional leadership is "No More Accidents."

Let's become more intentional, together.

CONTENTS

Forward

Introduction
The Argument from First Principles

Rule One
Leaders Are Linchpins Before They Are Anything Else

Rule Two
Leaders Eat the Apple Pie of E/I

Rule Three
Leaders Study Sales and Marketing

Rule Four
Leaders Know the Three "C's"

Rule Five
Leaders Cannot Always Build a Maserati Out of Toyota Parts

Rule Six
Leaders Do Not Confuse "Liking" with "Agreeing"

CONTENTS

Rule Seven
Leaders Resolve the Mismatch Between Science and Business

Rule Eight
Leaders Know Why Most Diversity Training Fails

Rule Nine
Leaders Avoid the Blame/Credit Trap

Rule Ten
Leaders Remove Barriers to Trust, They Do Not Erect Them

Rule Eleven
Leaders Find Their Team's "Zero"

Rule Twelve
Leaders Take Time Away to Avoid Becoming Pagliacci

Conclusion and Final Thoughts
The Future of Leadership

Index

THE 12 RULES OF LEADERSHIP

INTRODUCTION

The Argument from First Principles

"At least Cincinnatus had a plow."
Jesan Sorrells

The Argument

It is hard to write this book about leadership, or quite frankly any book about leadership, considering the current pandemic in the world. COVID-19 simultaneously changed everything about how leaders operate in a world, and further exposed much of the remaining, tenacious, mental infrastructure of the Industrial Revolution that is still around in small, medium, and even large organizations. And most of that infrastructure is still on display in organizations:

Employees who are at the bottom of an organizational chart, believing they are the foundation on which the organization rests, yet feeling as though they are treated as basement dwellers.

Managers and supervisors are squeezed in the middle, believing they are the glue that keeps the top of the organization from flying away, and keeps the bottom of the organization in line. Yet the reality is, they are asked to care about something they did not initially build, and asked to give positive lip service to ideas, innovations, and approaches to change they know will have a low chance of success.

Upper management and executives are at the top of the organizational chart, believing they deserve the status they have. And that preserving that status is the only thing that matters. Yet feeling as though they are in a constant battle with forces (i.e., governmental regulations, organizational ennui, etc.) the people in the organizational chart below them could never possibly understand.

And that is just the infrastructure in our organizations. Then, there is the mental infrastructure we tend to ignore that affects leaders even more. How we teach leadership in academic settings, how we write about leadership in books like this, and how we position leaders in our organizations through promotion, compensation, merit, competency, and other factors, has not been challenged significantly in the way the COVID-19 pandemic challenged leadership assumptions and expectations, in many years.

When our organization had physical office space before the pandemic and the "knock-on" effects of social distancing, government mask mandates, and work from home regulations kicked in, I would drive to it every day. This office was down the street from the abandoned, industrial residue representing the company that stood, at least in the 20th century, at the pinnacle of Industrial Revolution assumptions about the intersections between work, life, leadership, and the corporate social structure. That company, the internationally known IBM, once located in Endicott, NY at its height employed 14,000 "IBM Men"—and they were majority men—who were notorious for wearing the IBM corporate outfit of a white shirt, a black tie, and appropriate slacks with even their hair trimmed neatly in a "corporate-approved" fashion. An endless conforming, but relatively well-paid, flood of men would course and spill through and down the street where my office used to be located during lunch hours.

Their mere presence stood as the primary example of what successful, thriving, and scalable leadership and management practices could accomplish in the 20th century. As did the presence of men working at Endicott-Johnson Shoe Factory, General Electric, Carrier Air Conditioning, and other Upstate New York 20th century corporations. When IBM relocated its vast infrastructure to Montauk from Endicott and disbursed its people more globally, New York State, for reasons both the New York State government and IBM dispute, fired or early retired, many of the people who worked in those buildings, the majority of which were abandoned by the time our office was located there twenty some odd years later.

This is what I am talking about when I refer to "mental infrastructure." The pandemic wrecked the mental infrastructure of assumptions, expectations, and attitudes of leadership at all levels in our global society and culture, and laid bare the frank negotiations between public health, public policy, private medical choices, the responsibility to make a living, and the responsibility to lead people to do so. Therefore, publishing a leadership book is dangerous in today's world. No matter what assertions I may make in this book, they could be frozen in time by the reader, or dismissed as being just a "sign of the times." Or, equally as problematic, they could be too easily embraced as the "Holy Grail" solution to all post-pandemic leadership problems.

The reality is there has never been a "silver bullet" for leadership. It has always been an active act, full of fits, starts, stops, self-doubt, and recrimination. Leadership in any intentional context resembles the heroic acts of Cincinnatus, the ancient Roman farmer who told the citizens of the Republic what they did not want to hear in a time of public crisis, and then led them, kicking, and screaming, to victory. Intentional leadership looks nothing like Adam Neumann, who bilked millions of dollars out of Softbank, before exiting from We Work in 2019 to a "Harvard MBA-level" of clapping and applause from "thought leaders," in the entrepreneurial space while leaving a broken trail of jilted followers, angry employees, and perplexed lessees. And yet, no one tells leaders that, or even bothers to tell them the truth about leadership, which is this: You must be intentional and thoughtful in your planning, strategy, and tactics, before you lead anyone, anywhere, and before you adopt a "style" or "approach" to leadership that will, in the end, only work for your specific situation. It is much more important to know why you are leading and be intentional about the "how" of leadership and worry a lot less about the crowd on social media, the rewards you might or might not get, and, of course, yourself.

This book lays out, not a formula, but a series of twelve practices—lessons, or principles if you will—I have found leaders always need to examine, mold, investigate, dissect, and question. How did I develop these principles? I have trained close to 15,000 people in a variety of management-level positions from entry-level to the CEO level across multiple organizations and industries over the last ten years. I have taught leadership theories and philosophies and pushed hundreds of students over the past twenty years to question them at small community colleges and large public institutions. I have read—not exhaustively, I am a practitioner after all—many of the academic writings that undergird leadership theories and approaches. And I try to read and glean everything about leadership from the Bible and other ancient writings, all the way to Jocko Willink and whatever Malcolm Gladwell is writing right now. I also serve as the day-to-day CEO of a digital and software platform publishing company, HSCT Publishing, now on our third pivot coming out of COVID, with partners, employees, contractors, interns, clients, fans, investors, and others who look to me to make leadership decisions in the practical every day. I also have a wife of eight years (as of this publication date) and four children ranging in age from four to twenty-four. I have led volunteer groups, story groups, online groups, and church groups. I have even played and coached the great game of rugby with teams that were not always winning. All those areas and arenas of life, both public and private, serve as incubators for understanding, examining, distilling, and questioning, the principles of leadership our mental infrastructure tacitly assumes will still produce optimal outcomes even as that same infrastructure rusts away unquestioned in leaders' minds. And all leaders have access to the same incubators I have had, across time and space.

This book should not exist as an artifact, something frozen in time for leaders. Instead, we would encourage you, Dear Reader, to think of this book as a volume you read slowly, absorb carefully, think about deeply, question robustly against your experience, and then have the courage to implement from. Leadership, effective leadership most importantly, is the most critical element our world is missing, pandemic or not. And the more leaders are exposed as being ill-prepared, blind, ignorant, or just innocently blissful, the more the dragon of chaos, destruction, and myopia must consume—and the increased amount of bad, toxic, mediocre, and worse leadership we will have to suffer through in the face of the next crisis.

The Structure

We start with a basic first principle: every problem in every organization—and by extension in our world—can be solved through the intentional application of effective leadership principles and practices. Building from this first principle are ideas that bind the chapters together into a coherent whole, and make the chapters easy to read as individual lessons. I have placed a summary of content at the beginning of each chapter; thereby providing the opportunity for you, as the reader, to make a larger determination—before reading the whole chapter—if that chapter applies to your leadership situation. This is part and parcel of leaders thinking intentionally, planning strategically, and responding tactically to the world in which they lead.

But what are the topic areas covered in each chapter?

Leadership Roles and Responsibilities—This chapter covers all the ways to behave as a leader because behavior is the linchpin act of a leader. This means more than just giving lip service to the idea of leadership. It means walking out the roles and responsibilities of leadership and genuinely understanding their effect on your followers. I combine insights from the work of the writer and marketer Seth Godin in his book *Linchpin: Are You Indispensable?* with the core ideas expressed in *The Leadership Challenge* by Barry Kouzes and James Posner to make a larger point than either individual volume of work does independently.

Leadership and Emotional Intelligence—This chapter focuses on the role of emotional intelligence, but not in the way many books on leadership focus on emotional intelligence, which is as if attaining emotional intelligence is a "given" for a leader. The point of addressing emotional intelligence is that if a leader does not know herself, her motives, or even why she is leading, how can she be intentional? I question that assumption immediately and move quickly to establishing practical methods for a leader to grow in self-awareness. The work and research of Daniel Goleman and many others deeply influence this chapter.

Leadership and Conflict Management—Here I address the intersection between leadership and conflict in practical terms for leaders. This is because leaders need to realize a core first principle: leading without conflict can be compared to the pleasant, dopamine-fueled delusions of a drug induced high: It is not real, it is a fantasy, and intentional leaders better be ready to navigate conflict. Leaders must be aware of the effect of conflict but not intimidated by the prospect of tackling conflicts in their teams, their organizations, or their cultures. The work of multiple authors and researchers influences the tenor and direction of this chapter, with a special focus on the work of Daniel Shapiro, William Ury, and Roger Fischer.

Leadership Communication and Persuasion—This chapter identifies ways in which leaders seek to persuade; however, intentional leaders persuade knowing what they are doing and why. Persuasion as a talent and skill is buried deeply in all acts of communication, from writing to speaking. However, persuasion begins in the mind of the leader before it exits the mouth or the pen and leaders who do not realize this fact may wind up leveraging the wrong type of persuasion with the wrong audience. This chapter leans heavily on the work of Dr. Robert Cialdini, author of *Influence: The Psychology of Persuasion* and *The End of Power: From Boardrooms to Battlefields and Churches to States, Why Being In Charge Is Not What It Used to Be* and multiple other authors and researchers.

Leadership and Team Building—This chapter focuses on the nature of building teams and the thinking leaders must engage with if they want to have a genuinely high-performance team. All teams experience transitions and knowing that a leader cannot make a sedan into a race car is the first step to building high performance teams. Understanding and appreciating team building can only come about if leaders understand the research behind building teams—even not-so-high-performing ones—and this chapter incorporates the work and research of Connie Gersick, Tuckman and Jensen, and the writing of Patrick Lencioni, author of *The Five Dysfunctions of a Team: A Leadership Fable* serves as a link between the previous chapters and the chapters to come.

Leadership and Dealing with Difficult Teams and People—Leaders should expect to encounter difficult people and this chapter addresses the problem for leaders in negotiating with difficult people. Rather than be dismissive, infuriated, or impatient, leaders must be curious problem solvers. This is challenging when difficult people, teams, and even situations resist the alignment that is necessary for them to function. Through the lens of the work of the *Harvard Negotiation Project* and the writing of Sheila Heen, Douglas Stone, and Bruce Patton, I break down how leaders can effectively diagnose motives and excel at managing tricky negotiations with difficult people they are tasked with leading.

Leadership and Building Morale and Encouraging Motivation—"No one ever talks about morale, except when it's lousy," was the trenchant observation from Dwight D. Eisenhower and leaders should take heed. This chapter covers how to think differently about motivation, morale, and the intersection between the two areas. Building morale is no easy task and leaders must be aware of how to motivate their teams intentionally and practically by understanding how drivers of behavior tightly link to outcomes individuals and teams want to achieve. The work and research of Daniel Pink in his book *Drive: The Surprising Truth About What Motivates Us* acts as a baseline for this chapter, which is also heavily influenced by the writing and research of Abraham Maslow and his insights into needs and their hierarchy.

Leadership and Diversity—This chapter focuses, not on the need for diversity, but instead, on the need for leaders to impassion their teams to engage in the hard work of leadership development by navigating the hardest form of diversity possible: diversity of thought. Problems of diversity and a lack of engagement—or outright fear of those problems even being proactively addressed can stymie even the most sophisticated and experienced leader. And, if leaders cannot even get their teams to talk about what kind of toner to use in the new office copier (or get them to "unmute" their video on Zoom), how can they possibly expect to address identity, worldview, or meaning and mattering friction, conflicts, problems, and difficulties when they arise? The work of several authors and researchers undergirds this chapter content, but I have taken the liberty of avoiding the typical shibboleths of the types referenced by writers and researchers in the fields of social justice, intersectionality, and diversity and inclusion to make larger points about the power of intercultural competency for leaders and the work of Amy Edmondson and her most recent book on psychological safety, *The Fearless Organization: Creating Psychological Safety in the Workplace for Learning, Innovation,* *and Growth*. Understanding the need for such measures is critical for leaders to establish to ensure inclusion efforts bear the intended fruit.

Leadership and Accountability—The "Holy Grail" of leadership, even in military settings, responsibility, accountability, ownership, and taking risks all go together and leaders must understand the psychology of accountability before demanding it from their followers. This chapter addresses the nature of accountability and the difference between accountability and responsibility, which is important for leaders to understand before they demand risk-taking and ownership from their followers. Three books that set the tone for this chapter, *The Oz Principle: Getting Results Through Individual and Organizational Accountability* by Roger Conners, Tom Smith, and Craig Hickman; *Extreme Ownership: How U.S. Navy Seals Lead and Win* by Jocko Willink, and Leif Babin; and *Skin in the Game: Hidden Asymmetries in Daily Life* by Nassim Nicholas Taleb.

Leadership Discipline, Feedback, Strengths, and Well-Being—The intersection of feedback, well-being, strengths, and discipline (meting out consequences based on authority when rules, standards, and practices have been violated) is tricky for leaders and many avoid it, preferring to kick the can of the issues down the road for another leader to address. This chapter covers why delivering on what you say you will do as a leader is critical to, not only receiving buy-in from followers, but also maintaining a long-term growth curve on the team. Positive psychology is an element of this, but there is also consideration given in this chapter to how providing feedback affects the position and attitude of the person providing the feedback, as well as the environmental factors that can lead to a dearth of feedback, including an absence of trust and a fear of conflict. The work of Patrick Lencioni and the writing of authors Tom Rath and Jim Harter in their book *Wellbeing: The Five Essential Elements* provides a foundation for this chapter.

Leadership and Adapting to Change—Volatility, Uncertainty, Complexity, and Ambiguity (VUCA) is the U.S. Army War College's way of addressing Black Swans and it works when leaders are in stable environments, where change cycles occur once every twenty years. And that is gone. Leadership requires effective intentionality in smaller and smaller groups of people in more and more uncertain environments. This chapter covers the reasons why adapting to change is preferable to just reacting to it—or even responding to it. And, the writing of the venture capitalists Peter Theil and Nassim Nicholas Taleb provide insights into the practical considerations leaders must build into their teams from the beginning to be successful at adapting to change consistently over time.

Leadership and Self-Care—It is essential for leaders to take care of themselves and stop giving "lip service" to the principles of self-care. Compassion fatigue, burnout, stress, and vicarious trauma all contribute to leaders not engaging well with their followers. This chapter provides a tough ending to the book and a call to action for leaders to engage in the work of self-care and to role model that to followers. Practically, providing environments where competency and empathy can be held in balance is critical for leadership success and for team development and growth.

This collection of chapters and insights distills the work I have done over the last ten years in training close to 15,000 middle managers, executives, and other leaders in organizations and represents my attempt to get to clarity and practicality for the reader. I am not seeking to formulate a theory of leadership in this book or through these chapters. Instead, I came seeking to provide a well written manual leaders can access to begin their leadership journey toward attaining higher goals, strengthening their focus, building their teams, inspiring their organizations, and being able to say, at the end of a long series of leadership experiences, they were able to bring the best of themselves to the most important, intentional work of our new century.

The Call to Action

Intentional leadership matters in the 21st century, for numerous reasons, but two stand out above all the others:

The first reason is that, as the jobs once done by humans migrate more and more toward the computer, the mobile phone, and whatever hardware innovation comes next (probably the cloud, virtual reality, and A.I.), the only question worth answering is: Can a computer, an algorithm, or a Deep Fake do your job better than you can?

When the "yes" answers to that question outstrip the "no" answers, the Industrial Revolution based infrastructure of leadership assumptions, ideas, and even opinions about work will be radically altered. If they are not, if leaders bitterly cling to past notions, continually hag-ridden by re-imagining a past to which they cannot return, they will fail to take advantage of the positive parts of our increasingly complex mental maps, to address the complexities of a wild future whose outcomes and drivers they cannot fully predict, and may not have the sensitivity to care about.

The second reason is that as an ever-increasing number of individuals and companies become human-centered rather than technology-centered, the only acts that matter are acts involving understanding the effects of the promise of the Internet on our lives, engaging with emotional intelligence, performing intentional leadership with increasingly smaller groups of people, and leading others with courage and resilience. Organizations of the past century indicated, either explicitly or implicitly, that those traits were not very important considering where leaders found themselves on the organizational chart.

But that is no longer true. And it has not been for a while.

The leadership work that matters will be the work that values these traits above all else. And there are some fields (the human services most of all) poised to take advantage of this shift in what is valuable in the future from what was valued in the past: the complete demolition of the mental and emotional infrastructure tenaciously residing in the minds of employees, managers, executives, board members, shareholders, academics, and others.

The genuine tragedy COVID-19 revealed (or maybe poured accelerant over) is that the demolition work is plentiful, but the leaders to do the work are few.

Sure, an assertion can be made that there have always been leadership challenges. The assertion can be made that pandemics are nothing new, and future disruptions whose effects are more long-term and will require leadership to be just as savvy as it proved to not be during the current pandemic, will be even more telling in the world of leadership. However, this moment right now is the one in which we are living and I think that, if anything, the COVID-19 crisis should have taught all leaders everywhere, that trying to live in "the tomorrow" is a fools' errand.

This book is for leaders who have the curiosity, the will, and empathy to increase their competency in the work of leadership. This emotional labor of leading others toward better versions of themselves requires leaders to have the courage to embark on the journey, the clarity to understand what the stakes are, and the candor to admit when the work of leadership is not for them; and then, dare to help the leaders who need the help.

Let us start on our leadership journey.

CHAPTER ONE

Rule 1
Leaders are Linchpins Before They are Anything Else
Leadership Roles and Responsibilities

"Leaders must be linchpins. There is no other way."
Jesan Sorrells

This chapter focuses on helping the reader understand that the challenges of leadership that arise when leaders lack clarity, the ability to be candid, and the courage to act should not come as a surprise. It tees up the Three C's model (CLARITY-CANDOR- COURAGE) as a leadership schema. We stress the schema's importance and outline for leaders the nature of roles and responsibilities to followers. We lay out a case for thinking about leadership roles beyond merely performing the acts that position or power demand and getting to the "next level" with leadership as an intentional leader.

Introduction: Critiquing Some Assumptions

The mindset undergirding most practical leadership practices is chaotic, unfocused, reactive, and only occasionally—and miraculously—effective. If you do not believe this statement, think back to the last time someone led you to do something you did not want to do, or that you did want to do; it makes no difference. That person was probably as ill-prepared to lead you as you were ill-prepared to follow them. Leadership, when executed in this way, as it is in offices, workplaces, families, churches, and other organizations across the country, inevitably fails.

The reason the thinking behind most leadership practices

fails so spectacularly in the face of harsh reality is not rocket science, nor do we need empirical research—or academic research for that matter—to understand why. The reason it does not work in the living, practical, world is that thinking is based on four commonly held, yet deeply flawed, premises:

- Everyone can lead.
- Everyone should lead.
- Everyone has a right to lead.
- Everyone recognizes and seizes leadership opportunities.

When we think critically, even for a few minutes, about these assumptions, we realize why they are flawed and how deeply they embed themselves into the American—and increasingly global—mental models of how leadership "should be done," which then translates into academic models of leadership, which then translates into lived out models of leadership and on and on in an ever-expanding, ineffective, yet glorious sounding feedback loop. Often with disastrous results.

Furthermore, leaders, followers of leaders, and observers of leadership practices scratch their heads, or their chins, about leadership and why it does not seem to work, resulting in walking rhetorically in increasingly larger circles around the same eight theories of leadership that worked for the people who initially created them; but do not work for anyone else.

There must be a better way of translating leadership to action. And what follows in this text is a blueprint for how to lead better, but first we must "clear out the cruft" and reset our assumptions and expectations about what it takes to be a leader.

First, we break down these flawed premises. Then, we address what really matters in leadership and how to be intentional about engaging in the acts of leadership that matter to followers. Finally, we discuss what it means to be a linchpin—that is, a person without whom the organization, the team, or the system cannot work.

RULE ONE

Everyone can lead—No everyone cannot. An individual must have the temperament, personality, and be sensitive to the opportunities to lead; not everyone has the temperament to lead. This goes back to the ancient and valueless argument of whether leaders are born or made that distracts leaders within a dichotomy that does not exist to, or is designed to avoid thinking about the second factor: personality.

Not everyone has the personality to lead. In fact, everyone does not have the focus, drive, ambition, or even the internal desire to pick up the baton and lead from the front. But when this is stated as an observable fact, rather than a well-heeled opinion, individuals are lambasted for the narrowness of such a consideration. Leadership suffers when people are supported who display detrimental personality dysfunctions in positions of leadership in those positions because they happened to be the one person still left standing after the dust settles from a promotion, or as the result of a positive outcome to a difficult project or task.

Not everyone recognizes leadership opportunities. Leadership opportunities may be everywhere, with more arriving every day as entrenched incumbents fall ignominiously by the wayside. However, the person watching the opportunity may not be sensitive to the nature of the opportunity before them. They may not recognize the moment to act and take up leadership; therefore, the opportunity to lead passes many people by.

Everyone should lead—No everyone should not. An individual must be oriented psychologically to lead. From personality researchers to clinical psychologists to behavioral scientists, the evidence is clear: every individual is not blessed with the mindset, attitude, knowledge, experience, internal character, and confidence to lead other people. The belief that everyone should lead springs from ideas, concepts, and assumptions about the power of political and civic stories about egalitarianism and democracy. Such stories may work in the realms of politics and civics, but they rarely attain traction in the world as we live in it—and lead in it—daily. There are powerful hierarchies of dominance at play in all systems and environments in the world. This is clear from research by evolutionary biologists and others; humans respond, react, and play eternal games with each other to constantly jockey for position within those hierarchies. Few genuine, competent leaders emerge at the top from these brutal emotional, spiritual, and psychological battles. Our stories provide little guidance to leaders in the trenches of these battles.

Everyone has a right to lead—No everyone does not. Once again, the ideas of egalitarianism and democracy we want to be enshrined and preserved in law, politics and through the court system to preserve the ability to play a hierarchical game do not play out in the same ways in the world of leadership and hierarchies. Many people may have a desire to lead. They may even have the intention to lead. The position of "leader" may be granted to some in their hierarchy. However, the assertion that there is an inherent "right" to lead—whether that assertion is based on race, gender, socioeconomic status, or national origin is irrelevant—creates a slippery and tricky environment. It creates the circumstances that lead to the installation of bad leaders (because it was "their turn" and they were not emotionally, psychologically, or spiritually prepared for the stress and strain of leadership) or the installation of mediocre leaders (who are infinitely more toxic in their behavior and approach to leadership than even bad leaders are) and only rarely leads to the installation of good—or even great—leaders.

Everyone recognizes and seizes leadership opportunities—No everyone does not. There are far more opportunities to follow leaders than there are to lead others. Many individuals fail to recognize the glory and honor in following a good—or great leader—until after the moment of glory is achieved, the mountain is climbed, and the result is heralded—at least in the 20th century. Before the 20th century, people wrote about and enshrined the virtues of good followership into their children, their peers, and their communities through ideas and admonitions of religious discipleship, martial discipline, and good, old-fashioned hard work. However, as the 20th century spun out, the rise of bad nation-state leaders, coinciding with the increase of academic and pop-culture writing on leadership, the democratization of failure, and the perceived elitism of successes led people to question the very nature and infrastructure upon which the opportunity to follow other people rested. It is essential to understand, following matters just as much as leading—if not more so. Furthermore, recognizing and accepting when to follow and when to walk away is a distinction with a difference many leaders themselves struggle with.

The Three C's Methodology

The methodology of communicating with clarity, candor and courage, or the Three C's, was developed and teased out through research and development from the work we have done with teams and leaders over the last ten years and was meant to clear up

PRACTICAL LEADERSHIP DIFFERENCES	
What Behavior We Say We Want from Leaders	**What Behavior We Reward from Leaders**
Authenticity (we say that we want our leaders to "tell the truth" and engage with us about all the information regarding what's going on in an organization)	**Inauthenticity** (putting on a "good" show, engaging in enabling behavior, practicing disengagement, etc.)
Honesty (consistently listed as the number one most desired trait in leadership surveys of employees)	**Lying, Corporate Deception, Manipulation, "Shading" the Truth** (lies of omission)

PRACTICAL LEADERSHIP DIFFERENCES	
Transparency (often confused with authenticity, transparency has been demanded more and more by employees as social media has grown in prominence)	**Opacity** (employees do not want to know too much about their leaders, they want them to be "effective" when "hard" decisions must be made)
"Non-Toxic" Work Environments (much leadership training is focused on fixing work environments that are already broken)	**Employees try to advance** and/or get promoted in toxic work environments headed by leaders who reflect the overall work culture.
Resiliency to Absorb Failure (employees claim to laud and value leaders who "take risks" and "push for innovation")	**Employees do not want leaders to be "failures"** and if they are, then the employees lose respect for the leaders.

the tendency among organizational leaders to communicate with themselves, their teams, and their organizational structures with obfuscation, deception, and insincerity.

This is a trend that has continued to grow in the realm of thought leadership and has achieved heights of scale never seen before or experienced because of the prevalence of social media platforms. However, leaders need to understand, wrestle with, adopt, and practice intentionally and ruthlessly the Three C's

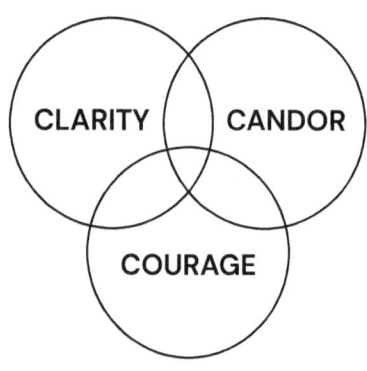

methodology. This is to have greater success in defining their roles and responsibilities to the team, the organization, and the culture. Leaders can extract higher levels of productivity and performance from teams and organizations through the application of the Three C's. This will ensure lower levels of false (and real) conflict, less political wrangling over decisions, more accountability, and higher levels of genuine trust.

In the first step, the leader defines what the problem is they are facing with themselves, the team, and/or the organization by first clarifying the issue.

Clarity in conversation, thinking, speaking, and writing to make thoughts, feelings, and motives known to the other party is critical. Clarity applies to both thinking and communicating. Establishing clarity as the shared organizational goal of all individuals requires ensuring team members feel comfortable with communicating until a shared understanding is established. A leader's commitment to transparency contributes to clarity.

To achieve clarity on identifying the problem accurately to solve it, a leader must ask the following questions:

- Am I seeing the problem clearly?
- Am I using the right identifying terminology to define the problem?
- If I had to tell the story of the problem to someone else not on the team, could I explain it to them?

Candor in a conversation—being candid with empathy and a focus on intentionality are critical for success. Candor contributes to an individual's credibility and trustworthiness. Your employees and colleagues must believe you are honest, forthright, and sincere. This means they must believe you are speaking your truth (and THE truth...or at the least not lying about circumstances and conditions, no matter how difficult they may be), and that you are doing so with their best interests—in balance with your interests and the organization's interests—in mind.

To be candid about the problem with themselves, the team and/or the organization, a leader must ask the following questions:
- Am I ready to be truthful and honest about this problem with the other person?
- Am I ready to hear their perspective on the problem?
- Am I willing to work with them to reach a solution, or do I want them to just "stop" whatever it is they are doing?

Courage in a conversation—having the courage to neither delay, nor avoid the conversation, is critical to achieving success. Brené Brown (2007) describes courage as a "heart word." (The Latin root means "heart.") Although contemporary definitions focus on bravery and heroism, Brown encourages us to remember the "inner strength and level of commitment required for us to speak honestly and openly about who we are and about our experiences—good and bad."[1] To be courageous about confronting the problem with themselves, the team, and/or the organization, a leader must ask the following questions:

- Am I ready to confront the other party without escalating?
- Am I offering a solution to the problem or just providing feedback with no solution?
- Am I able to emotionally address the reactions and consequences of this confrontation in a healthy way?

Identifying the problem with clarity, candor, and courage will help the leader accurately describe the effect of the gap between the expected behavior and the actual behavior without confusing the other party in the conversation.

Many leaders struggle with the basics of establishing clarity, engaging with candor, and responding and planning intentionally with courage for many reasons; however, the number one reason is ego. Leaders' egos cloud their inner monologues causing a lack of clarity in their thinking, which leads to a lack of clear writing and clear speaking. A sure sign of a leader who has abandoned their roles and responsibilities is the presence of jargon-heavy language that serves only to confuse, misdirect, and obfuscate an issue.

Ego rears its head when leaders are pressed to be candid, and usually about small issues or matters at hand. Being candid requires having a healthy dose of self-awareness. Furthermore, leaders struggle when they lack the clarity in themselves necessary to accomplish the goals they seek, and the honesty to talk about them. Candor is also a problem because it is often mixed in with the desire to be liked and not offend. This desire then results in hard conversations being avoided, hard decisions being made at the last possible moment, and allows people to elevate themselves in status, rather than being directed to do the hard work of emotionally maturing and growing, or leave, the organization. Being candid also requires a measure of vulnerability and exposure, which means trust must be reciprocated. If the leader is covering up, so will every other subordinate leader.

Finally, the courage, or heart, to think, write, say, and act in an ethical, moral, and social fashion means more than just bending to the whims of the crowd; sometimes the crowd is wrong. The team often needs to be led to where it does not want to go. Sometimes, the courage to lead in this way results in burnout, personal acrimony, hazing, appeals to the dominance hierarchy and all other manners of commonly accepted social and political negative outcomes. Keep in mind: the courage to lead in this way sometimes results in excellence, achievement, and moving the team past the mere accomplishment of a result and toward the accomplishment of something greater.

If leaders do not have the Three C's methodology in their toolbox, then all the leadership knowledge about theories, postures, and approaches to leadership is irrelevant.

If leaders do have the Three C's methodology in their toolbox, they can make the monumental decision about what type of leader they would like to be and then move to the last critical point of what behaviors and attitudes they will role model for their followers—the end-users if you will—of their leadership development product journey.

On Being a Linchpin Leader

For leaders, what really matters to being an intentional leader is knowing what the role of leadership is in the system in which leaders happen to find themselves, and then coupling that knowledge with understanding the responsibilities—and the depth of them—the leader is tasked with upholding. Rarely is this role of leadership well-defined, or even articulated; however, the role of leaders can be broken down into four categories, originally defined in the book *Linchpin, Are You Indispensable?* by the marketer, author, blogger, and general ruckus maker, Seth Godin.

- A leader can be a *bureaucrat*.
- A leader can be a *whiner*.
- A leader can be a *fundamentalist* zealot.
- A leader can be a *linchpin*.[2]

A *bureaucratic* leader is recognizable to everyone, everywhere, across time and space. From the realms of ancient Mesopotamia to the glittering steel buildings housing Silicon Valley's Wizards of Smart, there have always been bureaucrats. A bureaucratic leader does not have the passion for caring about her work. She shows up and does just enough to collect her check, go home, and begin to enjoy the things, the hobbies, that really make her life tick and move. The trouble is, with time, she loses clarity on why she continues as a bureaucrat. She just knows she does what she is paid to do. And she is highly emotionally and psychologically aware of where the invisible line is of "doing more," in her work, and she is not going to cross that line—not for any external motivation in the world. Money and status are uninteresting to her, because she knows the headaches of money and status do not lead to more power to make the kinds of changes she once wanted to see in the world. She believes in her heart of hearts that the power more status and a higher income and fancier title brings are more of the challenges she is not passionate about failing at any longer—the challenges of shepherding people to their best selves despite the circumstances rather than because of them.

A *whiner* leader is hide-bound to the past. Politically motivated to always be dissatisfied with the now, but unable to make plans and execute intentionally to build a better tomorrow, the whiner cares about the past and how it was yesterday, but he is not going to put his shoulder to the wheel to attempt the work of turning the wheel back. Instead, he will stand in the road of progress, complaining about the people, the process, the decisions being made by other motivated leaders under him, but will not lift a finger to move out of the road. As leaders, whiners complain up and down the hierarchy, they are not respected—except as far as the context of their position allows them to be—and they typically are abandoned by their positional followers emotionally and materially the moment a better, more competent, and quieter leader is discovered.

A *fundamentalist* leader is the same as a whiner leader, but the differences are: she has a plan, she is passionate about it, and she is executing on it. All the while wrangling team members, followers, and audience members to her side. At the heart of the fundamentalist leader are their most attractive features—talents of charisma, persuasion, and performance, particularly of spectacle. Fundamentalist leaders in religion, politics, the arts, and culture lead and perform very well, to human standards—at least for a time. However, all passion fades (no one can be excited at a very high level for an extended period, even basic biology will not allow it) and eventually, fundamentalist leaders fall. Usually very hard, very fast, and land even harder. Fundamentalist leaders meet everyone they stepped on, irritated, betrayed, and ignored on the way down the ladder of status and hierarchy, their passions and zealotry about whatever process or idea they lead with, convinced them to climb. Their end is ignominious, unclever, and quiet.

The last type of leader is a *linchpin*. This is a leader who understands internally that whining, zealotry, and bureaucracy are "non-starters" for leading people, changing culture, or influencing an organization. He understands that leading people involves both the sacred act of changing people and the mundane acts of small, daily transactions of emotional labor. A linchpin leader renders himself indispensable to the organizational culture he serves, not by only doing what is expected (what a bureaucratic leader would do), not by bemoaning the arrival of what is unexpected (what a whiner leader would do) and not by doing what is flashy at the moment (what a fundamentalist leader would do). Instead, a linchpin leader renders himself indispensable to the organization by *making the daily, mundane work of leadership so intentional, culture-changing, and impact driven, that it would be a hassle to replace him in the structure.* He performs this linchpin work intentionally, practically, slowly, and responsibly, focused more on his followers and their development than his advancement up the hierarchical chain, or applause from the audience watching. Finally, a linchpin leader realizes that mediocre leadership is more toxic to the team, the organization, the culture, and the hierarchy than polarized leadership; therefore, he works every day to make sure his leadership acts are polarizing and thus effective no matter who he is leading and no matter what context he is leading in.

A leader who understands her role can be defined in one of these four ways will be more intentional about choosing the strategies and tactics that will get her—and her followers—where she wants them to go.

Knowing Your Roles and Your Responsibilities

It is essential leaders understand their responsibilities. The responsibilities of a leader are many, but James Kouzes and Barry Posner in their book, *The Leadership Challenge: How to Make Extraordinary Things Happen in Organizations*, most succinctly define the responsibilities of a leader. They articulate that the responsibilities of leaders include engaging in the following responsibilities:

- A leader has a responsibility to role model the behavior they would like to see.
- A leader has a responsibility to inspire followers by articulating and defending a vision clearly, succinctly, and repeatedly.
- A leader has a responsibility to challenge the process, or the "status quo" of the system they are in.
- A leader has a responsibility to enable others to act through intentional delegation and intentional follow-up.
- A leader has a responsibility to encourage the heart through celebration and recognition.[3]

There is much talk about rights and very little focus on responsibilities in leadership literature; yet, a leaders' focus on responsibilities establishes an ethical tone for leadership. Such a focus also establishes boundaries a leader must struggle with to draw the best from themselves and their followers.

Let us break down Godin, Kouzes and Posner to see where the intersections are, and then we will walk through a case study that demonstrates some of what we are asserting here.

A leader has a responsibility to role model the behavior they would like to see.

The linchpin leader does not view the responsibility of role modeling the behavior they would like to see in their followers as a cross to be carried or as an environment to be avoided. Instead, they view role modeling as a natural outgrowth of their maturity and development as a leader. If the leader cannot role model the behavior she would like to see in her followers, a linchpin leader may ask, "Why bother leading at all?" Role modeling generates buy-in from followers, which allows followers to become leaders of themselves first and then others on the team in a virtuous circle that rarely breaks. If leaders desire success, they must role model what they want to have happen before it occurs.

A leader has a responsibility to inspire followers by articulating and defending a vision clearly, succinctly, and repeatedly.

The linchpin leader views the responsibility of articulating a vision, whether it be in writing or verbally, as a sacred act. Beginning with small goals and a limited vision, or beginning with a big vision, full of scary propositions, the linchpin leader makes sure he begins articulating a shared vision by first having clarity on what that vision is. Then he has the candor to express that vision in terms his followers can understand. By the way, he is not looking for agreement with the vision. A linchpin leader knows that chasing consensus or pursuing certainty at this stage of the game is a fool's errand. The linchpin leader speaks out the vision with courage repeatedly—when times are tough and when times are great. The linchpin leader performs this task repeatedly, defining the roles of the followers and the leader, but also co-creating the reality of the vision with his team members.

A leader has a responsibility to challenge the process, or the "status quo" of the system they are in.

The linchpin leader is relentless in the pursuit of opportunities to challenge the system in which they occupy and to shake things up. If there is no status quo to upend, the linchpin leader may get so restless that they seek out opportunities from outside the system and bring them back, reshaping, reframing, and reconditioning their followers to bigger and better heights and pushing them toward further horizons. The words "we have always done it this way" are poison to the linchpin leader and she knows any system she is in, the second those words are stated, a choice is on the table: battle the status quo, or leave the system. There are no other two ways to go about it. The linchpin leader is open to challenges, feedback, and questioning of her decisions, but she also knows that once a decision has been made to go forward; going backward and re-litigating the decision is not helpful; it is toxic, and is a practice that can lead to blame-gaming, and could lock up real innovation. She welcomes the rough and tumble exchanges that go along with challenging the organizational process.

A leader has a responsibility to enable others to act through intentional delegation and intentional follow-up.

The linchpin leader ties his growth in vulnerability, empathy, and humanity to the growth of his followers, and he knows the best way to ensure growth is to give away power. He also recognizes autonomy only truly works when the person is well trained, well-motivated, and well-empowered to make decisions, try new and alternative approaches to solving problems, and take on responsibility for failures and mistakes. Delegation is not a "set and forget it" system of leadership, nor is it a function of leadership that can happen without trust. However, when delegation is engaged appropriately and the boundaries of delegation are defined clearly and articulated repeatedly, mastery increases, work satisfaction rises, and the need for follow-through and micro-managing diminishes.

A leader has a responsibility to encourage the heart through celebration and recognition.

The linchpin leader encourages the heart. She knows the two simplest words of recognition and appreciation are "thank you;" and when they are lacking, productivity declines. She knows fair pay, time off, flexible working hours, telecommuting, appropriate working technology, time away from email and constant messaging from work are not perks of the modern office environment. She knows they are the baseline for the modern office environment, and she fights through advocacy for her followers to get every baseline feature available to them. She also knows recognition and celebration are sometimes not about Zoom coffees, 1:1's, and constant checking-in. She knows sometimes these come from offering followers the space to accomplish the task they were originally assigned without micro-managing through electronic means. The linchpin leader knows such behavior encourages the heart and opens the door to conversations and observations about the work that might not have ever occurred before.

Practical Tips for Becoming a Linchpin Leader

Tip #1 - Listen to others more than you talk. A linchpin leader knows there is a significant difference between speaking and listening and seeks to create leadership environments where listening more than talking can occur with mercy and grace. The linchpin leader is not afraid of the space of silence and what that space can bring, and knows that people like to talk about themselves more than they might enjoy hearing about others. This is a discipline the linchpin leader seeks to develop with time to find opportunities for the team to develop and for individuals on the team to see role modeling of linchpin behaviors. Deeply listening to others requires quieting the mind, engaging with focus, eliminating distractions in conversations (i.e., the presence of cell phones), and caring about the other person in the conversation enough to demonstrate you care.

Tip #2 - Assumptions and expectations reflect a particular worldview and it is better if they are discussed rather than imposed. A linchpin leader is constantly checking in with the team about expectations and is looking for the answers to four key questions:

1. What are your expectations of me and my performance as a leader?
2. What are my expectations of you as a follower and your performance?
3. What are the ways in which you experience success or failure?
4. How do you accept—or reject—feedback from me and others on the team?

Asking and answering these four key questions can help a leader reveal the expectations a team has, but they can also help reveal how to lead the team in a linchpin manner. Such leadership also requires understanding that the "bucket" of assumptions—the unexamined and accepted definitions and proofs everyone carries in their head and hearts about how the "world should work"—individuals have can lead to the creation of solvable problems, creative narratives, and vexing issues. When leaders fail to care about where and how the assumptions their team members are carrying in their mental and emotional "buckets" come from, they fail to become linchpin leaders and remain mere managers of people as a process, or worse, supervisors of people performing tasks. And while supervision and management are necessary, they are not the highest goal of a linchpin leader.

Tip #3 - Be aware and conscious of the dichotomies of leadership. Every team problem has a leadership solution, but not every team problem needs to be solved by the leader. Leaders who fail to understand the nature of leadership dichotomies fail fundamentally at larger aspects of the journey toward being a linchpin leader. These dichotomies are everywhere; in relationships with superiors, in dealing with difficult team members, in the fact of needing to influence without having authority, and in the space of leaders having to grow in self-awareness and negotiate effectively. Linchpin leaders are unafraid of these dichotomies and they understand that addressing them effectively requires patience, experience, and intentionality.

Tip #4 - Following is part of leading. There is very little practical, tactical advice about how to be an effective follower. According to the Ivey Business Journal, "Followership is a straightforward concept. It is the ability to take direction well, to get in line behind a program, to be part of a team, and to deliver on what is expected of you." [Source: https://iveybusinessjournal.com/publication/followership-the-other-side-of-leadership/].[4] In the Western world in general, and in the American context of leadership from which this book is written, followership may seem like a "non-starter," but linchpin leaders know when to lead and they know when to get out of the way and follow. This is not based exclusively on following individuals in the hierarchy who may have attained authority, position, or power, or who may demonstrate tactical competence but little else. Following as a part of leading requires many of the same traits a linchpin leader seeks to develop, including competence, courage, honesty, loyalty, and good judgment. However, wrangling and controlling the ego and maintaining humility in the face of challenging circumstances is the most important part of being a linchpin follower.

Tip #5 - "It" can always happen without you. A leader's ego—just like the ego of a team member—can lead a person with the capability of becoming a linchpin leader into the morass of emotional and psychological weeds of selfishness rather than into the growing forest of self-awareness. Ego can lead to leaders believing—as we see with many chief executive officers in many organizations—that the work of leading, growing, or expanding the people, the enterprise, or even the industry itself, cannot happen without them. Linchpin leaders know they are indispensable because all that work can happen without them, and they know the work that is essential to get right is the work of removing themselves from the structure of leadership with time, intentionality, and without a victim mindset. This requires making plans for succession and following them, placing a time limit on how long they stay engaged with the team and remaining focused on leading the team during the time they are there, and not falling prey to the temptations of golden handcuffs, or the siren songs of "Yes" people who may surround them. Linchpin leaders are clear on the limits of their abilities and know-how to consistently sidestep the temptations of ego by asking and answering this question for themselves: "Is my presence providing the maximum level of value to the team I am leading to accomplish the goal we are seeking to get to?"

CHAPTER TWO

Rule 2
Leaders Eat the Apple Pie of E/I
Leadership and Emotional Intelligence

"Leadership requires being able to withstand withering emotional fire. Not from your followers—but from yourself. Leadership requires dancing with your own fears before even thinking about dancing with the fears of others"
Jesan Sorrells

This chapter focuses on helping readers understand the complexities of emotional intelligence and why it is critical for leaders to understand the effect of the power of emotional content on their own leadership approach and on their followers' ability (or interest) in acceding to individuals in leadership positions. It outlines for leaders the importance of monitoring their own emotional state and "checking in" intentionally when emotions are running high. We make the case for leaders considering the long-term ramifications and consequences of unintentional emotional reactions rather than intentional responses.

Introduction: Emotional Intelligence is the Ice Cream to Leaderships' Apple Pie

The links between leadership and emotional intelligence have been explored repeatedly. Everyone "knows" what emotional intelligence is. Many trainers, consultants, writers, and "thought leaders" claim to know how to access emotional intelligence to accomplish business goals and jump-start defunct leadership.

And in a world where physical labor (and even logic-based labor) becomes less expensive (and thus less valuable in the marketplace), emotional labor—labor driven by the work of leveraging emotional intelligence to accomplish business outcomes—will become the "gold standard" for what organizations can pay for—and make money from—in the remainder of the 21st century and beyond.

Thus, understanding the how, why, and what of emotional intelligence—and how those areas intersect with what leaders do and the stories they tell themselves about what they do—becomes critical to workplace and leadership success.

Emotional intelligence (or E/I), first derived in 1964 from the research of Stanford University professors Peter Salovey and John D. Mayer, and their "Ability Model" and later popularized by the work of researcher and author Daniel Goleman, has been the most elusive subject to master and justify outcomes for in the world of hard-charging, revenue-driven corporations, cash-strapped nonprofits and politically driven government organizations and agencies. Goleman in 1990 described emotional intelligence as "a form of social intelligence that involves the ability to monitor one's own and others' feelings and emotions, to discriminate among them, and to use this information to guide one's thinking and action." [1]

Many researchers, coaches, facilitators, and trainers popularly assert that an individual's E/I matters more than their personal IQ; nonetheless, as a trait of leaders and others, it often is discussed as a tool used to manipulate people to advance in an organization. However, E/I is more than just expressing a few words of empathy (or sympathy) for someone else who is depressed, sad, or angry. It describes the interactions at a biological and psychological level between five elements: self-awareness, self-regulation, motivation, empathy, and social skills.

Salovey and Mayer also initiated a research program intended to develop valid measures of E/I and explore its significance. For instance, they found in one study that "when a group of people saw an upsetting film, those who scored high on emotional clarity (which is the ability to identify and give a name to a mood that is being experienced) recovered more quickly. In another study, individuals who scored higher in the ability to perceive accurately, understand, and appraise others' emotions were better able to respond flexibly to changes in their social environments and build supportive social networks." [Source: https://www.emotionalintelligencecourse.com/ history-of-eq/].[2]

Emotional intelligence includes all the behaviors people engage in that allow them to become better people. Leaders would do well to pay attention to the value of emotional intelligence, primarily because of the leadership attitudes prevalent in this quote from *Emotional Intelligence: Why It Matters More Than IQ* by Daniel Goleman:

> "The cost-effectiveness of emotional intelligence is a relatively new idea for a business, one some managers [and leaders] might find hard to accept. A study of 250 executives found that they felt their work demanded "their heads but not their hearts." Many said they feared that feeling empathy or compassion for those they worked with would put them in conflict with their organizational goals. One felt the idea of sensing the feelings of those who worked for him was absurd—it would, he said, "be impossible to deal with people." Others protested that if they were not emotionally aloof, they would be unable to make the "hard" decisions that business requires--although the likelihood is that they would deliver those decisions more humanely."[3]

Researchers have argued that E/I and job performance are intimately linked and, of course, Kouzes and Posner in their book *The Leadership Challenge* assert that all five of their elements of leadership are tied directly into it. E/I is the fuel that will drive workplaces in the future because emotions and emotional labor are the only thing left in the human experience that cannot be turned into an algorithm or programmed into the interface of a robot.

However, what has not been explored are the links between E/I and self-deception in leadership. Many of the areas of E/I tie directly into the stories, myths, and legends leaders tell themselves about the work they are doing in leadership and that works value to the people who are following them. And, many leaders are self-deceived.

Self-deception in leadership is nothing new. Without a strong dose of self-awareness and self-reflection, and a high level of emotional intelligence, many leaders cannot successfully navigate their own internal emotional lives, much less the lives of their followers. Self-deception occurs when leaders—or anyone else—"drinks the Kool-Aid" about the effectiveness of their own leadership approach and style. Self-deception occurs when leaders refuse to grow intentionally and challenge themselves to the process of growth gaining genuine E/I requires. Self-deception occurs when leaders underestimate the level of burnout or compassion fatigue on their teams. It also occurs when leaders fail to encourage the building of morale on teams in the face of retention issues and poor treatment.

Many leaders are self-deceived and there is one way for them to overcome this self-deception: accepting feedback, internalizing it, and then changing—genuinely changing—their behavior.

This is some of the hardest work emotionally intelligent leaders engage in, and it is also the most rewarding.

Emotional Intelligence: A *Very* Short - and not "All Inclusive" - Primer

There have been multiple volumes written and much research during the 20th Century about the various aspects of E/I. Much of that research is excellent and leaders should read and absorb as much of it as they can. However, we are interested here in exploring the broad strokes of E/I and its application to the work leaders engage in daily. We have included multiple resources and links to work on E/I for those interested in exploring more of this topic.

E/I includes all the behaviors people engage in that allow them to become better people. Self-awareness is paramount among these behaviors and many people lack self-awareness for a wide variety of reasons:

- They ignore wise advice,
- They choose to act in their own best interests rather than the interests of others,
- They make bad/poor decisions intentionally,
- They ignore outcomes, believing those outcomes will not happen to them because of the uniqueness of their situation or other personalized particulars,
- They ignore the cognitive dissonance a decision sometimes requires,
- They pursue goals diametrically opposed to what they say they want,
- They fail to emotionally engage with their own inner lives and inner voice, and thus, are not attuned to the emotions of others in a meaningful way, or their own emotions.

There are many more reasons people lack self-awareness. Psychologists, therapists, mental health professionals, and others have spent countless years, hundreds of millions of hours on research, and many millions (probably billions) of tax and private donor dollars worldwide studying why people fail to engage with self-awareness. They have developed terms, theories, and propagated ideas that seek to explain, in academic terms, what any average person knows for someone else, but may fail to know for themselves.

The reason is that the elements of self-awareness lie in opposition to the elements of pleasure-seeking, immediate gratification, self-fulfillments, and selfishness. However, without self-awareness, without having an inkling of how personal and professional actions and decisions can affect others, many people—and many leaders—cannot begin to attain the other elements of E/I, from motivation and empathy, all the way to self-regulation and empathy.

Therefore, at a fundamental level, a great deal of research is being developed to explain the links between narcissism—selfishness involving a sense of entitlement, lack of empathy, and a need for admiration, as characterizing a personality type—and psycho-pathological behavior—a neuropsychiatric disorder marked by deficient emotional responses, lack of empathy, and poor behavioral controls, commonly resulting in persistent antisocial deviance and criminal behavior.

After self-awareness is attained—and in many people, self-awareness comes to the forefront in its nascent stages between birth and ages four or five—then the harder E/I traits begin to develop and grow at the same time, in no order. Researchers insist that E/I formation occurs all at once and we are all born emotionally intelligent. However, empathy is critical, after self-awareness, for people to have success.

Empathy comes about when people are sufficiently self-aware and self-regulated (more on that later) to not only be in tune with others' emotional states, but also to be interested and care about the effect their actions have on others. Empathy can be divided into two levels: personal empathy and corporate empathy.

Anthropologists know that work relationships tend to consist of what is known as "second-level" relationships, following from the idea that the further afield a person develops relationships with others, the more distant those relationships become (weak ties) and the easier it is to harm or damage another human being. In sociology, the presence of weak ties versus strong ties helps make clear how information flows through social networks, and how trustworthy—or faulty—that information can be or perceived to be.

At the level of empathy, the presence of strong ties would lead one to believe empathy would be stronger in a familial unit, and weaker in a work unit and so on, up through the neighborhood to the locality, to the state. However, recent research debunking—or at least strongly questioning—the outcomes of the Milgram experiments in the 1950s and 1960s in America around authority and obedience, indicates people will stand up for others out of a rudimentary sense of shared empathy. This reveals the presence of corporate empathy—that is, empathy writ large and used to leverage and acquire social capital.

The presence of empathy in leaders is a critical component beyond just the personal empathy leaders sometimes leverage to make claims to power, authority, and control. Furthermore, empathy combined with self-awareness is great. However, many leaders perceive themselves as being more empathetic or caring than they are.

Following empathy, probably the most important E/I trait is self-regulation. In the 1970s, a researcher from Stanford University named Walter Mischel conducted a series of experiments in his study on the effect of delaying gratification. In these studies, "...a child was offered a choice between one small but immediate reward, or two small rewards if they waited for a period. During this time, the researcher left the room for about 15 minutes and then returned. The reward was either a marshmallow or pretzel stick, depending on the child's preference." [Source: https://en.wikipedia.org/wiki/ Stanford_marshmallow_experiment].[4]

This study has been replicated and critiqued in social science for many years and many reasons, but the outcomes of the experiment have been replicated across many different variations of this study. "In follow-up studies, the researchers found that children who were able to wait longer for the preferred rewards tended to have better life outcomes, as measured by SAT scores, educational attainment, body mass index (BMI), and other life measures. A replication attempt with a sample from a more diverse population, over ten times larger than the original study, showed only half the effect of the original study. The replication suggested that economic background, rather than willpower, explained the other half. [https://en.wikipedia.org/wiki/ Stanford_marshmallow_experiment].[5]

The question for leaders is this: does self-regulation lead to more optimal outcomes, or does immediate gratification (regardless of other factors) lead to more optimal outcomes?

In the context of both self-awareness and empathy, self-regulation becomes a necessary—and under estimated—aspect of E/I. Being able to not lash out at a co-worker, not spend money in the budget on frivolous items, to stare defeat in the face consistently without losing focus, drive, or perseverance are all aspects of self-regulation. And in leaders, self-regulation also leads to more empathy and increases the feedback loop into self-awareness.

From self-regulation, we move into the space of motivation. Motivation has been studied by researchers repeatedly in the 20th century and, as Daniel Pink, the author of *Drive: The Surprising Truth About What Motivates Us*, states in his TED Talk on the topic of motivation: "there's a mismatch between what science knows and what business does."[6] There is even more of a mismatch between what science knows and what leaders do. Motivation includes all the acts, both intrinsic (internal) and extrinsic (external) that drive people to commit to action in a particular direction. In leadership, the extrinsic things that motivate leaders include: money, wealth, and other acquisitions of material items. The intrinsic things that motivate leaders include acquisition of status, power, mastery, and, in some cases, purpose. Sometimes attaining and preserving increasing autonomy might be the driver that pushes leaders to higher success.

The last area of E/I that drives leaders is the all-encompassing area of social skills. Many leaders do well in this area of understanding and managing social situations. Managing social situations and the keys to managing and, in many cases manipulating, social situations is the one area from which many leadership theories spring: "Great Man," trait, charismatic, contingency, situational, behavioral, participative, management, and relationship. At the core of these theories is the idea that social skills matter more than anything else. The ability to tell a story, appear charismatic, or to even build relationships, all focuses around attaining and developing social skills. Social skills also include the ability to influence and handle other people's emotions effectively.

With this last trait of E/I, we come full circle to where we began at self-awareness, and the core idea of this chapter: that leaders are self-deceived.

Self-Deception: The Gift that Keeps on Giving

Self-deception is a personality trait and an independent mental state, [that] "involves a combination of a conscious motivational false belief and a contradictory unconscious real belief" (von Hippel and Trivers, 2011).[7] In essence, this means when a person holds two opposing thoughts in their heads at the same time, they are self-deceived. Leaders are especially prone to this state of mind if they do not have three types of systems designed and built to scale that cover three areas:

- Systems for Attaining and Maintaining Self-awareness,
- Systems for Attaining, Retaining, and Acting on Feedback,
- Systems for Scaling Empathy for Others to Change Personal Behavior.

But let us talk more about self-deception. Stories drive mental states and influence mental states in an internal feedback loop that leaders need to take the time and trouble to break. This is the assertion made many years ago by the Arbinger Institute, which wrote the seminal book on self-deception and leadership, *Leadership and Self-Deception: Getting Out of the Box.* "Self-deception actually determines one's experience in every aspect of life." (Arbinger, Introduction)[8] In essence, the presence of self-deception creates a box whose borders and boundaries bind leaders into a straight-jacket of contradictory actions and behaviors, contradictory thoughts and feedback loops, and contradictory directions and scattered focus for followers. Getting out of the straight jacket of self-deception requires creating systems that allow leaders the space to self-reflect, the courage to listen and act on feedback and the ability to listen to others and take them seriously enough to care about their humanity to change themselves.

Ray Dalio, in his book *Principles: Life and Work*, extols the value of designing and implementing systems for feedback loops for leaders to battle all types of workplace, organizational and leadership behaviors that lead to an overall lack of trust, the absence of conflict, and a lack of overall organizational accountability.[9] However, we are not going that deep. This entire book is built on the idea that there are twelve areas leaders can build systems in to practically address leadership problems effectively and intentionally. However, in the space where E/I overlaps with self-deception, there are only three systems leaders need to intentionally arrange and then scale to success in other areas across the organization.

Three Systems for Combating Self-Deception with Emotional Intelligence

Systems for attaining and maintaining self-awareness always begin by engaging in the process of journaling and self-reflection. They follow from leveraging principles inherent in the GROW Coaching Model to help leaders practically attain self-awareness.

The GROW acronym stands for Goal, Current Reality, Options, and Will or way forward. Goal means answering the question as a leader: what outcome do I want to achieve with self-awareness first? Goals must be Specific, Measurable, Attainable, Realistic, and Time Sensitive.

Current reality means taking the time to critically examine the reality of where a leader is at in the space of the five areas of E/I and may require the use of a personality trait examination and assessment tool. Too often, leaders attempt to solve a leadership self-deception problem or reach the goal of combating self-awareness without fully considering their starting point; often, they are missing—or blind—to some information needing comprehension to reach their goal effectively.

Options means addressing the choices available to a leader in the space of the organizational culture of the group they happen to be leading. The leader must create and list as many alternative courses of action as possible to self-deception and gain self-awareness. The quantity of options is more important than the quality or feasibility of the options when attempting to grow self-awareness through establishing a system of self-reflection. From a broad range of creative possibilities, the leader may be able to derive specific action steps toward combating self-deception.

Finally, Will, or Way Forward, means a leader must be self-aware enough to realize there are personal limitations to their own growth in the space of combating self-deception and they might need help—or the feedback of other people—to move forward. Leaders must note the costs and benefits of engaging with growth around self-deception, and they must be able to convert their thoughts around self-reflection to the actual action of journaling—writing out the way forward, because seeing ensures forward movement.

There are several prompts on which a leader can write that can help a leader begin the process of journaling, which sits at the root of the GROW model, some of which are below:

- What are your strengths?

- What do you do best?
- What do you not do well?
- What are the positive words people who know you would use to describe you?
- What do you enjoy most about your current role?
- What do you enjoy the least?
- What do you believe you are compensated for in your position at work to do?
- What do you want to accomplish in the next month?
- What do you want to accomplish by the end of the year?
- What do you think your followers expect of you this year?
- What do you expect of yourself this year?
- What do you find the most satisfying about your leadership role?
- What about your leadership role motivates you the most?
- When you achieve a leadership goal or goals, how would you like to be recognized?
- When you are successful, whom do you want to know about it?
- What leadership skills would you like to develop in the next year?

A daily journaling practice, based on the GROW Coaching Model, can help leaders begin the process of growing toward self-awareness and can establish a baseline for success. The next step in the process is creating a feedback loop for followers to engage with leaders.

Systems for attaining, retaining, and acting on feedback are the hardest systems for leaders to set up; this is because organizational ennui, team fear of conflict, political considerations, and personal ego all stand as factors that can block even the best efforts of leaders to establish open feedback loops that are self-sustaining and vibrant. This is where the advice from Ray Dalio on the value to leaders of arranging a feedback loop in a company can come in handy:

"Learning is the product of a continuous real-time feedback loop in which we make decisions, see their outcomes, and improve our understanding of reality as a result. Being radically open-minded enhances the efficiency of those feedback loops because it makes what you are doing, and why, so clear to yourself and others that there cannot be any misunderstandings. ***The more open-minded you are, the less likely you are to deceive yourself and the more likely it is that others will give you honest feedback.*** If they are "believable" people (and it is very important to know who is "believable"), you will learn a lot from them. Being radically transparent and radically open-minded accelerates this learning process. It can also be difficult because being radically transparent rather than more guarded exposes one to criticism. It is natural to fear that. Yet if you do not put yourself out there with your radical transparency, you will not learn" [Source: https://www.linkedin.com/posts/ raydalio_learning-is-the-product-of-a-continuous-real-time-activity-6415592291729186816-6XMe].[10]

To set up a feedback loop to combat self-deception and increase self-awareness—as well as to increase the opportunities for self-awareness among followers and in the organization overall—leaders must perform the following steps:

- Request qualitative feedback from followers about behavior, outcomes, and goals around emotional intelligence,
- Collect qualitative feedback via email, and not via survey, and the feedback must be collected anonymously, with all identifiers scrubbed from the feedback.
- Read the qualitative feedback and absorb all the emotions around it in the first reaction, which will include all seven stages of grief all at once, including shock and denial, pain and guilt, anger and bargaining, depression, followed by the upward turn, reconstruction and working through,

acceptance and hope. These emotional reactions to feedback should probably take no more than 24 hours to fourteen days.

- Respond to the qualitative feedback, not with explanations, defenses, or combative anger (as many leaders do) but instead, with a commitment to action and a plan to move forward away from self-deception.

Establishing a practice for responding to the feedback rather than reacting to it can help leaders not only grow in E/I, but can also help them combat self-deception and add an important step around feedback that can be replicated and role-modeled for followers as a way of growth moving forward.

The final step in evacuating the self-deception box as a leader is to create a system for scaling empathy for others to change your own behavior. Empathy at both levels, the corporate and the personal, can be manipulated by clever psychopaths and the opportunistic leaders who are looking to merely make a profit. For leaders to scale empathy, they must care about their people and genuinely be committed to growing as leaders in the positions they have been placed. Leaders need to remember the following—Caring costs.

- It costs to be empathetic to your employees' emotional needs.
- It costs to be mindful of the non-verbal messages from your role modeling.
- It costs to be engaged in the act of actively listening all the time.
- It costs to develop connections that gain you nothing in the short-term.
- It costs to care when that caring may not be "enough" for the other party when what was really desired by the other party was a transactional act, not a relational one.

I repeat…Caring costs. But where else are you going to

invest your emotional energy in as a leader?

Practical Tips for Growing in Emotional Intelligence as a Leader

Tip #1 - Own your own emotions. Leaders must understand and exhibit emotional intelligence in a variety of circumstances and then leverage that understanding. The first thing to do is own your own emotions as a leader. Leaders clearly define their emotions and if they cannot, they pursue self-awareness work to better understand themselves. When leaders are unaware of their own emotions, unaware of the effect of decisions made based on those emotions, or just do not care about their own emotions and their effect on others, they drive their teams into the proverbial ditch. Leaders own their emotions.

Tip #2 - Audit where most of your emotional leadership energy is going. Leaders understand that 80 percent of their emotional energy at a leadership level should be focused on the 80 percent of people on the team who can be led. The other 20 percent of their emotional energy can be focused on the 20 percent of the people on the team who will resist being led, undermine the leader, and potentially damage the team because of their dysfunctional behavior. Leaders audit the direction of their leadership energy to be on the lookout for compassion fatigue, burnout, apathy, and passive-aggressive behaviors. When leaders fall into the emotional areas that lead to a lack of appropriate direction of their leadership energy, they risk falling into self-deception. Leaders avoid self-deception as much as possible and audit where 80 percent of their emotional energy is focused on the team.

Tip #3 - Intentionally role model the boundaries you want to see. Leaders are role models. Even leaders who believe their leadership acts, as defined by the words "management" or "supervision," make their daily leadership acts meaningless and innocuous. When leaders embrace role modeling, they role model all the parts of leadership, even the ones that appear to be less than exciting. Role modeling boundaries go directly to Doing What You Say You Will Do as a leader. If leaders fail to role model boundaries of emotional intelligence, communication, negotiation, and other areas, they can effectively and intentionally lead the team. Leaders intentionally role model the boundaries they want others on the team to demonstrate.

Tip #4 - All emotions can be "toxic" if they are out of balance with the team, the organization, and the culture. Leaders know that all emotions—even those defined by others on the team as being positive—can become toxic if they are out of balance on the team. That toxicity can scale up to an organization and a culture. Leaders work intentionally to create and maintain environments where emotions and emotionally charged decision-making can be kept in balance without tipping the scales in a negative direction. The intentional work requires leaders to be aware of the problems their teams are facing, but also to be aware fundamentally of the substrate—or subtext—that lies below not only those problems but also the individuals' mindsets on the team. Leaders are vigilant and aware of changes in the team environment that can lead to out-of-balance emotional responses and reactions at scale.

Tip #5 - Be clear on what you "owe" the audience. Leaders know, emotionally, what they "owe" the team and what they do not. Leaders are aware and able to articulate the "why" behind their boundaries and can balance that "why" with other important factors in the team environment. They also are not self-deceived into believing they, as leaders, can "do" or "have" it all. They are patient, and while they may suffer from bouts of Imposter Syndrome, they do not allow self-doubt to destroy their capacity to lead others. Leaders know that the team, the organization, and the culture are always watching them and their behavior, and they know that such constant surveillance is a two-way street, not a one-way alley. They are watching the culture, the organization, and the team. Leaders are clear with themselves first, and every one second about what they "owe" and are confident in their ability to negotiate, and renegotiate, the terms of payment.

CHAPTER THREE

Rule 3
Leaders Study Sales and Marketing
Leadership Communication and Persuasion

"Leadership requires pulling people along where they may not want to go. Leadership requires challenging people when they do not want to be challenged. Leadership requires engaging with people in ways that will make them uncomfortable."
Jesan Sorrells

This chapter focuses on the importance of understanding and applying persuasion tactics and choosing such tactics intentionally to motivate, persuade, and convince other people (followers) to act. It asserts that leaders are marketers and sales professionals fundamentally and that no sales professional or marketer succeeds "by accident," even though it may appear that way to others outside the situation. The chapter makes a case for engaging in intentional acts of persuasion rather than allowing persuasion to "just happen" and introduces the Three C's model (CLARITY-CANDOR-COURAGE).

Introduction: Persuasion as the Jiu-jitsu of the Mind

We are all deceived.

Or at least, most of us who are not involved in the marketing industry are deceived constantly.

From billboards to banner ads, we are constantly being cognitively manipulated to buy, click, like, or advocate for ideas, products, or even positions in an argument we may not inherently believe in, but we have no choice but to act. The writer and researcher, Robert Cialdini, writes about it this way in his great book *Influence: The Psychology of Persuasion*:

> "I can admit it freely now. All my life, I've been a patsy. For as long as I can recall, I've been an easy mark for the pitches of peddlers, fund-raisers, and operators of one sort or another."[1]

Many leaders struggle with understanding the power of persuasion but struggle less with leveraging the persuasion of power. Many organizational leaders default to wielding titles, degrees, certifications, and other forms of authority they instinctively know followers respond to, but they do not know the "why." Leadership is hard enough without understanding the power of influence over others.

The unfortunate truth is, for many leaders, persuasion is not an active act, carefully considered and then leveraged. Instead, persuasion is an act (or a series of acts) the leader barely understands and, if she does, she performs them intentionally on a sporadic basis, and is surprised when those acts achieve the outcome she is seeking. In addition, leaders fail to consider deeply the role of power on influence and how that power is wielded via position, style, and approach. Finally, many leaders want their followers to "just do what they are told (compliance)" while also wielding authority badly, and then leaders wonder why motivation (See Chapter Seven on Morale and Motivation) is lacking and morale is low among team members.

Leaders must understand that, in areas of persuasion, power, influence, and the darker areas of humiliation, deception, and face work, there are a few simple tactics that, if intentionally leveraged repeatedly, can yield results that can move the world of a team, an organization, or even an individual. Influence, persuasion, and power all come together when leaders seek to engage people with whom they do not have direct authority over. Leaders in organizations that favor speed and competency do not always like to hear the following, but it is the truth: acts of collaboration (power with) allow more work tasks to be accomplished over a longer period than acts of coercion (power over). And, the reality is that it has always been easier to lead people with no authority through leveraging rewards and persuasion together.

It all starts, however, with understanding the roles of sales and marketing.

More Engineers Should Study Sales and Marketing

One of the more interesting types of people watching to do comes when working with groups of people who firmly believe they cannot be persuaded by emotional appeals, and from that belief, immediately move mentally to the space of not being able to "fall" for persuasion tactics at all. The definition of persuasion is about combining power and influence to get people to act as the influencer wants them to act.

And when watching what "works" with audiences who stalwartly claim they are immune to the power of persuasion, one realizes they all are consumers at the end of all the arguments, assertions, protestations, and denials. Every person, who claims to be immune to the "click, whirr"–to borrow from Dr. Cialdini–of persuasion tactics has a house, a car, a favorite "toy," and, at a deeper level, has a belief system to which they cling, a series of opinions they have convinced themselves that are correct, and a series of identifiable behaviors to which they blind.

Thus, everyone who believes they are logical and reasonable should study the fields of sales and marketing closely. Leaders who come from those fields--or who have closely studied and applied the psychological lessons from marketing and sales--tend to do better as leaders than those individual leaders who stalwartly state that those fields are all "manipulation" or "deceitful."

For those individuals who come from the fields of sales and marketing and are seeking to become leaders, there is an important caveat to this thought, and it is this: marketing is about changing minds, changing postures, changing attitudes, and changing lives. Manipulation is getting someone else to buy something they do not need, that will not benefit them, whose value is amorphous (if it is there in evidence at all) and is unnecessary to their development as an individual in the marketplace, not of ideas or money, but of a relationship. Manipulation serves ideology, control, compliance, and obedience, and transforms autonomous people into sheep. Marketing, genuine, open, psychologically aware marketing, does the opposite. It opens doors, creates a compelling vision of the future, tells a story without covering up the hard and ugly parts, and unites people and groups rather than seeking to divide them.

Leaders who seek to change lives for the better study the tactics and strategies of persuasion, and determine how best to apply those strategies to move people toward a better and more sustainable and hopeful future, while also making their followers aware of the pitfalls that such tactics hold.

This is genuine power, and leaders should be wise to its use.

Let Us Talk About Power for a Minute…

Leaders engage in the use of power all the time to make their followers obey, comply, and bend their wills toward the actions that need to be taken to get work done. However, most leaders do not think too deeply about power, whether its use is culturally-based or situationally-based, or both, and leader fail to fully appreciate the behavioral ripples that occur in the pond of followers' actions when the rock of power is thrown in. Some leaders who are intentional with their use of power, and very often, as a leader rises in the ranks of an organizational hierarchy, they begin to consider power and its uses less and less instinctively and more and intentionally. Kenneth Cloke, noted mediator and lawyer, and the author of *The Crossroads of Conflict*, quotes the Polish sociologist, Mihaly Csikszentmihalyi:

> "...One feature that distinguishes humans from other animals--perhaps as characteristic as speech or upright posture--is the fact that we find so many ways to oppress and exploit one another. Distinctions of wealth, status, and knowledge make it possible for some individuals to live off the psychic energy expended by others. "Power" is the generic term to describe the ability of a person to have others expend their lives to satisfy his or her goals. [Emphasis ours] Under this construct, there are only two possible types of power leaders can leverage, "power over" others with strong positional authority within a staggered hierarchy with plenty of organizational boundaries, or "power with," that is collaborative power, as in a small group with a relatively flat hierarchy and little organizational boundaries, that is self-governed and autonomous in its decision making and actions."[2]

Power is defined by Moises Naim, the author of *The End of Power: From Boardrooms to Battlefields and Churches to States, Why Being in Charge Is Not What It Used to Be* as, "the ability to direct or prevent the current or future actions of other groups and individuals."[3] Naim also notes that "precisely because power is primordial, elemental, in our daily lives, we rarely stop to address it analytically—to identify exactly where it resides, how it works, how far it can go, and what stops it from going further." Naim asserts that power is a dynamic between multiple people, situations, cultures, and other forces that we do not completely understand, reflecting the famous quote from Alice Walker, the poet and social activist, that "The most common way people give up their power is by thinking they do not have any."[4] The seminal 1959 research of French and Raven in the space of power, focused on the intentions of the wielder of power and determined five bases of power: reward power, coercive power, legitimate power, referent power and expert power: for all five types, the stronger the basis of power, the greater the level of power. Any attempt to utilize power outside the range of power will tend to reduce the power (French and Raven, 2005).[5] French and Raven researched their categories of power within a decidedly Western context and without looking substantially at the intentions; instead focusing on the effects of power on the target of the influence. However, Naim updates this thinking by focusing in his book on the channels, or how power is expressed in the real world outside the world of researchers and Polish social scientists.

According to Naim, the first channel of power people typically leverage is force--or the threat of force—backed by the will to engage in actions another party might not be physically able, or emotionally willing, to engage in. Force is a blunt instrument and used by many in authority only in extreme situations. The impact of muscle, or force, ultimately lies in acts of coercion. The researcher Mary Parker Follet suggested power is usually conceived of as power over another entity, or force. Force can exist in the following areas:

- The ability to bankrupt someone else.
- The ability to fire someone for not performing in a role.
- The ability to make someone comply against their will with an order.

Typically, many people cease thinking about power very deeply after they have considered, and leveraged, force over others. For leaders, this lack of consideration would be a mistake, and great leaders very rarely leverage force until they absolutely must—and even then, reluctantly.

The second channel of power is the code—or the rules established within a hierarchical structure over time. The code, according to Naim's work is the combination of the effect of values, morals, traditions, cultural norms and mores, social expectations and pressures, and religious beliefs and values handed down from generation to generation. The effect of the code lies not in coercion; it lies in activating a sense of moral duty. Leaders leverage the power of artifacts including:

- The design and layout of physical environments
- Symbols, signs, and logos
- Vocabulary, language, and stories
- Celebrations of events

Leaders use these areas to shape the cultural rules and structures in which their followers operate subtly and intentionally. This is a highly sophisticated leveraging of power and leaders must be hyper-aware of ways in which the code is often redefined once it interacts with the people it seeks to mold and change. The management theorist Peter Drucker recognized the power of followers interacting with leaders' best intentions around building a code in his assertion that "culture eats strategy for breakfast."[6]

Naim indicates the third channel of power is the pitch, or the ability to influence, persuade, and ref ram power for followers so the actions they take seem to be their ideas, rather than the leaders' ideas, or will. The pitch lies at the core of the power of persuasion and is exemplified most notably through advertising, marketing, and sales. This is the core reason it would do well for leaders to deeply study the research and work of marketers, particularly as the fields of cognitive neuroscience, big data, and machine learning begin to overlap and inform persuasion and nudging techniques at a mass social level. The pitch does not require the bluntness of force, nor does it require appeals to a moral code. Instead, the pitch is about persuading followers, and anyone else, that one action or behavior is demonstrably better than another. The effect of the pitch is in persuading others to see the situation in a way that leads them to advance the persuaders' goals or interests. The pitch alters our perception of a situation. In many situations for leaders, the pitch only works if the leader understands the principles of persuasion and how they "lock" together to effectively govern relationships. However, leaders must be aware that followers are always seeking to pitch them as well, and that the "dark side" of the pitch is manipulation, deceit, lying, and self-deception.

Finally, Naim asserts that the fourth channel of power is the reward, which lies deeply in the control of resources, some of which may be material, but very often are psychological or emotional. The research behind leaders-member exchange theory is all about the power of rewards, where the leader provides more rewards to those closest to her, and fewer rewards to those not in the "inner circle." It turns out, that with power, familiarity may breed contempt, but it also ensures that the follower and the leader will both wind up with some material, emotional, or psychological gain, rather than a loss. The power of reward lies in the ability to provide rewards (i.e., promotions, pay, etc.) to get others to behave in ways that align with the reward providers' interests. The effect of reward lies in being able to deploy material benefits to induce behavior.

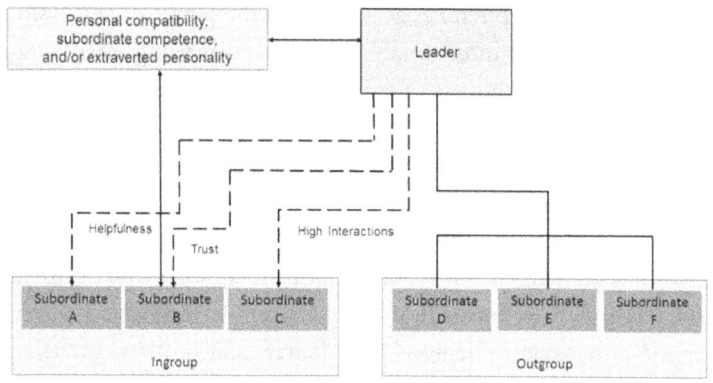

Leaders must understand the following points about power if they want to leverage the power they possess to attain the outcomes they desire:

- Everyone has a measure of power, from the boardroom to the kitchen table, and from the youngest baby to the oldest adult.
- The systems of power hierarchically constructed over time must be questioned, examined, and—in some cases—torn down and rebuilt, but only when there is a compelling vision of what another system would look like in the future for followers.
- A leaders' power is organic (granted) and shared with followers as well as being inorganic (thrust upon them) and selfish to the leader. This means a leader must wield power carefully, judiciously and from a deep core of moral and virtue that can only come about from an understanding of their level of self-awareness, and through attempts at personal reflection, apology, and being willing and able to handle consequences of decisions.
- Power, and the systems constructed around it, from cultural to emotional, must be open to change; if they are not, the systems and the power must be flexible enough to adapt, but not break, in the face of challenges to that power and its systems. (See Chapter Eleven, Adapting to Change.)

Principles of Persuasion

There are seven areas of psychology that effectively "lock-in" to each other in a hierarchical, top-down structure governing human relationships. These areas are broadly defined and there have been endless reams of research that delves into the nature and function of each of these areas. However, it is important for leaders to note that all seven of these areas create the context where persuasion and influence can be effective between a leader and their followers. For any persuasion efforts to work, contextualizing the persuasion effort is hugely important because, without appropriate context, the psychological tactic will not work, will be seen as shocking or unnatural, and will probably be ignored.

Think about it: as a leader, you would never attend a serious meeting with people whom you need to persuade to take an action at a serious time during a team or organizational crisis, in a clown outfit. Not unless your organization was a clown company, and even in such places, there is an upper limit on fake noses, cake makeup, and funny multi-colored wigs. By the same token, as a leader, you would not show up to a party where a clown was expected to appear in a business suit.

From the work of Robert Cialdini, author of *Influence: The Psychology of Persuasion*, influence is defined as "the ability to make people say "yes" without them thinking about it," and persuasion is defined as "the process aimed at changing a person's (or a group's) attitude or behavior toward some event, idea, object, or other person(s), by using written or spoken words to convey information, feelings, or reasoning, or a combination thereof."[7] For leaders, this is an important definition to absorb, because what it means is that writing, speaking, and showing up matter more for moving a team forward toward action, or to the side, or backward, than any other element of leadership. Leaders who fail to think well, fail to write well, fail to speak well, and then fail to show up well to lead. However, there is a place of grace: leaders who work on at least one area (thinking, writing, speaking, or presenting) tend to do better at leading others than those who work on none of those areas at all.

There are seven parts to influence and they lock together in a hierarchical structure when attempting to persuade another party of a point:

- Reciprocity
- Commitment and Consistency
- Social Proof

- Liking
- Authority
- Scarcity
- Consensus

Reciprocity—The principle of reciprocity is based on the idea of giving something in exchange for something else. Could be an idea, an emotion, a product, a service. For example, a marriage is supposed to be based on reciprocity, as is a business relationship,

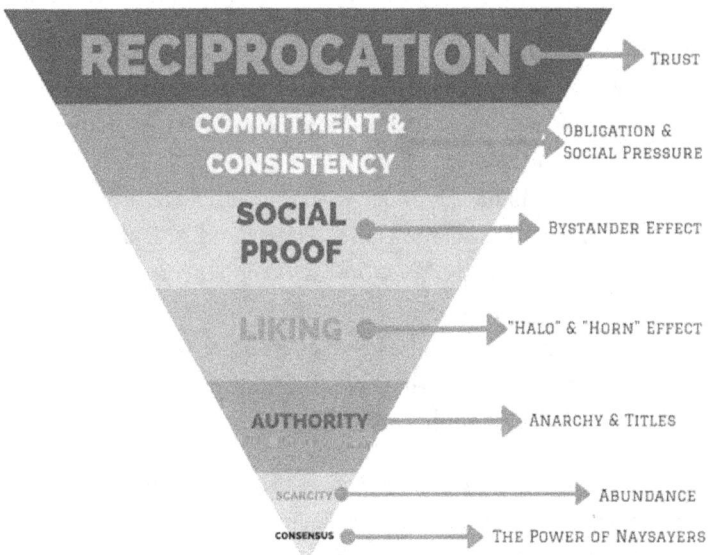

the rule that states we should repay, in kind, what another person has provided to us. All reciprocation is based on a transactional exchange of trust between the leader and the follower. Many leaders use reciprocation last and most often view this influence through the lens of either salary and benefits, or through the lens of recognition and reward. Intentional leaders reverse this and offer trust, and open hand, and personal vulnerability first, but in the appropriate context and they give away something (for example trust) in exchange for nothing, (for example compliments, rewards, favors, courageous emotional engagement, etc.) to grow trust on the team. Leaders engage in the three following acts to prove and deepen the likelihood of reciprocity being returned:

- Leaders clarify roles and responsibilities during critical team building or team transition periods to facilitate the formation and growth of effective teams and they intentionally create teams capable of problem solving within an atmosphere of trust and collaboration.
- Leaders demonstrate and practice attentive listening—without interruption, with pauses to consider salient facts, and with patience when it feels as if decisions must be made quickly and without much thought—and they work to convey understanding to others.
- Leaders manage conflict without avoidance, fear, power plays, or accommodation. They clearly and quickly identify sources of conflict and seek to turn conflict into a constructive exchange of ideas in a psychologically safe space while keeping the energy of the conflict focused on achieving desired outcomes, rather than avoiding conflict, escalating conflict, or ignoring conflict.

Commitment and Consistency—The principle of consistency says that once a position, message, or idea has been stated or obtained, the person stating the position should support it unconditionally. The rule states that once we take a stand, we will encounter personal, interpersonal, and social pressures to behave consistently with our position. Followers enforce this rule automatically with themselves, leaders, and even other followers, even if it would be better for people to be inconsistent and uncommitted—to change their minds. Leaders understand that commitment and consistency, as a method of persuasion, happens mostly under the radar and followers glean impressions about the level of commitment and consistency from empirical observations about leaders' characters rather than necessarily hard data about the outcomes of critical decisions taken in critical moments. Leaders work to grow in commitment and consistency in personal areas first and then scale that to the team when role modeling can be effectively leveraged for support of hard decisions:

- Leaders develop a plan and commit to changes over the long-term rather than the short term. They work to develop the support of allies and understand that the aggregate of decisions over time grows position and persuasion with stakeholders in drips, not floods consistently and committedly.
- Leaders ruthlessly follow up on promises they have made and commitments by following plans through to closure, persisting in the face of obstacles, and keeping their word.
- Leaders engage with effective time management by setting and following efficient work priorities. They eschew the seduction of working on many tasks simultaneously, and they intentionally balance the importance and urgency of tasks.

Social Proof—The rule states that we determine what is correct by finding out what other people think is correct. One of the easiest ways to determine what is correct is by doing what other people are doing. Or to say what other people are saying. Or to think what other people are thinking. This creates a sense of obligation and social pressure to keep individuals in line because individuals like to be part of a tribe. People do not want to be alone and cast out into the "outer darkness." And the lack of effort we put into social proofing proves its power; because we put so little effort into socially proofing people that, from the time people are born, they automatically seek the subtle social signals that come from parents first about what it means to really "fit in." Social proofing—which leads inevitably to bonding around social norms, which eventually transforms at work into policies and procedures—is powerful, but not so powerful that leaders cannot intentionally break it and remold it with a little bit of work. This is where, for leaders, business storytelling becomes an intentional act of organizational culture building the rewards and sanctions behaviors as they become apparent. And, it becomes less an act of verbally telling a story, and more an act of actively living a story. To leverage the power of social proofing, leaders perform the following actions:

- Leaders engage with followers with courage to break social pressure and redirect power and influence from where it is usually focused—with the strongest personality, or positional authority in the space—to where it needs to go. Social proof is easier to break with allies, but it can be shifted by engaging committedly and consistently with breaking up of power and position-based cliques that exclude outside points of view, fail to innovate, and who are in danger of becoming sclerotic in their thinking.
- Leaders provide coaching via timely, specific, and constructive feedback while also acting as "front line" developers of followers. They "walk the talk" and are constantly internally questioning the culture of the team and the organization they are in.

Liking—The principle of liking states that personal power, charisma, fascination, or some other intangible characteristic will cause people to follow leaders and/or create movements. The rule states that we would prefer to say "yes" to those whom we personally like. Attribution theory states that "we try to find reasons to support our preconceived notions."[8] Cognitive dissonance creates mental and emotional "friction": when two thoughts do not match up either logically or emotionally, we attempt to reduce this friction by finding things we like about people or a situation. The Halo effect of the "halo and horn" effect comes from this rule. Leaders are not confusing the draw of liking with the power of authority, the trade-offs inherent in reciprocity, the power of other people and culture, or the desire to have commitment and consistency. Leaders are wary of liking other people too much, but they also counterbalance this with the understanding that there are going to be people they like and people they do not. Instead of searching for cognitive surety and avoiding cognitive friction, leaders move toward that friction, examine it, and address it both emotionally and rationally. In the practical, effective leaders engage with liking in the following ways:

- Leaders intentionally engage with the purposeful understanding of body language cuing, active listening, and the impact of signs, symbols, and the physical environment in which they are seeking to influence others.
- Leaders provide clear direction to followers, set clear priorities, and foster a common vision. And when the circumstances demand a change, either in strategies or tactics, effective, intentional leaders abandon their egos and are willing to let go of the tactics and strategies they "liked" that did not produce the desired results.

Authority—The principle of authority is rooted in the idea that certain people, organizations, ideas, or cultural/political/social tropes have power over other ideas that have been "discredited." It also refers to the formal rights of not only leaders, but also followers, to marshal resources and make decisions to accomplish goals and achieve outcomes. The rule states that individuals follow orders when they are issued by people who are perceived as being higher in the hierarchical chain. Questioning authority through criticism, feedback, or even outright rebellion is seen by compliant followers and ego-driven leaders as welcoming anarchy. Leaders know the appearance of authority based on titles, clothes and other trappings is enough to get the obedience of followers.

Leaders also realize innately that the crushing jaws of social proofing, consensus, and authority—nonverbally signaled through titles, symbols, and other visible trappings of power—are enough to ensure compliance among even the most recalcitrant followers. However, appeals to authority as the initial means of persuasion are always traps for leaders, and leadership communication based on compliance and obedience almost always erodes into hierarchal resentment, embedded resistance, and a reduction in overall productivity. In the practical, effective leaders engage with authority only when necessary and in the following ways:

- Leaders intentionally choose to avoid opening their leadership communication with overt appeals to authority. They tamp down the trappings, clean up the non-verbal signaling, and actively resist the temptations to "power over" that authority brings.
- Leaders lead with respect first. They open leadership communication with appeals to empathy, shared vision, common goals, and a modicum of strategic vulnerability.
- Leaders expect resistance, (See Chapter Three, Leadership and Conflict Management) and when that resistance manifests, they do not push for compliance with authority until their back is to the wall and the options for resolution are genuinely exhausted.

Scarcity—The principle of scarcity is based on the idea that we live in a finite world with finite resources such as time, energy, people, and products and that the fewer the resources, the more that they are valued, in terms of trade-offs and negotiation. The rule states that opportunities seem more valuable to individuals, leaders, and followers alike when access to them or their availability is limited. Followers and leaders want what they cannot have and desire, plot, negotiate and fight over opportunities (such as for recognition, praise, more money, promotion, etc.) when those opportunities are perceived as being rarely available. Unintentional leaders who lack self-awareness and social empathy leverage the lack of access to resources to ensure compliance and obedience when social proofing, authority, and consensus fail to do the job. However, intentional leaders think through scarcity and examine their teams closely to determine accurately what the resources are that are scare, and what the resources are that may be abundant. To leverage scarcity with heart, leaders perform the following acts:

- Leaders systematically determine, through empirical observation and acquired data through anonymous employee engagement surveys and other means, what is the scarce trait, resource, or energy on the team (i.e., emotional intelligence, people with skill sets, or positivity in the face of failure, etc.), and then make an intentional plan to address those scarcities.
- Leaders systematically determine, through empirical observation and acquired data through anonymous employee engagement surveys and other means, what is the abundant trait, resource, or energy on the team (i.e., hubris, poor training levels, poor levels of accountability, etc.) and then make an intentional plan to address those abundances by curtailing an action or behavior.
- Leaders understand that performing in the areas that are scarce rather than engaging in doing more things that are abundant moves the team forward toward accomplishing goals.

Consensus—The principle of consensus states that people need to "be on the same side" (or at least enough of them) to be able to create an environment where agreement can occur and forward momentum is generated. However, endlessly seeking consensus can be a trap for unintentional leaders because if they have not secured confidence from their team in the other six areas of persuasion, then seeking consensus becomes a rhetorical cul-de-sac. For leaders on the other end of the spectrum, seeking consensus can be a way to hide from culpability and accountability and avoid doing the hard things that make leadership inherently undesirable for many people. Leaders may also tend to believe they need to get everyone "on the same side" to accomplish goals. However, naysayers can sometimes have more value than those in the group who agree with everything overall. In the practical, effective leaders navigate the shoals of consensus in the following way:

- Leaders relentlessly get to know their team members. And when the pressure to grow (or scale) the team comes from the organization, the followers, or others not involved in seeking consensus for decisions, leaders advocate up, out, and across the hierarchical structure by asking the question "Why?"
- Leaders rely on honesty and vulnerability to explain to their followers what the environment is signaling, and they work to challenge followers' cognitive biases around data, while also being open to challenge themselves.
- Leaders develop channels for motivation by encouraging followers to achieve results with commitment, focus, and discipline.

The Magic Bullet Store is Out of Business

And it has been for a while.

A lot of the success leaders have at leveraging all these principles of persuasion to motivate, move, and get work out of followers, lies in a deep understanding of how people operate in the realm of storytelling and emotional engagement at a psychological level.

There are no "magic bullets" for that.

The work of communicating effectively through narrative structures, or through communication, goes beyond leaders if communication has happened and goes toward leaders tirelessly restating the narrative so followers hear the narrative, internalize the narrative, and then act on the narrative.

The real issue for leaders around persuasion and the work of leadership is that the current systems we have for the education of our children (school), getting money to adults in an exchange for labor (work), and taking care of both the Earth (capitalism) and the people on it (health care), grew up over the last 100, 200 or 500 years. And those systems of persuasion were based on assumptions that grew up over the same period about what constituted a narrative, who could make that narrative "work," and who even got to speak the narrative.

This is where concerns about who has power and who does not come into play in the modern world.

Now, those systems are in flux and are changing and many leaders resist the call to narrative for the same reasons people with an engineering mindset fail to appreciate the inherent power in sales and marketing: they believe that, while everyone else may "fall" for a narrative, they are immune to its powers. This is a fallacy (most known as the narrative fallacy) and it permeates leadership thinking and mindsets still, despite all contemporary evidence to

TWO POINTS TO REMEMBER:
HOW we talk about what matters (the language we pick) matters more than **WHAT** (the goals we are trying to accomplish as a team) we talk about.
HOW we talk about what we talk about, matters more than **WHAT** we talk about.

the contrary. The response from intentional leaders should be to act to put their hands on the levers of the systems in the sphere of influence they can control (family, work, community, finances, social life, etc.), and begin to push the levers of change intentionally, purposefully, and deliberately.

And to do so with winsomeness, kindness, and grace.

But to do it tenaciously.

After all, as Nassim Nicholas Taleb notes in his seminal book, *The Black Swan: The Impact of the Highly Improbable*, "Ideas come and go. Stories stay."[9]

Persuasion Tactics—The Top Five

Persuasion, conflict management, active listening, responding to advance the conversation rather than to advance yourself, engaging without judgment to pull allies to your side—these are all skills that can be learned, taught, and passed on hand-to-heart, generation-to-generation.

If the prospect of doing even one percent of that is too daunting for you as an individual inside of your sphere of influence, then you should be asking not "Now what?" but "What is it that I really want to accomplish in this limited life I have now?" Here are the top five tactics for leveraging persuasion, being a good steward of power, and telling a narrative that moves followers to action:

- Understand your own internal variables; i.e., how you understand power, relationships, etc.
- Develop a compelling story to tell others that will override the story they are telling themselves about you
- Control anger and negative emotions and avoid escalation
- Approach situations and circumstances honestly and without fear
- Be willing to give a little to get a little, but be firm in what you will accept and reject

Fortunately for all of us, we were born at the beginning of a revolution in human affairs, human systems, and human motivations.

And all revolutions are scary and destructive before they are enlightening and hopeful.

Look for work first, and hope will come.

Practical Tips for Leveraging Persuasion

Tip #1 - Study the principles of sales and marketing as if your leadership life depended on it. Leaders should be open to learning from everywhere; the ideal place to learn how to persuade others is from the best practices of sales and marketing. Sales processes have transformed from a field that employs high-pressure, pushy tactics (although some still use those tactics) to a field that employs relationship-building practices. More united with marketing than ever before, sales is a field driven by the ability to create emotionally intelligent relationships with customers and clients. It is also a field where having the courage to ask for a sale (a variation of asking for help) without also applying emotional pressure is the key to success. These are valuable skillsets for the practical, intentional leader to absorb.

Marketing is about persuasion as well. And not the kind of marketing that gets a person to "click" on an ad, a video, or a piece of writing on the Internet. Marketing in its best form encourages people to change, act, or become better versions of themselves. This is the type of marketing leaders should study with enthusiasm and apply the lessons from that marketing to their real leadership lives with verve and winsomeness.

Tip #2 - Know and be able to talk about your "why." Leaders who fail to articulate the reason they are acting, making decisions, or accepting consequences for action, fail a major test of leadership. Followers should never be left wondering what a leader wants to pursue or why. For many leaders, the "what" is easier to address with clarity than the "why," because the "what" is easy to contextualize and depersonalize. However, the "why" is filled with emotions, historical experiences, hard-learned lessons, and all manner of information leaders prefer followers not know.

But if followers do not know a leader's "why," the contextual "what"—a goal, a vision, etc.—will not have enough power to drive the team beyond accomplishing the goal at the lowest possible level. Leaders who are comfortable with the authenticity that talking about their "why" aloud provides will have more success in driving the team to accomplish continuously larger goals in the future.

Tip #3 - Persuasion tactics are just that: tactics. Leaders understand that the aspects of persuasion are always tactical. They may inform the overall strategy of growing influence, deepening team bonds, building relationships, or just getting a task done, but they are not the strategy in and of themselves. The leaders who fail to understand this distinction can get caught in the weeds of reciprocity or may become consumed by aspects of groupthink on their teams emanating from the power of consensus and social proofing. Leaders learn the philosophy and psychology behind these tactics and layer the tactics together while recognizing their presence in a communication interaction with others. But intentional leaders avoid the temptation to make the tactics the whole strategy in leading their teams.

Tip #4 - Be aware of nonverbal communication and influence based on subtext, not always context. Leaders know that nonverbal communication and influence rely heavily on the power of unstated assumptions, unexamined expectations, and commonly accepted norms of leadership behavior. They also know that all of these can be violated, supported, questioned, or developed at will and that this is the work of intentional leaders and intentional leadership. Subtext—the stuff floating around the bottom of all communication interactions—can drive influence more effectively than all the contextual interactions in the world. Human beings relationally switch from subtext to context without thinking, but leaders examine subtext closely and calibrate their tactics of influence intentionally.

Tip #5 - Avoid self-deception. Drinking your own Kool-Aid will poison you first. Leaders avoid self-persuasion via the seduction of both self-deception and other deception. Lying, manipulation, deceitfulness, and other destructive behaviors may be rewarded because the outcome is accomplished and the goal is achieved, but that reflects a leadership mentality more focused on the short-term gain of a goal than the long-term pursuit of a relationship. Leaders cannot deceive themselves because fundamentally, leaders must operate at a higher level than their followers. Although we are all deceived, leaders must be aware but not self-deceived.

CHAPTER FOUR

Rule 4
Leaders Know the Three "C's"
Leadership and Conflict Management

"Not every follower you have is going to "whistle while they work." As a leader, you might have more trouble with your followers than those who are resisting your efforts. Keep yourself humble and aware." "

Jesan Sorrells

This chapter focuses on the role of conflict in leadership and asserts that conflict is the "coin of the realm" for leadership success and that no great change or great leader is made without conflict. The chapter asserts that conflict is a natural situation on a team or in an organization and can be positive if the leader directs the conflict rather than allowing the conflict to railroad them. This rule makes a case for shifting mindsets around conflict rather than merely applying one more tactic in the hope that it will "work" to "resolve" the situation.

Introduction: Peanut Butter and Jelly Sandwiches

Leadership and conflict go together like peanut butter and jelly. And because leaders face conflict just about as often as they eat a peanut butter and jelly sandwich, they should probably have the strategies to address conflicts within themselves, on their teams, and in their organizations down pat. We have not found this to be so. Instead, what we see in our work with leaders at all levels of an organizational hierarchy is the tendency to address conflict (or not address conflict) in the same way many of their followers do. To compound the issue, leaders tend to blame or place accountability for the outcomes of the conflict in other areas.

Not all leaders do this act, as you may be thinking right now. Some leaders rise above the conflict fray, manage problems, attempt to valiantly resolve issues, and try mightily to do everything in their power to move themselves, the team, and the organization forward despite resistance, pullback, push back, ennui, disinterest, and bureaucracy. And yet, even excellent leaders are still stymied by conflict and have been since time out of mind.

Why is this?

Conflicts happen for a variety of reasons, but the biggest reasons tend to be around the perceived inequitable distribution of limited resources, rather than merely over people, time, or the perennial favorite as a conflict driver, money. Conflicts happen not because of people's employment positions, their emotions, or even their differing ideas, although all those areas can be drivers to escalate conflicts past the point where they can be successfully negotiated. Leaders will discover, if they listen closely to the people in conflict, and give subtext as much attention as they tend to grant to context, that many conflicts are driven by stories. Stories that are structured around control, power, merit, competency, emotions, and other elements become the contextual soup leaders find themselves in. Stories followers tell themselves, each other, and the leader lead to systems of beliefs and values that inevitably create the cultures in which conflicts thrive. Just in case leaders believe the presence of no conflict means there is nothing to worry about, Patrick Lencioni writes in his book, *The Five Dysfunctions of a Team: A Leadership Fable*:

> "It is important to distinguish productive ideological conflict from destructive fighting and interpersonal politics. Ideological conflict is limited to concepts and

ideas and avoids personality-focused, mean-spirited attacks. Ironically, teams that avoid ideological conflict often do so to avoid hurting team members' feelings and then end up encouraging dangerous tensions." (Lencioni, 202-203).[1]

Indeed.

The stories leaders hear about conflict are also nonverbally communicated through actions, behaviors, assumptions, choices, preferences, and responses to information and other people's stories participants may not like. Leaders must choose how they will address conflicts on the team, in the organization, in the culture, and even conflicts within themselves. Therefore, self-awareness, empathy, delaying gratification, and more are critical to the success of leaders in conflict within growing relationships, creating alliances, dealing with enemies, and being an effective and intentional ally to friends. This is all no easy feat.

Fortunately, there are many, many good, great, and excellent books on the market today about conflict in difficult conversations (*Difficult Conversations* by Shelia Heen and Doug Stone), how to have conflict conversations (*Crucial Conversations Tools for Talking When Stakes Are High* by Kerry Patterson, Joseph Grenny and Ron McMillan), how to negotiate a conflict (*Never Split the Difference* by Chris Voss and Tahl Vaz), and how to manage even the worst conflicts (*Negotiating the Non-Negotiable* by Daniel Shapiro). There are many, many good, great, and excellent courses, podcasts, videos, lectures, and colleges at the undergraduate, graduate, and doctoral level on how to navigate conflict, parts of the conflict, and even how a leader can deal with conflict effectively. The problem with all those podcasts, books, academic and non-academic courses, videos, lectures, and other tools is that when leaders are in the midst of a conflict, unless they have immediate access to those tools, that advice, and that information at the moment, in the context of a particular conflict moment, they default to their natural, learned behaviors that have been ingrained and practiced long before podcasts and online courses took the world by storm.

The fact is, leaders are people and people forget: they forget their posture and their positions in a conflict. They forget their place in their very carefully crafted scripts. They succumb to the range of emotions inherent in the conflict moment. They fall prey to the tactics and skillsets of amateurs and other dangerous opponents in a conflict and they forget—or put down—the power they had. They rely on their positional authority to bring weight to conflicts where their positional authority, to paraphrase from leadership author Marshal Goldsmith, will not get them where they want to go with the other party, even though it got them to where they are right now. The researcher Hermann Ebbinghaus described the propensity to forget as follows:

> "Ebbinghaus forgetting curve describes the decrease in ability of the brain to retain memory over time. The issue was hypothesized by Hermann Ebbinghaus in 1885, which is why it is called Ebbinghaus forgetting curve. The theory is that humans start losing the memory of learned knowledge over time, in a matter of days or weeks, unless the learned knowledge is consciously reviewed time and again. A related concept to the forgetting curve is strength of memory, which states that the time period up to which a person can recall any memory is based on the strength of the particular memory." [Source: https://www.psychestudy.com/cognitive/memory/ebbinghaus-forgetting-curve].[2]

The presence of ego, the power of emotional context, the trend toward forgetfulness, feelings of entitlement or victimization, resentment, and a lack of accountability all can guide the leader inevitably toward ruin in a conflict scenario. Many leaders instinctively default to the idea that more or clearer communication will somehow be their savior in a conflict scenario. Or, they hold to the false belief that a tactic or "hack" will drain the messy emotions from a conflict scenario and will somehow make the other party reasonable and compliant. Then some leaders believe they will overcome another party's objections by sheer force of will, or through leveraging charisma to avoid problems.

In the short term, those tactics may yield fruit. They may work for the leader to "unstick" the team and to move them toward accomplishing an immediate goal. However, the long-term effects of those tactics, and the unquestioned, unexamined, and unchallenged philosophies, assumptions, and expectations undergirding them, can create team environments where suboptimal outcomes in the long term that appear to create optimal outcomes in the short term, become the norm. This then leads to a death spiral of cultural decline, a lack of team cohesiveness, a constant churn of productive followers and other signs of dysfunction. These outcomes drive the leader crazy and retention of non-productive, dysfunctional followers drives the leader crazier, as do many other outcomes. These outcomes do not have to be immediate and loud. They can be quiet and grow slowly in the dark like fungus, metastasizing below the radar of even the most seemingly competent leader. As the author, educator, researcher, and speaker Dr. Kenneth Cloke points out in his seminal conflict management book, *The Crossroads of Conflict: A Journey into the Heart of Dispute Resolution*:

> "A…rarely identified component [of conflict] consists of the presence of an adversarial, bureaucratic, or highly competitive system, context, culture, or environment—be it psychological, relational, familial, organizational, social, economic, or political. Systems manifest their dysfunction through chronic conflicts that may appear purely personal [emphasis ours] yet emanate from deeply systemic sources (Cloke, p. 22).[3]

It is the role of leaders, and leaders alone, to forge new ways of addressing systemic conflict that appears to be purely interpersonal and of no interest to resolve to the team, so individuals, teams, and cultures can be stewarded well through inevitable changes and disruptions. It is also the role of the leader to determine whether a conflict needs to be resolved, as in ended with no hope of it returning, or managed, meaning constantly revisiting the same topics, problems and triggers with perseverance, empathy, and focus. Because most intractable—or seemingly intractable—conflicts tend toward having a relational element buried within them, we take the position that leaders would be better off managing conflict, rather than searching vaingloriously for a solution to tensions, frictions, and even conflicts that might make the team more productive, more focused, and more effective. But this is where intentionality and self-awareness about their own personal conflict management style acts as the driver of a leader's responses to conflict on the team.

Some Basic Conflict Management Principles

We have found in our work with leaders for many years that there are a few basic principles leaders must adhere to when they attempt to navigate a conflict. These principles then build into philosophical approaches to conflict and tailored strategies for managing conflict, which can then lead to scalable tactics that work over the long course of time. These principles, when laid out in practice and executed with ruthlessness, can assist any leader in accomplishing their conflict management goals on the team.

The following is the list of principles we flesh out during this chapter, with practical explanations illustrating each principle and its application to leadership:

1. Conflict is a process of change.
2. Conflict creates resistance.
3. Conflict scales in the length of time to resolve in direct

proportion to the emotional difficulty of the people, the subject, or the outcome involved in the conflict.

4. Conflict strategies and tactics begin with understanding your own conflict management style and intentionally applying specific methodologies internally first.

5. Conflict requires applying principled negotiation practices to navigate effectively.

These principles, while ordered from number one to five may appear as though they are a checklist; a closer reading reveals they wind up together with each other and they merge. However, multiple tactics and approaches can "spin out" of each one of these principles, which can make a leader's job of managing conflict significantly easier.

In addition to understanding the impact of principles on addressing conflicts, leaders must be sensitive and aware of their own conflict management style and the basic tendencies of people to navigate conflict in a deeply personal way first and then move to the tactical and practical aspects of addressing conflict. Proximity plays a role in that many relationships between team members (unless they are also family members) tend to be second-level relationships; that is, they are relationships where the parties are not intimately related and yet there is a relationship there.

The Principles of Conflict Management: A Breakdown

The first principal leaders need to address and internalize is the idea that conflict is a process of change.

No matter how many ways a leader may decide to fight the assertion, conflict always either results in a change of some kind in the team, the individual, or the organization, or a conflict is embedded inside of a change-based process the leader has some control over. The principle belief about conflict as a process of change opens the leader to two ideas at once that can be combined into one powerful idea that will determine a strategic and tactical posture toward conflict the leader can then leverage for success.

The first part of the idea is that conflict is a process, with rules, standards, and principles it runs by. There is an operating system for conflicts and for navigating them. They are not just "one damn thing after another." Leaders must be sensitive and aware of the ebbs and flows of conflict to make the best of the situation at hand, but also position themselves and their team for success in the most principled manner possible. Great leaders like General George Washington or Mohandis Gandhi understood this principle innately and they used this understanding to commit to tactical acts that, in the short-term looked foolish and even dangerous (i.e. surrendering and retreating repeatedly from key strategic positions or challenging the salt trade in India by the British directly), but that in the long-term accomplished goals and achieved outcomes (i.e. independence from Britain by both America and India) both leaders envisioned initially.

The second part of the idea is that conflict equates to change by generating the same emotional resonance around volatility, uncertainty, complexity, and ambiguity (VUCA)[4] that any change process would normally generate. Multiple transformative moments happen to parties in conflict, whether they are comfortable with those moments happening or not. Resistance to change is a space leaders must negotiate as well and knowing conflict is at the core of that resistance can allow leaders the space to choose different tactics. In science, the Hungarian researcher and physician Ignaz Philipp Semmelweis knew that hand washing would save the lives of thousands of pregnant women and the scientific establishment (the bureaucracy) at the time in the late 19th century categorically rejected his findings because the procedural changes his research would have created in how births were facilitated was too much to handle. Semmelweis was a leader who understood that every time he advocated for his research position, with principle, he was creating a conflict to generate change—and to save lives.

And, as I write this in the fall of 2020, everyone everywhere is sanitizing their hands repeatedly, whether they are pregnant or not.

The second principle leaders need to address and internalize is the idea that conflict creates resistance. We already mentioned the volatility, uncertainty, ambiguity, and complexity that change brings. VUCA was a concept developed by the researchers Warren Bennis and Burton Nanus and furthered fleshed out through the work of the U.S. Army War College. The idea behind VUCA is that leaders must learn from failure and learn from the types of failures that change itself creates. We will explore VUCA more in-depth in another chapter, but suffice it to say, VUCA creates resistance. Resistance, as defined by the American author and ruckus maker, Seth Godin, lies at the intersection between what we would do, what we could do, and what we should do, as people, but do not do. Resistance has both a biological root and a psychological root. The biology of resistance is based on the amygdala. The amygdala is the oldest part of the human brain and it drives all of people's deepest most natural compunctions: to eat, to sleep, to procreate, to breathe, and so on. The amygdala likes safety and security and calm. It dislikes—or becomes active—around disruption and change. Because change is dangerous.

Change—of any kind—disrupts an individual's ability to perform basic survival functions. If this were a fact of mere biology it could be overcome in the 21st century. However, the amygdala is sneaky because it communicates with the higher order functions of the human brain to generate justifications for a lack of action in the moment. The amygdala fools the higher order functions of the brain located in the pre-frontal cortex and the neocortex that come up with dreams, ambitions, aspirations, and visions, into believing all manner of lies, untruths, and outright stories.

And when a conflict is on the horizon, the amygdala is quick to get the information to the higher order functions to avoid, to skirt, or to blow up and engage overwhelmingly in reaction to a conflict. Leaders must be wise to the tricks of the amygdala and the power of resistance in themselves and others to overcome that power.

The Map is not the Territory - Conflict Management Styles

Intentional leadership of parties through conflict requires leaders to have a basic understanding of themselves and a curiosity as to why they do what they do within a conflict context. Unfortunately, many leadership trainings, books, and other types of content skip past this hard part of navigating conflict, because it is neither sexy nor interesting to anyone other than the leader who needs help. Plus, the fact is many leaders lack self-awareness in general about even their own most basic motivations to lead. In addition, they work in dysfunctional, toxic cultures that support "getting the job done," all the time sacrificing people for the process. Then, when advice is sought, it is given in the form of a theory that worked for someone in a different context, with a different personality, leading a different group of people to accomplish different goals. Leadership will call this jockeying for power and hierarchical influence "natural" and, to some degree, they are correct. Human beings and the human experience are oriented toward extracting sense and meaning from chaos. Thus, human beings, to solve this chaos problem that too much competition and choice brings, have created hierarchies. These hierarchies allow people with competency to jostle for all types of influence, from status to control, and inevitably, this jostling will cause friction and friction creates conflict, which leads to either positive optimal outcomes or negative suboptimal outcomes. These systems foster more competition in the pursuit of determining relative merit and negotiating reality toward a manifestation of the absolute good.

In this understanding of the conflict world, it becomes imperative for leaders of all types to examine with a critical eye what their own triggers are that can lead to conflict scenarios and to examine critically the conflict culture of their teams and organizations at scale. The presence of psychological and emotional triggers, combined with contextual circumstances, historically unresolved conflicts, and the presence of a dysfunctional or toxic culture, can lead even the best leaders away from conflict and toward the seductive ease of apathy, accommodation, avoidance, and either false compromise, or fake escalation. Leaders must know themselves if they are to navigate the treacherous waters of conflict with themselves and their teams, but they also must realize the map of their inner triggers and outer reactions to conflict cannot possibly encompass the entire territory of conflict on their teams.

However, a map is helpful as a thumbnail guide to reaching a destination, and the role of conflict responses and behaviors is important to acknowledge. Leaders address conflict in teams and cultures in multiple ways, but the six most common ways are through aggression, collaboration, compromise, surrender, avoidance, or an appeal to a higher authority. These reactions and responses can be mapped and tracked, providing leaders with clarity about how they are engaging, or disengaging, with conflict, the tools to be candid about conflict and its positive and negative effects, and the courage to act when no one else will. From the assessment work performed by researchers at the Leadership Center at Washington State University and the writing of Jay Hall, *Conflict Management Survey: A Survey of One's Characteristic Reaction to and Handling of Conflict Between Himself and Others* (The Woodlands, Texas: Telemetrics International 1969)[5], comes a map of the conflict management styles leaders and others employ.

From the image above[6], we can see the dominant considerations in any conflict focus on negotiating at the intersection of relationships with other people and the pursuit of self-interested, team interested, or organizationally interested goals. The line between these two considerations runs through the heart of every leader and follower, and where a leader chooses to fall on the line determines their conflict management style. Many leaders will reject this framing of the conflict map and will point out that many conflicts that happen daily have no relational element

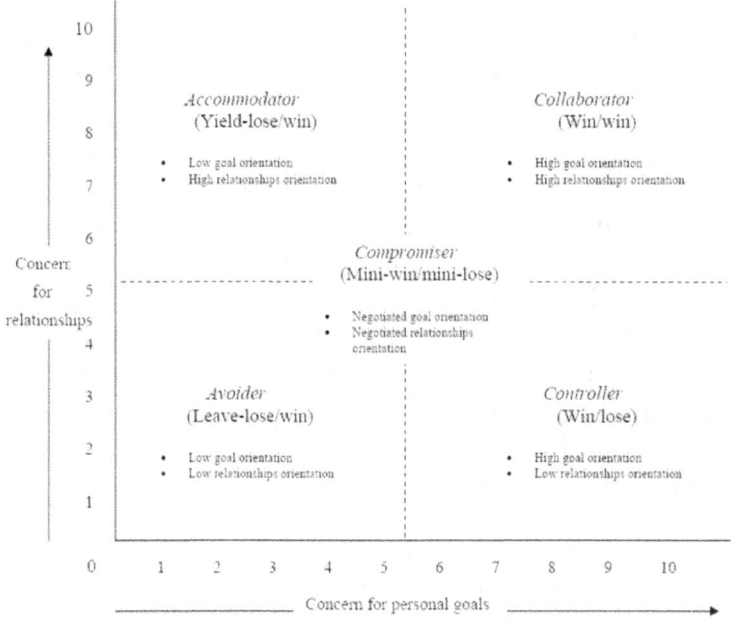

(c) The Leadership Center At Washington State University

to them whatsoever. And they would be correct. Many conflicts that focus on tasks, processes, or systems can be resolved without resorting to fancy tactics or psychological two-stepping. However, the conflicts the map is designed to elucidate are not the easy, task-oriented ones. The map shows where leaders and others fall in their conflict response when the solution to the conflict tension is non-obvious, the problems at hand are complicated and emotionally messy, and the resolution is not easy to find—if indeed there is one in the first place. Let us examine each style and provide some practical tips for navigating the territory the map of styles explains.

Accommodating—In the upper, right-hand quadrant, leaders who adopt an accommodating approach to conflict tend to value cooperation more than assertiveness in a conflict scenario. They want to engage in the process of saving the relationship in exchange for losing the goal. Accommodating can take many forms but usually the element of self-sacrifice, obedience, or just surrendering to the other party in the relationship are characteristics of this approach to managing conflict. When leaders are seeking harmony, stability, and the maintenance of relationships—even toxic and dysfunctional ones—with allies or enemies, accommodation will be the tool used to make that happen. At a practical level, accommodating is a fine approach when a situation, a person in authority or of a higher actual or perceived status, or the overall environment is hostile to a leaders' goals. But be warned—the seductive teddy bear of accommodation can easily slip into powerlessness and give the appearance to others not "in the know" of tacit approval of poor behavior.

Avoiding—In the lower, right-hand quadrant, leaders who adopt an avoiding approach to conflict tend to value diplomacy, sidestepping problems, and "tip-toeing through the tulips" of conflict. Leaders in the avoiding space tend to understand deeply the effects and influences of conflict outcomes, but may feel powerless to do anything about them. Leaders who are not avoiding but will do so as a tactical act tend to imitate passive behavior and appear to give up on accomplishing personal goals, as well as give up on the maintenance of the relationship with the other party. At a practical level, avoiding is an appropriate approach if the stakes of a problem are not high or the problem at hand is trivial. When there is little chance of changing another party, situation, or process, avoiding is critical for surviving long enough in a leadership position to act when the time comes. Finally, leaders know that disruption is not always an overall good, and thus avoiding can delay disruption, but only for a season.

Collaborating—In the upper, left-hand quadrant, leaders who adopt a collaborative approach to conflicts are adopting the "gold standard" in managing team conflict. Leaders who manage conflict with a collaborative approach want to have it all: a great relationship and goal accomplishment at the same time. They do this by digging into issues, exploring disagreements deeply, and confronting problems before they even become problems. When leaders are seeking to be creative and compelling in a conflict scenario, they will pursue a collaborating approach. However, leaders, followers, and others may grow impatient with a leader adopting a collaborative approach primarily because of the time issue, but also because many times, collaborating is employed as a ruse while other actions are deployed. At a practical level, collaborating is a fine approach when time is not of the essence, when peer-to-peer conflict is at the heart of the problem, or when consensus building is the point of the conflict in the first place.

Compromising—In the middle quadrant, leaders who adopt a compromising approach to managing conflict genuinely see both sides of the conflict and seek mutual grounds for all parties involved to resolve the problem. Leaders in the compromising space do seek expediency through exchanging concessions, splitting the difference (which certain conflict management advocates and writers recommend leaders not do), and seeking middle-ground positions. The drawback to compromising is that when seeking the middle-ground, sometimes there is no middle ground position or outcome to pursue. The resolution to certain problems is black and white. And many times, leaders misunderstand and mis analyze the opportunity for an ideal outcome and become trapped in an endless cycle of playing rhetorical, emotional, and psychological games with another party. At a practical level, compromise is often either ignored as being a naive approach to addressing conflict, or it is overweighted as the only way forward out of a conflict scenario. Both extremes are incorrect. Compromise works best for leaders when the problems are complex, time is not of the essence, when positional status between participants and resources are relatively equal, and when the goals are clear.

Competing and Controlling—In the lower, left-hand quadrant, leaders who engage in competing and controlling conflict tend to be viewed as either strong leaders through conflict, or as insensitive bullies. Because other people's feelings, the context of the situation, and even the nature of the relationships between the people in conflict take a back seat, leaders who deploy a competing and controlling mode in a conflict scenario very often are forced into a power, or status, oriented mode of resolution. Polarizing and seen as disagreeable, leaders who adopt this mode may cut a wide swath through the organizational culture, be perceived as dominant and domineering, and may have their conflict mode confused with competency. Competing controlling leaders make quick decisions to "resolve" conflicts, not realizing they have destroyed relationships and trust in the process. At a practical level, there are times when a decision must be rendered, a consequence accepted, and a team, organization, or culture dislodged from where it has been stuck in conflict. When leaders want to implement an unpopular decision, anticipate aggressive behavior from another party, or when there is a crisis, competing and controlling take center stage.

With the modes explained and the map illuminated, there are a few other considerations for leaders to keep in mind when approaching conflict: knowing what your default conflict approach is on a conflict-to-conflict basis can help leaders determine how to best break or build new conflict management habits so they can adapt when the territory shifts. The ability to shift from a default reaction or response to conflict requires deep intentionality, the skill set of silencing the internal voice of disruption and argumentation leaders sometimes have, and practice. Leaders who practice shifting from their default mode to another mode and back again welcome the comfort and control such a shift provides, and they grow in self-awareness so they are not surprised when a new challenge arises. They lead their people to engage in the same shifting behavior and coach them explicitly by providing feedback about how to resolve and manage conflicts more effectively and intentionally while doing it with clarity, candor, and courage.

The Three C's Methodology—A Redux

When leaders understand themselves and their personal approaches to conflicts, they can understand and listen closer to their followers, their team, and to other stakeholders in the structure of an organization. However, this does not mean they are ready to tackle conflict immediately. There are several areas leaders need to intentionally focus on to achieve the outcome they want from conflict while ensuring the parties involved also manage to keep working on the task at hand. From active listening to stopping the internal psychological resistance and objections to considering the rhetorical value of external viewpoints, leaders must realize that successfully managing conflict in organizations begins internally in the leader and works its way outward, rather than starting externally and moving to change parties from the outside. By acknowledging this, applying the Three C's Methodology becomes useful because it forms a practical communication foundation for leaders engaging with parties in a conflict.

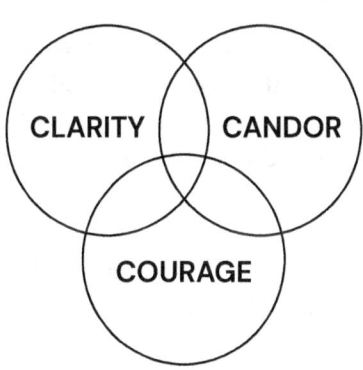

As we looked at in Chapter One, Leadership Roles and Responsibilities, the Three C's Methodology leverages the pillars of clarity, candor, and courage to move leaders to a powerful understanding and appreciation of the value of communication as a type of connection when leading people in general. In the specific realm of managing conflict, the Three C's can guide leaders toward a deeper understanding of themselves and others in conflict if it is practically and intentionally applied in the following fashion:

Clarity—In general, leaders need to be strategically clear in their minds, their speech, and their actions to be successful in any leadership pursuit. In the specific realm of managing conflict, this goes double. When managing conflict, clarity of thought includes actively listening, not only to what the other party is asserting as their position, but also parsing internal voices—also termed "white noise"—that may distract the leader from focusing on what the other party is saying. This "white noise" acts as a form of amygdala driven resistance at a psychological level and creates a mentality of defensiveness, a loss of focus, and confuses both the context of the conflict as well as the subtext of the conflict for the leader. At a practical level, leaders need to clear their minds through a habitual mindfulness practice such as meditation, personal journaling, or prayer to attain clarity before, during, and after addressing a conflict with other people.

Candor—In general, leaders need to be candid with followers after being clear with them. Being candid means leveraging hard-headed empathy with a focus on targeted intentionality to build bridges and cross divides even in non-conflict scenarios. In a conflict, being candid with parties means telling the truth after diagnosing the motivations of the parties in the conflict as accurately as possible. Leaders may consider the idea of being candid in a conflict to be the most dangerous of the Three C's and they would be correct. However, candor is the linchpin that links clarity to courage. Without candor, leaders cannot even hope to plan to manage a conflict successfully, much less bring it to any sort of resolution. At a practical level, leaders need to work to prepare themselves emotionally and psychologically for the perception in the other party in conflict that their candor is hurtful, demeaning, noncontextualized, or just a "non-starter" in the face of the context they, as the other party, are focused on. They also must stay focused and determined in the face of withering emotionally driven feedback delivering a candid message to another party about their behavior or speech, invariably will produce.

Courage—In general, leaders need to be courageous to face conflict in the first place, particularly if their conflict management baseline style leans more toward avoidance or accommodation. Even if the leaders' style leans toward confrontation and collaboration—or toward the quick decision making that competing controlling is known for—there must be awareness on the part of leaders about the level of courage required to act. For leaders, taking action to address a conflict while also clearly assessing the conflict environment is at the core of courage. Without courage linked by candor to clarity, leaders cannot hope to make more than superficial and temporary changes to their own conflict approaches and will experience deep disappointment in other parties when conflict does arrive; as it always will. At a practical level, leaders need to have their "ducks in a row" before jumping into a conflict, and they also need to have the courage to recognize when they have avoided, accommodated, or confronted poorly in the past, take accountability for the consequences of past actions, and bravely lead through the conflict toward change.

The prime reason leaders do not address conflict on their teams is they do not have a strong understanding of the Three C's, or they ignore their influence and potential willfully. However, if leaders want to be successful in resolving and managing conflict, rather than be stuck maintaining the political status quo until an external crisis appears, then they must exercise the Three C's intentionally and thoughtfully. Without intentionality at every level, there is no success at all in managing conflict, much less addressing resolution. This results in a spirit of indefinite optimism reigning in a dysfunctional team and organizational culture. As the venture capitalist and author, Peter Thiel points out in his book *Zero to One, Or Notes for Start-Ups and How to Build the Future*, "To an indefinite optimist, the future will be better, but he does not know how exactly, so he will not make any specific plans. He expects to profit from the future but sees no reason to design it concretely."[7] This lack of planning, or design, combined with willful or accidental blindness can cause leaders to fail spectacularly when conflict—which fundamentally begins and underlies the process of change—appears on their teams and in their cultures, usually around specific narrow issues and then spreading quickly to other, dormant challenges. This phenomenon occurs everywhere, from families to societies and cultures. The essence of leadership in conflict and crisis requires intentionally planning and addressing the dragon of conflict before the fires burn down progress, impede growth, and stymie the development of competency and merit in organizations and cultures.

Practical Tips for Managing Conflict as a Leader

Arguments, disputes, disagreements, and differences of opinion are the cornerstone of any leadership journey. Without a doubt, conflict rears its ugly head more and more often on teams as the dynamics of the workplace shift, and as workplaces become more decentralized, less homogeneous, and more egalitarian in even their physical design and conception. Any discussion of the "future of work" must include considerations of the future of how people will get along (or not) at work and the steps leaders can take to ensure workplace efficiency and productivity continue to rise, even as the number of actual humans involved in disputes and conflicts continues to fall.

The dynamics created by having smaller, more diverse teams, with sharper hierarchies, or no hierarchies at all, have not been thoroughly examined, and this is a shame. It is almost as if the assumptions with which the "smart" people are approaching the presence of conflict in the future at work are almost utopian in nature. Leaders do not have the luxury of engaging with such assumptions; for when conflict comes, as it most surely will, utopia usually does not come with it. This is where leaders must understand some basic principles for navigating conflict on workplace teams, but in general, everywhere else in their leadership lives.

Tip # 1 - Do not be shocked, surprised, or stunned by the presence of arguments, disputes, disagreements, and differences of opinion between people on your team. In fact, be shocked when equanimity and peace seem to reign. That can be a sign of trouble. As Patrick Lencioni points out in *The Five Dysfunctions of a Team: A Leadership Fable*,"...conflict is considered taboo in many situations, especially at work. And the higher you go up the management chain, the more you find people spending inordinate amounts of time and energy trying to avoid the kind of passionate debates that are essential to great teams (p. 202)."[8] This is not to say that leaders should encourage conflict, in particular leaders should be incredibly sensitive to destructive interpersonal conflict and watch out for conflict over ideas that can descend into conflict over people. If a leader is surprised by conflict because "everything seemed to be going so well" that leader hasn't been paying attention to the temperature and climate of the team for a while.

Tip #2 - Be prepared to address conflicts at the lowest possible level first. Escalation of destructive interpersonal conflict, to either you as a leader, to a leader above you, or horizontally to the rest of the team, is a sign that lower-level leaders have not been adequately prepared with tools to manage and, occasionally resolve, conflict, and that there are issues with trust and relationships on the team. Leaders should prepare other leaders through a combination of training and coaching to address conflict at the lowest possible level first. This requires that leaders empower others; which also means, leaders must give away the power to micro-manage out of a sense of mistrust or misplaced trust. This is a tough line to walk and the best leaders understand there are conflicts they must address at a higher level and there are conflicts lower subordinates can address at a lower level. However, the intent of the leader must be communicated, unambiguously, and repeatedly, while also maintaining consistency and fairness in meting out consequences based on leadership authority.

Tip #3 - Know your own conflict style and that of your team. Teams and individuals have their own conflict styles and approach. Individuals will associate outcomes from conflicts with their overall identity. Teams will associate the outcomes of conflicts with their overall approach to accomplishing a goal or getting a task completed. If leaders personally are oriented toward accommodation, they may struggle with the need for effective confrontation, which is required to make things change on a team. If leaders are oriented toward competing and controlling, confrontation may become a space of ego-driven aggressiveness and punishment of recalcitrant subordinates. If leaders aren't aware of their own conflict style—and aren't humble enough to own it and act around it for the benefit of the team overall—the story of conflict will become a story of leadership failure, marred by miscommunication, mistrust, micro-management, and psychological exhaustion.

Tip #4 - Get your thinking clear as a leader. If you are not thinking clearly, you are not speaking or writing clearly. This opens the door on the team to ambiguity and miscommunication and confusion. Team leaders—and leaders overall—try to get as clear in their heads about what to accomplish and why, and when there is conflict, they are prepared to actively listen, consider other possibilities, and put their egos in the right spots. The leaders who do that become effective; the leaders who do not, muddle through and may have a few successes based on repeatable processes, established sclerotic systems, or highly competent followers, but they will not be great leaders. Adding a daily habit of writing and journaling helps with clear thinking, as does competent coaching, and even long-term mentoring relationships. Leaders need to establish clearly defined habits and strong interpersonal relationships with others to navigate confrontation—and the emotions conflict sometimes brings—as well.

Tip #5 - Communicate persuasively, listen actively, and be candid with yourself about your ego. When leaders communicate persuasively and work on developing the relationship patterns inherent to well-developed emotional intelligence, they do better at the practical, tactical elements of negotiation, arbitration, and even mediation. Reflecting, reframing, active listening, patience, looking for non-obvious and counterintuitive answers, behavioral mapping, as well as genuine curiosity and care about other people and how they are performing lead leaders to success in many areas. The last area, ego, is the hardest for leaders to manage and overcome and will rear its ugly head when we address dealing with difficult people, team building, accountability, motivation, and feedback. Success in these areas lies in a leader harnessing and directing her ego rather than letting the ego harness and direct her. But just as with everything else for a leader, it all begins with herself.

There are a multitude of books, guides, websites, courses, podcasts, and YouTube videos online, and in-person courses and seminars that can teach a leader the tactical, day-to-day strategic tools needed to navigate conflict effectively. Any training that involves case studies and role playing with a higher level of interactivity will be more beneficial to a new or experienced leader than just passive content consumption. Coaching must be added to any training or knowledge gathering effort because coaching closes the gap between hearing and doing. It also creates a neutral relationship that allows for feedback to a leader around best practices. At HSCT Publishing, we believe our trainings, books (like this one), and guides are the best on the market to teach leaders how to incorporate conflict management and resolution into their overall leadership practice. However, there are many other good ones out there in the market that are focused on developing industry-specific competencies and can provide a leader with answers to specific team-based questions and concerns. Leaders should seek to refresh their skillsets in conflict management with competent skilled facilitators and coaches every year to stay sharp and to continue to grow on their leadership journey.

CHAPTER FIVE

Rule 5
Leaders Cannot Always Build a Maserati Out of Toyota Parts
Leadership and Teambuilding

"Leadership requires pulling people along where they may not want to go. Leadership requires challenging people when they do not want to be challenged. Leadership requires engaging with people in ways that will make them uncomfortable."
Jesan Sorrells

This chapter focuses on helping leaders understand that team building is more than throwing people together and hoping they become task-oriented, collaborative, and cooperative. It also addresses the importance of rituals, standards, practices, and expectations as the "glue" that binds groups together so they can accomplish the act of being on a team. The chapter lays out a compelling case, which demonstrates that, without many of the previous aspects of leadership, the environment for psychological safety can never produce any viable fruit.

Introduction: Every Leader Wants a Sports Car That Costs as Much as a Sedan

Professional jealousy, organizational envy, and industry covetousness blind many leaders in their team-building efforts, and invariably lie at the heart of many team-building failures leaders continually experience. Leaders want the "sports car" of a high performing team that gains an award in their industry—or even outside of their industry—but they do not want to put in the work to build their own "sports car." Or, even worse, they seek to apply the principles of a high-performance vehicle to the reality of a "sedan." These failures come about because leadership in many organizations, and leaders, generalize—external to lived context—from the individual examples of leadership success in team-building they read about to the particulars of their own situation. In other words, they seek to shove a square peg into a round hole.

And let us be even more honest, many leaders, when confronted with the task of rebuilding a team broken by mistrust, communication dysfunction, false conflict (which can look and feel real but is merely a convenient distraction from the hard work of confronting and eliminating bad behavior on the team), lack of accountability, and little to no results, shrink at the prospect of such a rebuild effort. This is because it takes time, effort, and a good dose of the apocryphal "blood, sweat, and tears" to rebuild a wrecked sedan, much less transform it into a sports car the organizational hierarchy and shareholders may lust after, but may not want to get their hands dirty in making.

There is only one Jack Welch, or IBM, per industry.

The other factor that creates conditions of difficulty for leaders when building a team is two factors that link together inexorably: diversity and difficult people. There is no doubt a diversity of individuals on a team creates a diversity of opinions, perspectives, and approaches to performance, results, goals, and accountability. It's not only diversity of country of origin, race, creed, or culture, but also diversity of mindset, which can create the environment where people are not compliant or obedient, and many times, cannot be coerced or convinced to become so. It is clear from a wealth of research that collaboration and trust are the two factors that combine to ensure high performance among a collection of individuals. However, there is a little remarked upon transition that has happened in the global culture, driven partially by the rise of democratic societies in the formerly totalitarian parts of the world, and the rise of access to information, data, and entertainment in the parts of the world that have long since historically adopted democratic norms, however imperfectly. And this transition can best be summed up in an analogy to games, specifically the sports of American football and American baseball.

Until the 1960s and the rise of television culture, football was considered a hooligans' game, closer in philosophy—if not practice—to its violent cousin rugby, or even Australian rules football. This collision sport, played at the highest level, relies invariably upon each member of the team subsuming themselves to the whole to win the game, win the championship, or win the day. Hockey and other team sports rely on the same ethic. However, baseball, a sport attend to by many Americans from the 1920s through to the 1960s when it began its long and ignoble decline (partially driven by the fact baseball does not translate well to the television medium and works better on radio where the mind can image what the eye cannot see) is a sport where individuals can do well, but the team can lose. Or individuals can have poor athletic showings, and the team can still manage to pull out a win.

This transition, from a culture of individuals whose performance and success are predicated on their own talents and skills showing up despite how the team performs, to a culture of individuals motivated to make sure the team performs behind the leadership of one individual, goes mostly unremarked upon in America, and it's very un-remarkableness means leadership culture in America, and increasingly globally, is less focused on the individual and more focused on the team.

And leaders know. From the questions asked during the interview process for a job ("Are you a 'team player'?") to the reasons for firing an individual ("He was not a 'team player' or a 'culture fit' so he had to go") leaders, cultures, and organizations are focused more on the "why" than the "what" of building a team, and are missing several key factors that, if paid attention to more attentively, might result in the type of high performing sports car all leaders desire.

Or, at least, a better performing sedan.

Do We Even Know What We Want? –The Qualities of a Team Player

Every leader "knows" what they want as a team player, and what they want on a high-performance team. However, very few leaders can articulate in meaningful ways the practical traits they seek in their followers. Defining these traits requires leaders to be clear (clarity) about what they want, and then to have the ability to ask for what they want in others (courage) and to be clear with followers when they are not getting that which they seek (candor). Getting a team to respond and grow requires knowing the psychology of following (See Chapter One, Leadership Roles and Responsibilities) and knowing how far to push individuals past their own comfort zones. Each area, or quality, of a team player is hard to quantify in terms of financial outcomes; however, there are leadership studies (some of which are academic, some of which are commercial) that reveal the following tidbit:

> "In a presentation at the 2020 SHRM Talent Conference, Susan Collins, Director of Talent Acquisition and Employer Branding at Talbots, shared that 97 percent of employers surveyed reported that soft skills were either as important as, or more important than hard skills in their organizations. It is also important to note that 46 percent of new employees fail within 18 months, mostly due to a lack of soft skills such as professionalism, or ability to get along with others. In another study by Boston University, Harvard University, and the Ross School of Business at the University of Michigan revealed that training in self-awareness and soft skills, like interpersonal communication and problem-solving, produces a 256 percent return on investment, based on an average

rate of 12 percent higher team productivity and retention." [Source: https://crestcom.com/blog/2020/07/07/soft-skills-development/].[1]

And on high performing teams, the high level of tolerance of ambiguity, appreciation of differences, resiliency, self-awareness by individuals, goal orientation, independence and interdependence,

Responsibility and Accountability	Makes appropriate decisions regarding one's own behavior Recognizes and accepts consequences of actions Meets agreed upon expectations Follows through on commitments Willing to accept responsibility for personal errors Takes responsibility for one's own learning
Independence and Interdependence	Appropriately determines when to act alone and when to work or consult with others Demonstrates ability to initiate action and effectively engage others to enhance outcomes Works with minimum supervision whether it be alone or within a group Adapts behavior as appropriate in response to team or organization needs
Goal Orientation	Manages energy and behavior to accomplish specific outcomes Possesses and maintains sufficient motivation to achieve goals Has an understanding of how to use their talents and skills to contribute to the betterment of society Demonstrates effective planning and purposeful behavior Does not allow distractions to prevent timely completion of tasks Pushes self, when needed, to accomplish goals

Self-Awareness	Maintains and projects an optimistic perspective Expects the best from self and others Accurately assesses and articulates (when appropriate) personal strengths and weaknesses Shows interest in learning about others and their accomplishments Demonstrates ability to help others adapt to new situations
Resilience	Able to recover from disappointment or bad experience and continue to work successfully Able to learn from a bad experience and recover Able to work through disappointments (i.e., what caused them, what can be done to avoid them next time, and what can be done to repair them now)
Appreciation of Differences	Works effectively with others, despite differences; can respectfully discuss differences with others Recognizes advantages of moving outside existing "comfort zone" Seeks out others with different backgrounds and/or perspectives to improve decision making Appreciates the importance of diversity and conveys this value to others Understands and respects the values and beliefs of others
Tolerance of Ambiguity	Demonstrates intellectual and emotional ability to perform in complicated environments and the absence of standard operating procedures Can work under conditions of uncertainty [2]

and responsibility and accountability, is so pronounced that it lies under the surface of the interactions between individuals. It lies at such a high level that the diseases that plague lower-performing teams, regardless of the level of talent, transmute into other issues in other areas. The other place where these immutable skills appear is in the classic Bruce Tuckman theory of team formation; that is: forming, storming, norming, performing, and adjourning.

Developed during the pioneering days of organizational development, Tuckman and researcher Bruce Jensen, developed a theory that his student, Connie Gersick would later reject in favor of the Punctuated Equilibrium Model of team development. And while our writing here is more concerned with practicality than theory, it would be instructive to note that Tuckman's theory of team development has been adopted so deeply into the cultural language of organizational behavior that leaders seldom discuss it. And when the soft skills in the figure above are laid atop the team development structure, a leader begins to understand that a high-performing team can either be guided through stages, pushed through stages, or allowed to grow through the stages of team development.

Forming—This is the stage where individuals come together to form a team. If leaders aren't careful, the seeds of future issues and dysfunction are often planed here at this stage. At this stage, the risk of conflict is high, as is the tension around vulnerability. This stage can be compared to going on a first date with a prospective partner—everyone is on their best behavior, highly conscious of what is occurring in the environment, and ready to leap toward commitment—or away from commitment—as quickly as possible. This is a stage that takes teams a minimum of six to nine months to traverse, though it may take longer on teams where individual mistrust is high, where the orientation toward tasks over relationships is high, and where organizational culture favors speed to a solution over deeper connections among people first.

Storming—This is the stage where trust building begins. It is at this point the areas of concern around dysfunctional behaviors come into play. The writer Patrick Lencioni writes in his book *The Five Dysfunctions of a Team: A Leadership Fable*, about the five dysfunctions "truly cohesive teams trust one another, engage in conflict around ideas, commit to decisions and plans of action, hold each other accountable for delivering results, and focus on the achievement of collective results."[3] At the storming stage the opposite of those positive traits can develop on the team. In addition, "...participants form opinions about the character and integrity of the other participants and feel compelled to voice these opinions if they find someone shirking responsibility or attempting to dominate. Sometimes participants question the actions or decision of the leader as the expedition grows harder..." [Source: *Leadership the Outward Bound Way: Becoming a Better Leader in the Workplace* by Outward Bound USA, Rob Chatfield].[4] Indeed, leaders who are not paying attention at the storming stage will often find that conflict becomes the norm, hierarchical juggling for power (real and imagined) becomes the behavior of the day, and the qualities of being a team player take on a darker hue.

Norming—This is the stage where the phrase "We've always done it this way," begins to rule. At the norming stage, any dysfunctions not resolved in the storming stage are considered "normal," and it is at this stage the deeper elements of culture begin to appear from beneath the soil of the team. This is also the stage where, if conflicts haven't been resolved from the Storming stage, they become part of the "ditch" or "dip" of dysfunction on the team. When an outsider or a new person enters the team environment and begins to question the team culture, they are typically rejected at the Norming is the stage. Or, their advice is greeted with skepticism by team members about changing behaviors and dysfunctions based on the norms of their already formed culture. It is also at this stage that rituals, standards, practices, and habits of team members at an individual and group level become areas the team—and the leader of the team—no longer comment on or, if they are negative, may feel powerless to change.

Performing—This is the stage where competency, normalcy in the context of the team culture, and decision-making become the key elements driving success in the teams. At the performing stage, acknowledgment of cultural norms, respect for the hierarchy, and the nature of competency in decision-making in the context of the team culture matter significantly for individual and overall team success and accomplishing goals. In Tuckman's theory, performing has its own distinct stage in team development. However, where leaders live and lead, performing is demanded from team members at all stages of team development. An acknowledgment of this fact is critical to understand in terms of culture, conflict, dysfunction, the establishment of norms and culture, and competency in decision-making.

Adjourning—This is the stage, later added through the work of researcher Bruce Jensen, that describes the ways in which people separate from each other on the team. At the adjourning stage, team members may experience what psychological researchers and therapists call "felt separation." The ability for team members to separate well may be a necessary element in maintaining their professional focus and vitality. This phase in the teambuilding cycle is often ignored by leaders on the team and in organizations in general, and how it is usually handled sometimes involves ceremonies and rituals, but very often is ignored, resulting in potentially deleterious psychological effects. This adjourning stage not being dealt with well can also result in team members "hopping" from position to position, or from job to job, with no sense of loss or attachment.

For many team leaders, the Tuckman-Jensen Model of team development will resonate deeply. However, Connie Gersick's model of team development—Punctuated Equilibrium—is also instructive for those leaders who are seeking to practically align their leadership focus with the team overall. The Punctuated Equilibrium Model is based on the Darwinian concept of evolutionary growth, and the work of paleontologists Niles Eldredge and Stephen Jay Gould, who both believed evolution occurred in rapid, radical spurts rather than gradually over time. Gersick applied this thinking to teams: groups of people who are brought together by a leader, they are given a task, nothing happens for a long time, the leader motivates—or "gooses"—the group to action (an external stressor appears to motivate action), there is a burst of evolutionary energy that moves the group task forward, and then the group returns to stasis until another external stressor appears and the process completes itself yet again. Gersick postulated that time and task performance mattered more to team development across time and to the leaders' understanding of team development, than a focus on managing the team through a series of discrete, closed, steps via a finite process.

Both Gersick and Tuckman-Jensen have many overlaps in their thinking and approach to group development—and there are other elements that can improve—or detract—from successful team building, such as group cohesion, groupthink, social loafing, and the nature of roles (formal and informal) that the intentional leader must consider. But this is not an organizational behavior text and our desire to be practical and intentional in discovering how teams form is instructive only in that it informs how leaders search out and find the type of people who will engage overall with team culture to create a high performing team. To build a race car that works, understanding the theory of thermodynamics is fine, but it is more important to know what you want the car to do and why. So, here are some practical suggestions for building a high-performance team:

Establish team trust early by clearly articulating a team goal and a team vision—Trust takes a long time to build and moments to lose. Psychological safety (See Chapter Eight on Diversity) is a key factor in building trust, but so is role modeling, setting expectations, and following through on consequences for poor or misaligned behavior. There are four steps to building trust to create a high-performing team from day one:

- Incorporate the definition of trust into actions: "…the confidence among team members that their peers' intentions are good, and that there is no reason to be protective or careful around the group" (Lencioni, p.195).
- Role model vulnerability by talking honestly about the past, avoiding blame, and planning for the future.
- Be open to feedback you may not like to hear as a leader from your team about your performance. Read Ray Dalio's *Principles: Life and Work*, for more details on how to set up robust feedback systems.

Establish a foundation of psychological safety, based on articulated expectations, meaningful consequences, clarity, candor, and courage when times are tough.

Encourage growth throughout all the stages of tasks (Tuckman-Jensen) along with time and stress (Gersick) and stay focused on accomplishing the overall goal—High-performing teams are clearly solution-oriented and have a focus on accomplishing small goals. However, the leaders of high-performing teams must balance that small focus at the local level with clearly articulating a large, compelling, purpose and vision for the team. There are four steps to creating a high-performing team with a "small target" focus from day one:

- Repeatedly articulate a compelling vision and purpose for the team.
- Be clear about which goals are small, which goals are medium-sized, and which goals are large and "scary"—but also exciting.

- Keep the team focused on accomplishing small goals on a day-to-day basis and take the time to refocus the team on larger goals consistently.
- Consensus and certainty are great but are not necessary to accomplish goals.

Embed accountability into every level of the team formation process, and Do What You Say You Will Do; that is, no matter how talented an individual performer is, they are not higher than the overall team—High performing teams have a "no ego" rule that is typically unspoken, and while individuals do have outsized talents and outsized egos sometimes, they know when to put those away for the good of accomplishing team goals (independence and interdependence). Responsibility, accountability, ownership, autonomy, mastery, and purpose (See Chapter Nine on Leadership and Accountability for more on these areas), all link together on a high-performing team, where team members know what the goal is, understand the expectations of them, are highly trained and internally motivated by doing the work required of them, and know they can continue to improve at the work they are performing and see the results of that growth every day. There are five steps to embedding accountability to create a high-performing team from day one:

- Clearly define results for individuals first, the team second, and the organization last.
- Acknowledge that conflict is healthy and appropriate for reaching a solution to a non-obvious problem.
- Encourage team members in their autonomy to make decisions, but also to accept consequences.
- Ownership is an emotional act. If people do not feel "bought in," they will not be "bought in." Coach team members to buy into results but make it clear the team is moving forward.

Of course, without trust, as Patrick Lencioni notes in his book, *The Five Dysfunctions of a Team: A Leadership Fable*, not even a low performing team can leap over the bar of even the most moderately difficult task[5], which then lays the foundation for the linchpin of the team: the qualities of a team leader.

Qualities of A Team Leader

As we know, trust takes a long time to build and moments to lose. Any leader engaging in the process of building a high-performance team must have, at the baseline, a beginning grasp of the power of a leader's role and the basic responsibilities of leadership as we explored in Chapter One. Leaders must also have a grasp of self-awareness (emotional intelligence), humility (lack of ego), courage (the Three C's methodology), persuasion, and the strength to take on the weight of accountability when their followers cannot or will not. And to build a team that is high performing and allows individuals to come together in the full openness of all their own talents and skills, leaders must have two other qualities, not often acknowledged, or deeply addressed: knowing when, how, and why to say "no" and sticking to that answer, and knowing when to refrain from speaking and acting.

Psychological safety is a key factor in building trust, but so is role modeling, setting expectations, and following through on consequences for poor or misaligned behavior. And, at a practical and intentional level, leaders are responsible for establishing psychologically safe environments on their teams, contextualized to the work, the organizational culture, and the team members

Self-awareness	Understanding and acknowledging personal limitations
	Being open to feedback and actively changing because of it
	Engaging actively in critical self-reflection practices (i.e., journaling, meditation, prayer, etc.)

Humility	Willing to step back out of the limelight Understanding what the actual "work" of leadership is, versus what the "work" appears to be in the public eye Knowing when to disconnect from small outcomes to focus on large vision
Courage	Understanding when to step forward to take on accountability Being able to have "hard" conversations about performance Thinking, speaking, and writing with clarity
Persuasion	Knowing the rules and methods of persuasion and knowing which methods to use in what context Understanding that persuasion is an act of growth and communication, not manipulation Demonstrating patience without wavering in focus
Personal Strength	Grasping the difference between the leader "doing" and the team "doing" Having a strongly established locus of control external to the team's performance, situational outcomes, or organizational political pressure Being able to act without seeking permission
The "No" Factor	Being able to say "no" and mean it. Understanding that "no" is not a tool for every leadership situation. Being able and willing to contextualize with clarity, candidly, and courageously a "no" to anyone in the hierarchical structure.
Willingness to be Unlikeable	Knowing the power of being effective over the perceived importance of being liked Being vulnerable in the appropriate context and at the appropriate time Able to empower others to do "hard" tasks, and being able to support them

hired to do the work. From the work of Harvard researcher and author, Amy Edmondson, "Psychological safety [describes] an environment in which people believe that they can speak up candidly with ideas, questions, concerns, and even mistakes. Extensive academic literature on psychological safety has demonstrated its powerful association with learning and performance in teams and organizations." [Source: https://www.psychologytoday.com/us/blog/the-fearless-organization/202006/the-role-psychological-safety-in-diversity-and-inclusion].[6] Leaders must consider that there may be high levels of psychological safety on teams of people volunteering to perform a task and low levels of psychological safety on teams of people being paid to perform a task, because of the presence, or absence of emotional context. Leaders know psychological safety must be contextualized to the group setting and the dynamics of the group and the leader must be as deeply in tune with those dynamics as they can be from day one. There are four steps to building trust to create a high-performing team from day one:

- Establish trust "…the confidence among team members that their peers' intentions are good, and that there is no reason to be protective or careful around the group"[7] as part of the culture early by engaging in practical delegation of small tasks from you as the leader to followers before worrying about competency levels
- Engage openly in learning conversations as a group and avoid blaming or shaming
- Address issues, problems, and concerns immediately and follow up with individuals and the team consistently
- Keep the team focused on accomplishing near-term, mid-term, and long-term goals and maintain clarity on the distinctions between those goals

"All We Talk About is Culture, Culture, Culture…"

The reality of the importance of environment and team culture cannot be underestimated when leaders are thinking about how to align their teams intentionally and successfully with high-performance. Expectations, both verbalized and those provided via contextual clues, signals from the organization's support mechanism, and goals that are aligned to reality, all contribute to the development of an attitude of high-performance that transmutes into an expectation of high-performance, which creates a feedback loop that establishes a mindset of success—despite—not because of the current environment. For example, on high-performing college and university sports teams, the players, the coaches, the college administration and even the fans all have the same mindset towards success. On high-performing college and university sports teams, the coaches and the players co-create systems of expectations and aligned mindsets that allow them to cultivate a high-performance team environment and culture. The coaches and players are practical and intentional about this process from day one, player one, practice one all the way to the last day, the last player, and the last practice of the season.

These teams serve as an example of what high-performance "looks like" but they also demonstrate how leaders can work intentionally to build the types of high-performing teams they want to build that will work repeatedly and consistently over time.

Arguably, there is an assumption that underlies the development of a culture of a high-performing team, and that is an assumption of a level of talent, merit, and competency at accomplishing a task. If the organizational or team culture historically has failed to function at a high level, leaders must "reset" the team. If the organizational or team culture is not clear in defining what outcomes they desire from recruited talent before, during, and after the moment of recruitment, leaders must "reset" the team. If the organizational or team culture is focused on winning competitions and playing games that have nothing to do with the stated outcomes and that serve to distort, or change, the culture of a team, leaders must advocate for changes to that part of the culture while also advocating for building a different and better team. If the assumptions of team alignment, addressable failure, advocacy for systemic change, and the autonomy to build a functioning team structure are not in evidence, leaders have a responsibility to be clear about what their emotional, psychological, and even spiritual limitations are around building a better culture while also building a better team.

Here is where the steps to grow accountability on the team should be addressed more intentionally:

- Clearly define and communicate desired results of performance to individuals first, the team second, and the organization last. And understand this communication will be repeated until it "sticks" because of the tendency of humans to forget based on the Ebbinghaus Rule.
- Acknowledge that conflict is healthy and appropriate to guide a team toward a non-obvious solution to a problem. And understand this acknowledgment will not always be appreciated by team members who may view conflicts as something to be avoided, or quickly resolved. (See Chapter Three, Leadership and Conflict Management.)
- Encourage team members in their autonomy to make decisions, but also to accept consequences of those decisions. And understand this autonomy will result in decision making and reward flowing to followers while consequences and accountability flow to the leader of the team.
- Ownership is an emotional act. If people do not feel "bought in," they will not be "bought in." Coach team members to buy into results but make it clear the team is moving forward. And understand this level of ownership reaches its peak over a long period of time with many reversals built

into the progression and growth of ownership.
- Candidly communicate when team members are not accomplishing the work that will lead to results and courageously engage with consequences. And understand this means any behavior that could destroy the culture of the team cannot be tolerated.

All these areas produce dichotomies with which leaders will grapple. There is a tension between repetitive clarity to drive growth and harassing discourse. There are tensions between allowing conflict to occur and feelings to get hurt and making sure people can work together to accomplish a task. There is a tension between autonomy and consequences. There is a tension between ownership and accountability. Finally, there is a tension between candid communication to high performers (or even delivering feedback to middling and low performers) and tolerating bad—or just suboptimal—outcomes and behaviors. There are two responses to this tension: the first response is that the work of leadership is to navigate the tension and to be as transparent and clear about where the tension lies. The second response is for leaders to engage in the intentional self-awareness work required for leading and acknowledging their own weaknesses and foibles in the tensions and then to do the work to repair them. Understanding, accepting, and navigating this tension is part of the work of a linchpin leader, and at scale, is the work of a linchpin team.

The Work of Teams: On Being Indispensable

High-performing teams are indispensable. What this means in practice is that the team will go through all the growth stages and experience the problems that come from navigating those growth stages and they will come out the other side, appearing in their behavior and focus, to be scaled up versions of linchpin leaders we addressed in Chapter One, Leadership Roles and Responsibilities. Similar points about the assertions we made about linchpin leaders in Chapter One can be repeated here.

The linchpin team does not view the responsibility of role modeling the behavior they would like to see in their fellow teammates as a burden to be hoisted or as a situation to be avoided. Instead, they view role modeling as a natural outgrowth of their maturity and development as a team culture. If the team cannot role model the behavior they would like to see for each other as teammates, a linchpin may ask, why would they bother being a team at all? Role modeling creates buy-in among and between team members, which permits individual team members to become leaders of themselves first and then others on the team in a virtuous circle that rarely breaks. If teams want to have success, they must role model the changes in attitude, behavior, values, and culture before they occur.

The linchpin team takes on the responsibility of articulating a vision, whether it be in writing or in speaking, as a sacred act. Beginning with small goals and a limited vision, or beginning with a big vision, full of scary propositions, the linchpin team ensures there is first clarity on what that vision is. Then the team has the candor to express that vision—and drawbacks to accomplishing it—in terms everyone on the team can understand. By the way, the team is not seeking 100 percent consensus with the vision. A linchpin team realizes that chasing consensus or pursuing certainty is just another sophisticated form of hiding from the hard work of commitment. The linchpin team demonstrates and repeats the vision with courage regularly: when times are tough and when times are great. The linchpin team performs and defines the roles of the followers and the leader, but also co-creates the reality of the vision between team members.

Overall, the linchpin team is restless in the pursuit of opportunities to challenge the system they are in and to shake things up. If there is no status quo to upend, the linchpin team may get so restless that they seek out opportunities from outside the system and bring them back, reshaping, reframing, and reconditioning the culture, pushing, and cajoling it to better and better heights, and toward future horizons. The words "we've always done it this way" are a poison pill to the linchpin team and the team knows that any system they are in, the second those words are stated, a choice is on the table: battle the status quo, or leave the system. There are no other two ways to go about it. The linchpin team is open to challenges, feedback, and questioning of their decisions; however, they also know once a decision has been made to go forward, going backward and re-litigating the decision is not helpful, it is toxic, and a practice that can lead to blame-gaming, and lock up real innovation. The linchpin team welcomes the rough and tumble exchanges that go along with challenging the organizational process.

The linchpin team ties their own growth in vulnerability, empathy, and humanity to the depth to which team culture grows, and they know the best way to ensure that growth is to surrender power to trust. They recognize autonomy only truly works when individuals are well trained, well-motivated, and well empowered to make decisions, try new and alternative approaches to solving problems, and take on responsibility for failures and mistakes. Delegation is not a "set and forget it" system of leadership, nor is it a function of leadership that can happen without trust; however, when delegation is engaged with appropriately and the boundaries of delegation are clearly defined and articulated repeatedly, mastery increases, work satisfaction goes up, and the need for follow-through and micro-managing decrease.

The linchpin team encourages the heart through the intentional development of purposeful rituals, repeated stories, and defined practices. The linchpin team knows the two simplest words of recognition and appreciation on the team are "thank you" and when they are lacking, productivity declines. The team knows fair pay, time off, flexible working hours, work from home, appropriate working technology, time away from email and constant messaging from work are not merely perks of teamwork, instead, they stand as artifacts of how a team is recognized and applauded for its hard work. The team knows recognition and celebration are sometimes not about Zoom coffees, 1:1's, and constant checking-in. The team understands celebration and recognition come from offering fellow team members the space to accomplish the task they were originally assigned without micro-managing through electronic means. The linchpin team knows such behavior encourages the heart and opens the door to conversations and observations about the work that might now have ever occurred before.

There are two other areas high-performance teams focus on to create functioning organizations and cultures.

High-performing teams are clearly solution-oriented and have a focus on accomplishing small goals. However, the leaders of high-performing teams must balance that small focus at the local level with clearly articulating a large, compelling, purpose and vision for the team. There are four steps to creating a high-performing team with a "small target" focus from day one:

- Articulate a compelling vision and purpose for the team.
- Be clear about which goals are small, which goals are medium-sized, and which goals are large and "scary"—but also exciting.
- Keep the team focused on accomplishing small goals on a day-to-day basis and take the time to refocus the team on larger goals consistently.
- Consensus and certainty are great but are not necessary to accomplish goals.

High performing teams do two things well: they deliver feedback to each other and accept blame and they understand decisions provide options for actions. The Navy SEALs and the Marines in the US military have successfully developed feedback loops and action orientation that allows them to create high-performing teams. There are six steps to creating a high-performing team that can deliver feedback without delivering on the blame game and ensuring psychological safety.

- Understand a decision is better than no decision; encourage a bias toward action.
- When the team fails to accomplish a goal, engage in an after-action reporting system.
- Encourage team members to engage in the "solutions game," not the "blame game."
- Coach people and teams through encouragement and feedback to accept the responsibility toward finding solutions rather than wallowing in the defensiveness of blame.
- Engage in active listening and leverage patience to reduce your own defensive responses to feedback.
- Reject feedback designed to shame team members into silence and inaction.

Making a high-performance team can seem like a daunting task for leaders. However, if leaders understand their roles and responsibilities to the team, lead with emotional intelligence, navigate conflict effectively, and leverage communication and persuasion intentionally, they can become leaders who move their teams to greater success. There are drawbacks, problems, and minefields leaders must negotiate, and in the following chapters we address the power of these other forces and address how to not be overwhelmed by them and how to behave intentionally.

Practical Tips for Creating a Team

Tip #1 - Go to work with the team you have, not the team you want to have. Leaders understand deeply the following quote from the former Secretary of Defense, Donald Rumsfeld: "You go to war with the Army you have, not the Army you might want or wish you had at a later time."[8] The truth of leadership is that team building can sometimes be a luxury leaders can little afford to covet. Sometimes, leaders must lead first and build the team later. The Tuckman model of team development is accurate (as is the Gersick Model) and the fact is, teams are asked to perform to their highest level while they are in the process of still forming. And if there are outside stressors, environmental changes, or technological or logistical problems, they still must perform. Furthermore, usually, the unstated demand is they do so at the highest possible level. Yes, leaders are sometimes asked to forge a Maserati out of Toyota parts, but many times leaders must start a high-performance race with a sedan before they can get a sports car.

Tip #2 - Be honest and forthright with your leaders about the limitations of the team. Leaders must have the courage, clarity, and candor to be honest and forthright about the limitations of the people they are leading when they are speaking to their leaders. Every team has limitations and boundaries. Every team has individuals who have weaknesses. Knowing how to talk about those weaknesses without whining, complaining, or blaming is a skill leaders would do well to develop. Not every leader is going to be blessed with a team of high-performers and not every high-performing team on paper is going to demonstrate that promise in practice. Leaders must walk the line with their leaders in discussing limitations and weaknesses and figuring out creative solutions to the problems those limitations create. Leaders must also find the strengths in the team and individual team members and leverage those strengths despite weaknesses.

Tip #3 - Know where the team is in the development cycle. Leaders are aware of where their teams are in the team-development cycle. They know that if their team is trapped in the ditch (dip) between Storming and Norming, it is their responsibility to draw them out of the dip. Knowing there will be a dip, a downturn, or a Storming event that will occur in the team dynamic, but not knowing where or when that will happen in the team environment is the purview of the intentional leader. The intentional leader is attuned to the dynamics of the team and the vagaries of human engagement with the team. Leaders work to keep their leadership fingers on the pulse of team growth and they shepherd team members through the Forming stage by ensuring expectations are set and bonding occurs. Even in Performing, they realize the task is not nearly as important as the relationships between people. Finally, leaders set the table with their followers to ensure exits from the team are celebrated, intentional, and embedded with meaning and mattering.

Tip #4 - To have a linchpin team, you must have linchpin followers. Linchpin leaders are indispensable to performing linchpin work in environments that require engagement from teams with work beyond even accomplishing rudimentary tasks. Candle problems—that is, those problems that require solutions that leverage a higher level of cognitive ability and engagement—require creating and maintaining teams that are linchpins in and of themselves. Followers who understand that being a follower is about engaging with behaviors that are the same behaviors of being a linchpin leader—work ethic, competence (or proficiency), ego management, and more—engage with being a follower completely.

Tip #5 - Failure is always there, but not an option for stopping. Leaders understand what Gene Krantz and the flight controllers at Mission Control in the Apollo Space Program understood about dealing with problems in getting men to the Moon: "… when bad things happened, we just calmly laid out all the options, and failure was not one of them."[9] The quote, "Failure is not an option," is often misunderstood by casual leaders—and ego-driven ones—as being an admonition to do all they can to never fail. The potential risk of failure is always present when individuals get together to perform a task with each other. Leaders build into dynamic of teams the fact of failure and they lay out the options—which do not include quitting in the dip of failure. Leaders know teams who get to the other side of the dip of failure receive rewards that can only be compared to landing on the Moon successfully.

CHAPTER SIX

Rule 6
Leaders Do Not Confuse "Liking" with "Agreeing"
Leadership and Dealing with Difficult Teams and Individuals

"Leaders know that the large thing about small things comes down to how those things are handled."
Jesan Sorrells

This chapter focuses on the principles of dealing with difficult people, which is a little different for leaders when they are pushed into accepting positions they may personally and politically disagree with but may have to enforce with followers to make events happen and move projects forward. This is also a chapter that directly addresses the power of history and historical interactions with followers and talks honestly about the social proofing (Halo and Horn Effect) that leads to leaders sometimes misjudging difficult—or intransigent—distributive bargainers. The chapter asserts that if the leader fails to address the behavior of difficult people on the team, their destructive behaviors can scale and expand quicker than the leader may be able to address.

Introduction: The Problem That Will Not Shut Up

The fact of leaders addressing their followers' behavior—usually poor, but also good—is as inescapable in discussions of leadership as conversations about accountability, motivation, moral, and even discipline and feedback. Leaders receive advice from numerous arenas about how to effectively address behavior they find to be suboptimal, and many leaders default—despite the reams of advice—to "doing what I think is 'best' in the situation." Because, as leaders rightly presume, who can know all the "ins-and-outs" of a decision regarding how to sanction, address, or ignore a follower's behavior? How can a book, an essay, a YouTube video, or an experienced facilitator know the troubles the leader has already addressed with the followers? It is against this backdrop of thinking that the topic of how a leader should address the behavior of difficult people comes to bear.

Followers are difficult for a variety of reasons and motives, and it requires determination, grit, and a strong measure of courage to face those followers and their multifaceted, multi-layered, motives with clarity and candor. However, many times leaders are the blind guides who insistently, "strain out a gnat," of focusing on all the wrong behaviors, all the while failing to "swallow [the] camel" by addressing the immediate problem of the difficult person that is right before them (Matthew 23:24 *KJV*).[1] Followers rarely can describe their own motives for difficult or demanding behavior because they may be lacking in self-awareness, they may be self-deceived, or they may just be selfish and uncaring. When leaders suspect this is the case, they often attempt strategies to "save" the difficult person because they are a "high-performer" who "produces results," all the while tearing apart the collaborative fabric of the team. Finally, followers' psychology ranges across multiple areas; however, they may also exhibit the psychological trait of disagreeableness, where they may not be particularly well matched with other people in groups, but they are creative and conscientious about performing well on a task. Leaders—who themselves may exhibit a touch of disagreeableness along with a touch of extraversion—may not necessarily view the behavior of a difficult person as "wrong" until it begins to affect the accomplishing of their goals.

When leaders seek to deal with difficult people, they must look at their own triggers—the psychological areas that lead to emotional responses, determine the motives of the other party, and then determine the best steps forward strategically. This is not for the faint of heart, because all three of those acts must take place at the same time and with the same level of veracity and focus. But once they do, leaders will find themselves being taken off guard, and off their game, a lot less often when recognizing and addressing the behaviors of difficult people. But first, let us revisit courage.

Resiliency, Grit, and Courage

When leaders face confronting and addressing the behavior of difficult people, they have options. "They can engage with aggression (yelling, physical fighting, making another person feel bad, collaboration (problem solve together, talk it over, come up with a solution, negotiate), compromise (everyone gives something, no one gets what they want), give in (let someone else have their way, you do not care about the outcome, the other person has more power than you), avoid or delay (pretend it's not an issue, run away, avoid the other person) and/or appeal to authority (get someone up the chain to resolve the issue)." [Source: Gary Gam, Gam at Camp Services Inc.][2] Rarely do leaders explore these options fully, because many times they are trapped in the space of cowardice, fear, or real ignorance as to what actions to take. Plus, there is the desire for compliance. One of the great tragedies of the Industrial Revolution leadership training trap of the 20th century is the idea, promulgated through writing, research, and training, that compliance and obedience will come about from followers if tactics are applied and strategies are launched. The problem with this idea is that compliance and obedience present challenges for leaders when abundance, or the perception of abundance, trumps the need for competency and the clamor for obedience when resources—time, talent, money, and benefits—seem to be in never-ending supply. It is precisely at those moments when leaders must adopt a new set of strategies designed for the courage required to resist returning to demands for compliance and encouraging the development of collaboration. These approaches do not complement each other and they can create emotional friction for leaders; tensions that can lead to the development of grit.

When leaders are faced with the problem of reconciling the behaviors of difficult people in times of relative--but not absolute--abundance, they must develop grit. Grit is the quality, once described in Charles Portis's 1968 novel, *True Grit*, via the following exchange:

> "Mattie Ross: "Who is the *best marshal* they have?'
>
> The sheriff thought on it for a minute. He said, 'I would have to weigh that proposition. There is near about two hundred of them. I reckon William Waters is the best tracker. He is a half-breed Comanche and it is something to see, watching him cut for sign. *The meanest one is Rooster Cogburn. He is a pitiless man, double-tough, and fear do not enter into his thinking. He loves to pull a cork.* Now L.T. Quinn, he brings his prisoners in alive. He may let one get by now and then but he believes even the worst of men is entitled to a fair shake. Also, the court does not pay any fees for dead men. Quinn is a good peace officer and a lay preacher to boot. He will not plant evidence or abuse a prisoner. He is straight as a string. Yes, I will say Quinn is about the best they have.'
>
> Mattie Ross: I said, '*Where can I find this Rooster?*"[3]

Or, as the researcher Angela Duckworth, author of *Grit: The Power of Passion and Perseverance*, states, "Grit is passion and sustained persistence applied toward long-term achievement, with no particular concern for rewards or recognition along the way. It combines resilience, ambition, and self-control in the pursuit of goals that take months, years, or even decades." [Source: https://qz.com/work/1233940/angela-duckworth-explains-grit-is-the-key-to-success-and-self-confidence/].[4]

Grit comes as well from engaging with the tension of unresolved, and unresolvable, opposing viewpoints, perspectives, and even motives. When leaders participate in working with difficult people and difficult situations, they must be "pitiless [people], double-tough, and fear do not enter into [their] thinking." The fact is, many leaders do not already possess the depth of resiliency to address the challenges difficult people often confront them with. Too many times, they see the easy way, or the path with the least resistance, while mouthing bromides, talking tough, and doing little that is actionable in the face of the systems in which they are leading. It takes genuine courage to face difficult people on their own ground and to do so with "no particular concern for rewards or recognition along the way," because leaders do not get claps for addressing hard people, or dealing with hard situations. They sometimes do not even get to see the benefits of their good works.

Triggering Events and Their Antecedents

When faced with the trouble of dealing with a difficult person, leaders must face their own triggers and the other party's. A trigger is not a verb, as in the modern conception. A trigger is a noun. In psychology, "a trigger is a stimulus such as a smell, sound, or sight that triggers feelings of trauma." [Source: https://www.goodtherapy.org/blog/psychpedia/trigger].[5] Formed through the "fight or flight" response system in the amygdala, as well as short-term memory, unaddressed trauma, and a lack of appropriate therapeutic management, triggers are real, but their impact and how to address them have yet to be fully explored by scientists. There is a lot of talk in social science circles about triggers and trigger warnings receive short shrift from much of the work world outside of academic settings. Leaders must be able to successfully diagnose the source of those emotional and psychological triggers. And leaders must successfully defuse the triggers during conflict situations by leveraging clarity, candor, and courage. The fact is, leaders are at "ground zero" when addressing the effects of difficult people's behaviors in the work world. Leaders are charged, non-verbally and contextually, of course, with carefully managing the psycho-social cultural dynamic of various people and teams in organizations encountering populations, cohorts, and people of generations raised with differing conceptions of what constitutes trauma, triggers, violence (e.g., language use as violence), and what does not. This mix creates a confusing and challenging leadership environment constituted primarily of the perception of a landscape of virtual rhetorical eggshells, low work productivity, and constant visits to the human resource office.

If this reads as impossible, that's because on paper it is. On paper, any leader needs to have a degree and a license to practice psychology, psychiatry, mental health counseling, and therapy to even begin the process of facing their own triggers and defusing them, much less someone else's. On paper, a leader should have access to years of emotional, spiritual, and psychological data and analysis of the individual difficult person and have the ability and interest to dig into another person deeply and with years of time.

That's on paper.

The reality of addressing and diffusing difficult situations and people is that leaders often do not have the expertise, interest, or level of therapeutic care to apply to the long-term defusing of a trigger for just one situation, much less all the subsidiary potential situations that could arise when facing a difficult person. This lack of expertise leads to fear of dealing with a difficult person, fear of saying, or doing, "the 'wrong' thing," and encourages leaders to create and promulgate strategies for dealing with difficult individuals on teams with hope rather than substance. Many times, leaders lament that people cannot "just come to work, shut up, do the work, and go home." This is a callback to a perception of easy compliance and obedience to paternalistic authority that does not track with the reality leaders face in the present day. A leader's lack of expertise and comfort with the confrontation of triggers and their outcomes can lead leaders down the path to other ways of addressing difficult behavior that are equally ineffective.

Harvard researcher and editor of the *Negotiation* newsletter, Katherine Shonk, points out in her article "What Type of Hard Bargainer are you Facing?" in the 2013 *Harvard Program on Negotiation Dealing with Difficult People Report*, "When dealing with a counterpart who will not give us what we want, we tend to write him off as difficult or irrational. Yet negotiation scholars point out that few people are truly irrational."[6] Leaders intellectually know that few people are truly irrational. However, leaders intuitively know, in the political context of leveraging difficult behavior to achieve a desired outcome, people may behave in an irrational fashion for the context of the situation. This behavior is filtered through the perceptions, judgments, and assumptions of other people involved in the situation and can serve to erode a leader's position in the group if the behavior goes unaddressed, or is addressed incompetently.

Triggers are deeply personal and it's not always clear to people why they behave the way they do, even in an easy context. Leaders should expect people who lack self-awareness, or actively reject calls to what the leader believes is rational behavior, if what is presented by the leader is an option to behave clinically rather than to behave reactively. Leaders must be honest with themselves about their own perceptions and attributions of behavior and seek to achieve a higher analytical plane to assess character.

Understanding how and why a person behaves in the way they do is a powerful negotiation tool in the face of people who may lack self-awareness, maybe being manipulated by other people or circumstances of which you are not aware, or who are deliberately behaving in a difficult manner.

The Doctor is "In"

Diagnosing the behaviors of difficult people is the first step to leaders successfully negotiating with them. The clear-eyed leader negotiates with a difficult person by having the clarity and courage to observe their behavior, analyze the cause by asking questions and listening closely to answers, and then ruthlessly negotiating with the person rather than the behavior. The behavior of difficult people comes in three forms: accidental, reluctant, and intentional. From the 2013 *Harvard Program on Negotiation Dealing with Difficult People Report*:

> "Seasoned negotiators understand that mental shortcuts can impair our most important decisions without our awareness. Sometimes a negotiator's tough stance can be chalked up to constraints or interests of which you are unaware," write Deepak Malhotra and Max H. Bazerman in their book *Negotiation Genius: How to Overcome Obstacles and Achieve Brilliant Results at the Bargaining Table and Beyond* (Bantam, 2007). At times you will encounter negotiators who believe that hard bargaining is the most effective strategy. They may attempt to manipulate you by using displays of anger, hurt feelings, or even mental illness to get what they want," writes Northwestern University professor Leigh Thompson in her book *The Mind and Heart of the Negotiator* (Pearson Prentice Hall, 2005)."[7]

Individuals who are difficult because of internal biases, mental shortcuts, egocentrism, overconfidence, or who are interested in escalating circumstances to a conclusion that works for them, can be diagnosed as accidentally difficult. Once a leader realizes this, they can use this knowledge to move the situation in their favor. For instance, by recognizing that a difficult person tends to be rather egocentric and overconfident, thus making their behavior difficult to address, the leader can talk to the person behind the behavior—the subtext, rather than the context—and negotiate with that person. Negotiation in the space of biases, psychological behavior, or emotional puffery can come in the form of humor, de-escalation, distraction, or even just a reframing of facts to achieve greater clarity. Leaders should role model good negotiation behavior with this type of individual because if not, they might feel backed into a corner and escalate the situation. Or, they might react rather than respond to an offer with too little time given to them.

Individuals who are difficult because of constraints and interests a leader is unaware of respond well to questioning and listening. Primarily, this is because a reluctantly difficult individual wants to do a deal, but their level of power, authority, or competency is being threatened by larger extant forces than the leader can bring to bear. This makes any leader who listens and attempts to resolve those forces in favor of the individual in question an ally rather than an enemy. Leaders miss this all the time, in presuming the constraints the difficult person must overcome are a "them problem" and the leader has enough problems to address of their own. However, a reluctantly difficult individual is looking for a partner, not another enemy, and selfishly pursuing motives in a political manner will not yield the types of outcomes leaders are seeking from that difficult person. If the difficult person has a history and neutral experiences with a leader, they may not be basing their behavior on what is currently happening in the negotiation. Rather, they are seeking to psychologically balance outcomes from the past and potential outcomes in the future. Leaders are sometimes reluctant to bring up history, in the fear it will "muddy the waters," or "not go 'anywhere,'" but these fears may be unfounded.

Intentionally difficult individuals are the hardest individuals for leaders to address and negotiate with, because leaders can unintentionally escalate individuals who are reluctant or accidental in their behavior to become more and more intentional. Leaders who fail to reframe problems, actively listen, confront candidly, and de-escalate appropriately can lose the negotiation game with an intentionally difficult individual before the negotiation has even begun. On the other hand, intentionally difficult individuals rely on such behavior from leaders to continue to pursue their own goals and motives.

An example will be illustrative here. After a training a group of managers and supervisors on conflict, two participants approached us. They asked our facilitators about what the best way to address a difficult individual would be who constantly engaged in manipulative and borderline abusive behaviors. This individual would begin a relationship with a new person at work. They would find out what the person liked and bring them that thing on a repetitive basis. The individual would go out on cigarette breaks outside with people from work and pretend to be friendly. However, when the individual who was the target of all this friendliness and relationship building would attempt to get promoted in the organizational culture, the manipulative person would suddenly transform and become difficult to deal with. And not just for their former "friend," but also for everyone else who had to work with them. The two people who approached our trainers asked how to resolve this issue because they were now being tasked with dealing with the manipulative person on the downside of their career.

This is the perfect example of an intentionally difficult individual who leverages manipulation, "glad handling," friendliness, and other forms of behaviors that appear positive on the surface but, in truth, are negative underneath. Here is another example from the 2013 *Harvard Program on Negotiation Dealing with Difficult People Report*:

> "...in her book *The Mind and Heart of the Negotiator* (Pearson Prentice Hall, 2005), Thompson tells the story of AOL's advertising chief Myer Berlow playing with a large knife during a 2003 negotiation with Amazon.com CEO Jeff Bezos. When displeased by another AOL executive who was attending the meeting, Berlow reportedly threatened to stab him."[8]

This type of behavior appears irrational and as if it would be "one-off" or rare and leaders tend to dismiss the warning signs from an intentionally difficult individual; however, leaders need to understand this act of dismissal is counted upon by the individual in question. In the words of the Old Testament writer in the *Book of Daniel*, intentional individuals have taken a leader's measure—or a team's—and found it wanting. And they have successfully done so many times.

To address a tough negotiator who has been allowed to get away with manipulative behavior over time, a leader would be well advised to have a plan before interacting with the individual in question. To develop such a plan, leaders need to speak less than they listen. And it's not just avoiding speaking to have the silence act as an intimidating factor, or because they genuinely have nothing to say. Leaders must leverage silence to observe and calculate the actions of an intentionally difficult individual and document behavioral and communication inconsistencies carefully. After all, the person who has the most documentation when a confrontation occurs typically "wins" the engagement.

Intentionally difficult people engage in manipulation, gaslighting, and other forms of communication behaviors that can rattle even the most self-confident leader and sow seeds of doubt in their approach to working with others. Getting a reality check and seeking advice from a trusted, neutral individual is an element the best, most collaborative leaders leverage for success. Even they realize they may not know their own motives, much less the motives of another, equally flawed individual. Leaders examine their own biases, search for blind spots in their mental maps, and make sure they have "all their ducks in a row" before engaging with intentionally difficult individuals. Of course, leaders need to engage with courage and address behaviors and confront reality as quickly as possible while being clear about the boundaries of appropriate behavior. This requires firmness and conviction and can be even more difficult when an intentionally difficult person enjoys the fight, they believe they have set the table of circumstances to receive.

Individuals For Whom Conflict is a Way of Life

The social worker, lawyer, therapist, and mediator, Dr. Bill Eddy, has researched and examined for at least the last thirty years the behaviors of individuals for whom conflict, confrontation, and difficult circumstances are a way of life. He defines these individuals as high conflict people; that is, people for whom their pattern of behavior increases confront rather than deceasing it (management) or moving to resolve the conflict. High conflict people (HCPs) tend to engage in extreme behaviors on the conflict spectrum with out-of-control emotions, a strong tendency to shift blame to others, and engage in other behavior that would be considered more in the range of bullying and sometimes outright violence.[9]

For an HCP, "the juice is the worth the squeeze." Meaning how they view life and its various experiences is via the lens of conflict behavior. HCPs do experience personality disorders including narcissistic, borderline, antisocial, paranoid, and histrionic personality disorders or traits. However, leaders need to realize such mental health diagnoses are best left to the professionals. High conflict personality is not a diagnosis and one of the worst things a leader (or anyone) can do is "diagnose" an HCP based on repeated, observable patterns of behavior. Leaders would be better served to manage the relationship with the HCP rather than seeking to resolve a conflict, engage in a confrontation they cannot obtain a satisfactory conclusion to, or preparing emotionally to dig in for a year's long, twilight struggle around a conflict that should have been resolved immediately.

Dr. Eddy recommends having a "Private Working Theory" if a leader (or anyone) suspects they have encountered a high conflict personality. The cornerstone of such a theory rests on two areas: 1) do not assume you have all the facts as a leader and that you are "right" about the person's behavior and 2) do not tell the person your thoughts about them. Unlike other difficult bargainers, HCPs cannot gain insight into their own behavior and are merely triggered to escalation by insinuations—either verbally or in writing—that something might be wrong with them, or with their approach, to the world.

In his books, *It's All Your Fault!* and *5 Types of People Who Can Ruin Your Life*, Eddy describes the following steps for dealing with an HCP:

1. Connect with the person with empathy, attention and/or respect (unless it's not safe and you just need to stay away from the person).

2. Analyze your realistic options in dealing with the person (write a list of options, then decide which one makes the most realistic sense in dealing with him or her; sometimes it's best to slowly phase the person out of your life).

3. Respond to hostility or misinformation: use responses that are Brief, Informative, Friendly, and Firm (B.I.F.F.). Avoid advice, admonishments, and apologies—they will use these against you later.

4. Set Limits on dangerous or bothersome behavior by deciding when, where, and how you meet to discuss issues. Get assistance from authorities (such as the police), advocates (such as lawyers), and supportive persons (family and friends) to help you decide how to set limits. Avoiding harsh statements as an attempt to set limits because they just increase the HCP's bad behavior.

It's better to learn about the predictable behavior patterns of HCPs and ways to respond constructively. If you think someone is an HCP, use this information to focus on ways of changing your own behavior, not theirs. Manage your relationship primarily by managing your own anxiety and your own responses. [Source: https://www.highconflictinstitute.com/hci-articles/who-are-high-conflict-people].[10]

Leaders would be well advised to incorporate these practices into their pattern of leadership behaviors when dealing with an HCP. However, because many leaders are convinced that competencies and success in one area can immediately translate into competencies and successes in another area, they often make ego driven decisions about HCPs—and other difficult conflict types—that translate later into problems and greater issues. Humility, grace, and collaboration with the HCP, as well as engaging in emotional, psychological, and behavioral tactics that will "cordon off" the effects of the behavior of an HCP from the rest of the team—and from the leader themselves—is critical for success. Particularly when that HCP, or that difficult bargainer is higher in status or has more influence than the leader on the ground now.

Practical Tips for Dealing with Difficult People

Leaders must get real when dealing with difficult people, but they must get even more real when dealing with difficult teams. The signs of dysfunction on a team—or in a team's culture—are usually obvious, but many leaders ignore them, hoping vainly the problems will just go away. However, the leaders who face the signs, confront the behavior, deliver appropriate consequences, and document and follow-up on the process achieve far better results than those leaders who do not. Although this is not "rocket science," it does require the leader to have clarity on which dysfunction they are addressing with the team, the credibility and trustworthiness that comes from candor, and the courage to show vulnerability to people who might not appreciate the vulnerability, or who might weaponize such displays of vulnerability to advance their own selfish agendas.

The author Jeffrey Pfeffer, *Leadership BS: Fixing Workplaces and Careers One Truth at a Time*, holds to the idea that behaving in a Machiavellian fashion is not only the right option for addressing dysfunctional behaviors, but also that it is the preferable way that is expected by followers, and leaders should stop trying to subvert their followers' expectations.[11] On the other hand, the author Patrick Lencioni's *The Five Dysfunctions of the Workplace: A Leadership Fable* holds the opposite view: leaders have a responsibility to establish trust, remove barriers to healthy conflict, encourage accountability, and demand results.[12] And if these actions subvert the expectations of followers who are ill-mannered, dysfunctional, or unable to change, well then, they always have the option to pursue other avenues to success in other organizations.

What both authors miss (and the reason there are so many books on leadership, including this one, on the market today) is that leaders vary individually by temperament, character, focus, moods, level of wisdom, knowledge, life experience, and personality across the spectrum of not only the Big Five Factors of psychology, but also by numerous other metrics. One leader may begin their leadership journey by eschewing ruthlessness and, being unable (or unwilling) to change the environment around them, may become enveloped in the very dysfunctional behaviors they once devalued. Another leader may emotionally and psychologically struggle to lead a dysfunctional team and succeed in changing it over the long-term, to the detriment of pursuing other strategic victories. And yet another leader will ignore or dismiss difficult people and situations continuously and repeatedly, and plow ahead with accomplishing a task while dragging the dysfunctional crowd along with her.

What leaders off all stripes need is two things: 1) an acknowledgment that confronting difficult people and teams is hard and will never be an easy task, and 2) some simple steps to take to address the behavior of difficult people and teams that is replicable and scalable across time, people, and experiences, even though their mileage will vary. What follows is an attempt to distill the top five practical tips for dealing with difficult people that work, no matter what their bargaining style is, their personality quirks, or how dysfunctional they may be as individuals.

Tip #1—Engage in active listening. Just as with more general conflict management principles we outlined in the previous chapter, engaging with active listening is about more than just merely the actual act of listening. It's about turning off the "white noise" inside of a leader's mind and focusing exclusively, at the moment, on what's happening with the difficult person or team. The purpose of active listening at this level is to hear subtext, determine motives, suspend judgment of those motives, and gather information to have a plan of action. Many leaders ignore active listening or dismiss it when history, past experiences, attained wisdom, or speed to solution seem to take priority. However, the humility in actively listening requires leaders to engage not only with their minds but also with their emotions.

Tip #2—Accurately examine the difficult person's motives. Leaders must engage in understanding and quickly determining the motives of individuals who are presenting as difficult on their team. They do not need to understand psychology, the person's personal history, or their culture (that will come later), they only need to know if the person is driven by ego, circumstances of which they (the leader) are unaware, or if they are being intentionally manipulative. When leaders place their own motives for gain ahead of dissecting and determining accurately the motives of a difficult person, they wind up believing the person is irrational, foolish, or just uninformed. Those last two might be true, or might not, but actually, very few people are irrational. And just because their motives and the leader's motives are at cross-purposes in a negotiated interaction, does not mean they should not be approached with curiosity rather than escalation.

Tip #3—A firm "no." Leaders are all over the map on this one. However, when dealing with a difficult person, whether driven by ego, circumstances, or intentionality, leaders must be willing and able to render a firm "no." Sometimes leaders try to couch their "no" in a sandwich of other "yes" responses, and although this can make the other party feel good, many times amateur communicators screw up the delivery, like a person repeating a joke they heard on a sitcom and stepping on the punchline. Professional leaders give firm "no's" and can articulate clearly to their followers the "why" behind the "no." Many times, leaders will disengage at this point and move on to solving the next problem, but this is the point where follow-up is hugely important for leadership success in dealing with difficult people, addressing difficult situations, and managing difficult teams.

Tip #4 - Not confusing "liking" with "agreeing." Everyone wants to be liked. No human is so disagreeable in their psychology that they do not want someone, somewhere, at some time, to like them. Leaders are no exception to this rule. However, when dealing with difficult people, addressing difficult situations, and managing difficult teams, leaders must understand what is being negotiated in the hard moment. This understanding requires leaders to be focused on the present moment of the negotiation and to be sure they have a plan for follow-up and follow-through at the end of the interaction, no matter the outcome. Agreement with a difficult person is an act of supreme rationality and many leaders cannot get there because their emotional responses and reactions will not be tamped down. But just because a leader agrees with a difficult person, it does not mean the person is their friend, their colleague, their ally, or their buddy. And being clear about that is important, particularly for leaders who struggle with self-worth, imposter syndrome, or who are dealing with other, lower level, uncivil behaviors in the team culture on a day-to-day basis.

Tip #5—Not labeling people with whom we disagree. The author and former FBI hostage negotiator, Chris Voss, recommends labeling the other party in a negotiation in his book *Never Split the Difference: Negotiating as if Your Life Depended On*

It. He makes this recommendation as a way of engaging with, what he calls "tactical empathy."[13] We've often referred to this exact same tactic as "hard-headed empathy" and it works. However, leaders must avoid the trap inherent in understanding (but not agreeing) with another party's point of view that lies in two areas: 1). The trap of dismissing the other party as soon as rapport is established, and 2). The trap of abandoning skepticism to pursue a quick "resolution" to a difficult situation and thus setting up future problems down the road. These traps are not easy for leaders to spot and require diligence, engagement, intentionality, and a fair degree of trust, but not necessarily in the skills, abilities, motives, or knowledge of the other bargaining party. Instead, the leader grabs all of that to sidestep the trap.

CHAPTER SEVEN

Rule 7
Leaders Resolve the Mismatch Between Science and Business

Leadership and Building Morale and Encouraging Motivation

"Leadership requires expecting resistance from people, but not accepting it. Leadership requires expecting misalignment, but not accepting it. Leadership requires getting on people up the "chain of command" and down the "chain of command" to generate any sort of forward motion."

Jesan Sorrells

This chapter focuses on the sticky problem of how to motivate followers whose motivations are antithetical to the leader's motivations or goals. It also addresses the role of trust and awareness in knowing the people a leader is tasked with leading and being sensitive to their needs and ambitions while also counterbalancing the needs and ambitions of others. The chapter lays out a case for avoiding manipulation tactics, bullying tactics, or other tactics that might accomplish short-term goals, but will demotivate performers, reduce team morale, and block long-term growth.

Introduction: Our Abundance Problem

Leaders and followers alike in the Western world have too much.

And it is not just physical and material items (material prosperity) or even good health and long life (physical prosperity). Leaders and followers have too much free time, too few physical challenges (not including health-related ones) and too much money (those making between $32,000 and $50,000 per year

USD are ranked by economist as being in the top one percent of the wealthiest people in the world). For the first time in human history (at least in the post-post-modern nation-states of the United States, Canada, Japan, South Korea, and most European nations), people have an abundance of time where they do not have to be ruthlessly motivated by attaining or maintaining a basic need, such as food, clothing, or shelter, or where they aren't totally psychologically owned by ascending a hierarchy of needs, such as one described by Abraham Maslow.[1] For the first time in human history, a group of people has enough abundance, comfort, physical and psychological safety, and access to spiritual knowledge, that they can choose a path with almost no external resistance.

There is too much.

Too many choices.

Too many options.

Too many demotivators.

Too many dopamine-driven distractions.

There was a study conducted several years ago that estimated that modern, Industrial Revolution audiences formerly received 5,000 marketing messages in a week during the period of the middle 20th century. Now, those same people receive approximately 50,000 marketing messages a day. These messages are designed by intelligent marketers who deeply understand human psychology, to create a false sense of missing out, a sense of scarcity, in a time of overwhelming abundance if people would just open their eyes.

Leaders have always struggled with how to motivate other people. This is a two-fold problem, revealing both a leader's care for their people (empathy) and a leader's desire to control followers and move them around like widgets (controlling). Many times, leaders will ask "How can I motivate my people?", and the short answer is: you cannot. People must motivate themselves. Individuals at every level of the team and the organization must reach down inside of themselves and marshal the desire to accomplish a task, the decision-making skills about which task to take on, and the willpower to see the task through to the end. There is no outside force that can do this for an individual. Of course, the desire, ability, will, and focus to start a business, advance in an organization, or even engage in athletic competition exists in individuals who ultimately end up leading. Thus, leaders commit the cardinal sin of imputing their drive and motivation onto others and then are surprised when others resist.

With that being acknowledged, there are a few things a leader can do to make the struggle with motivation easier and to make the challenge of growing and maintaining morale less challenging. Leaders have a responsibility to understand the difference between morale and motivation. Leaders must role model the motivating behavior they would like others to replicate. Leaders should develop environments that do not allow for demotivating behaviors, attitudes, postures, or mentalities and be ruthless in rooting that behavior out of the team. Leaders have a responsibility to engage in the discipline motivation requires, have the humility to acknowledge when it is not working, and the courage to change it.

All in the face of an ever-expanding pile of too much.

A Distinction with A Difference

Motivation and morale are often put together like cheese on a ham sandwich; but cows and pigs rarely share much in common beyond the environments on the farm they find themselves in. These fundamental differences between motivation and morale aren't always understood by leaders in general, and so we must define the parameters of the discussion.

Motivation is the internal driver of an individual. Motivation can come about from external factors (extrinsic) or from internal factors (intrinsic), but many times develops from a fusion of both internal and external drivers. For instance, a farmer may want to be liked (external driver) by her fellow farmers but she also wants to feed her family and she is hungry herself (internal driver). So, when she goes to the market with her farm goods, she may haggle hard with some buyers, but with others she may take a soft touch. And that's after she's made the decision the night before to get up at 4:00 AM, feed the cows (and the pigs), make a thousand smaller decisions, and then proceed to the market to begin selling to peers, to strangers, and to friends. Motivation lies at the root of most goal-directed, or goal-focused, behaviors in people. The problem begins when leaders observe motivating behaviors that seem to be task oriented and profitable in one person, and then attempt to graft those behaviors onto another person without being curious about the differences in psychology, culture, gender, or historical background between the two people.

Beliefs and intentions matter when addressing and understanding the motivations of individuals. In his book *Liminal Thinking: Create the Change You Want by Changing the Way You Think*, author Dave Gray makes several points about the power of beliefs:

> "These six principles constitute a theory of beliefs: how they come into being, why they are necessary, how they are reinforced over time, and why people cling to their beliefs, even when they are incomplete, obsolete, or invalid. They are beliefs about beliefs.
>
> 1. Beliefs are models. Beliefs seem like perfect representations of the world, but in fact, they are imperfect models for navigating a complex, multidimensional, unknowable reality.
>
> 2. Beliefs are created. Beliefs are constructed hierarchically, using theories and judgments, which are based on selected facts and personal, subjective experiences.
>
> 3. Beliefs create a shared world. Beliefs are the psychological material we use to co-create a shared world, so we can live, work, and do things together. Changing a shared world requires changing its underlying beliefs.
>
> 4. Beliefs create blind spots. Beliefs are tools for

thinking and provide rules for action, but they can also create artificial constraints that blind you to valid possibilities.

5. Beliefs defend themselves. Beliefs are unconsciously defended by a bubble of self-sealing logic, which maintains them even when they are invalid, to protect personal identity and self-worth.

6. Beliefs are tied to identity. Governing beliefs, which form the basis for other beliefs, are the most difficult to change because they are tied to personal identity and feelings of self-worth. You cannot change your governing beliefs without changing yourself." [Source: https://liminalthinking.com/six-principles/].[2]

When considering motivation, leaders must understand that beliefs manifest in actions. Actions are driven by intentions. For instance, if the farmer mentioned above intended to sell her cow and sold her cow, she successfully realized her intent and her neurochemical responses will indicate that she is having greater motivation. If she intended to sell her cow but did not, her intention was thwarted and her motivation might decline. Motivation in this sense is driven by psychological beliefs the farmer had about her cow, the value of the decision to attend the market and sell the cow, the desire to make a profit from selling the cow and the past experiences she has had in the marketplace with cow sales. This is before we even get to the fact of her being a woman, a farmer, or any of the other identity structures that are granted enormous weight by modern day individuals.

Motivation all starts with the self. Leaders can, as the old saw goes, lead people to the river, but they cannot make them drink the water. This is a hard truth about motivation many leaders reject, so they spend an inordinate amount of time consumed with managing expectations around the external drivers of motivation. Those things that are embedded in the environment around followers, such as rewards, salaries, promotions, and rewards. This list also includes negative, or suboptimal, extrinsic motivators such as coercion, manipulation, persuasion, and other forms of influence peddling leaders get caught up in leveraging because either they cannot conceptualize a different way of motivating people, or because they are motivated by these types of external drivers and have a desire to make sure others are driven in the same way. Leaders who lack imagination, lack curiosity, who are genuinely driven by the accumulation of external reward, or who enjoy coercion and domination, are experiencing increasing frustration in the work world of today with the people they are leading at work, because the drivers of motivation that worked so well in the past are collapsing in the face of followers' beliefs about abundance.

Thus, from the individual, the emotional contagion of frustration, disappointment, fear, anxiety, and other negative emotions spreads and team morale suffers and declines. Morale can be defined as the total satisfaction derived by an individual from his job, his work group, his superior, the organization he works for and the environment. It generally relates to the feeling of an individual's comfort, happiness, and satisfaction within a team environment. Morale is a team and group level driver of actions, intentions, and beliefs. Morale is infectious and spreads like a disease. Morale shapes how the team communicates, negotiates, and rationalizes decisions, actions, behaviors, attitudes, and other responses and reactions to external factors with which they are faced. Edwin Flippo (1961) defined morale as, "Morale is a mental condition of groups and individuals, which determines their attitude." [Source: https://indiafreenotes.com/motivation-and-morale/].[3]

Morale is a combination of followers' attitudes, behaviors, and a manifestation of views and opinions—all taken together in their work scenarios. The environment drives morale. Leaders often do not think too hard about the work environment they lead in, as defined by language choices, non-verbal signaling, symbolic representations, and how policies, procedures, and processes are defined. Leaders in low morale environments may experience the following outcomes:

- Greater grievances and conflicts in an organization.
- High rate of employee absenteeism and turnover.
- Dissatisfaction with the superiors and employers.
- Poor working conditions/environments.
- Employee frustration.
- Decrease in productivity.
- Lack of individual motivation.

World War II General, Dwight D. Eisenhower infamously said, "No one ever talks about morale except when it's lousy."[4] Leaders often overlook the importance of culture when morale is high and objectives are accomplished. Culture as a driver for morale is the driver exhibiting the employees' feelings toward work, working terms and relations with their employers. However, leaders will note there are teams with a high level of morale and low level of productivity, where everyone is high-fiving each other and having a great time, but very little organizational value is being created. On the other side, there are multiple examples of companies and organizations where morale is low, but products are getting out the door to the customers. Culture, whether created in fear, in resignation, or in hope matters to leaders in getting the most out of their people and aligning followers' attitudes on and specific reactions to their jobs. Leaders in cultures with high morale may experience the following outcomes:

- A strong alignment to teamwork on the part of followers.
- Organizational commitment and a sense of belonging in the followers' minds.
- Immediate conflict identification and resolution.
- Emotionally healthy and psychologically safe work environment.
- Effective communication in the organization.

- Increase in productivity.
- Greater motivation.

When leaders recognize that culture, alignment, and morale lock together, they work diligently to make sure an ennobling vision and clear mission ring out across the organization consistently. They boldly question executive leadership and challenge the organizational structure to stay focused on results and stay out of the traps of the victim cycle, which can spiral a team into low morale. Leaders are ruthless in understanding that goals must be prioritized and may shift, but alignment and culture cannot move at all. Leaders are not impressed by high levels of individual motivation, nor are they depressed by low levels of morale on the team. They know emotions come and go, but focusing on the goal is critical for consistent success. They commit to doing the work of leadership around culture building and alignment and know morale will come along. Finally, leaders know the final backstop of morale is them. It's their fault if the morale is not working.

Leaders also know the culture of the world outside of the team is always changing and shifting and they pay close attention to the social and cultural inputs of entertainment, politics, media, and finance because they have their heads up and looking out across the horizon for threats that might develop that will cause slight shifts in culture inside the team that can result in long-term outcomes.

What Science Knows and What Business Does

In his TED Talk from 2009, Daniel Pink, the author of *Drive: The Surprising Truth About What Motivates Us*, states that "There is a mismatch between what science knows and what business does."[5] Leaders understand this mismatch well. The same science that brought us I-phones and the material abundance and prosperity mentality of the Industrial Revolution also brought research to management and research insights to leading people.

The issue is that cognitive biases and mental models of belief prevent many leaders from both understanding and executing on the insights scientific research brings to the realm of leading people. Here is what science knows: motivating people begins with paying them fairly for the work they do, and then moving inexorably toward motivating people based on intrinsic desires and drives that cannot always be financially quantified. Leaders with more than a few years of experience understand that leading people is about knowing them and what they want deep in their hearts before making a request of sacrifice from them. The dynamic driving teams in many organizations today are fueled by the collapse of the power of extrinsic drivers, the lack of courage of leaders to pursue different paths, and the reluctance of organizations as entities to acknowledge and critically examine cold, scientific realities, robustly researched.

Where does all this scientific insight begin? With the researcher Abraham Maslow, who began looking at the dynamics of human motivation in the 1950s and 1960s. Maslow created the principles of humanistic psychology to explain why people engage in the way they do with the world in healthy, rather than dysfunctional ways.

> "Maslow described human needs as ordered in a prepotent hierarchy—a pressing need would need to be mostly satisfied before someone would give their attention to the next highest need. None of his published works included a visual representation of the hierarchy. The pyramidal diagram illustrating the Maslow needs hierarchy may have been created by a psychology textbook publisher as an illustrative device. This now iconic pyramid frequently depicts the spectrum of human needs, both physical and psychological, as accompaniment to articles describing Maslow's needs theory and may give the impression the Hierarchy of Needs is a fixed

and rigid sequence of progression. Yet, starting with the first publication of his theory in 1943, Maslow described human needs as being relatively fluid—with many needs being present in a person simultaneously." [Source: Maslow, A. H. (1943). A theory of human motivation. Psychological Review, 50(4), 370–396. https://doi.apa.org/doi/10.1037/h0054346].[6]

Maslow asserted that a healthy individual was motivated to initially seek to satisfy basic needs (e.g., food, clothing, shelter). At work, these basic needs are typically framed at the monetary or compensation level. In a volunteer organization, these basic needs have a more subtle psychological and emotional tone because many of the people who are involved in the work of nonprofit organizations already have many of their most basic physical needs met. Once these physiological or basic emotional needs have been satisfied, they are no longer a motivator. The individual then begins to seek the fulfilling of needs at the next level, which include physical safety (e.g., protective clothing, protection against injury or health hazards), financial security at work (protection against unemployment, loss of income through sickness, etc.), and at an emotional level, psychological safety (team bonding with a feeling or sense of permanence, social proofing of acceptable and unacceptable behavior, and norming to the team environment). This overlaps with the next level of needs, which include social needs. Maslow asserted that many people are motivated by belonging to a group, or what the author Seth Godin would call a "tribe." Motivations at this level are driven by the need for love and belonging (e.g., working with colleagues who support you at work, teamwork, communication), as well as the need for acceptance and validation of self. This then leads to the individual pursuing satisfying needs focused on recognition and the respect of other people. They reflect the fact many people seek the esteem and respect of others. A promotion at work might achieve this but also doing work that has meaning or matters to other people and to the individual might accomplish this. Finally, Maslow posited that at the final level, individuals would be motivated by pursuing a state of harmony with the world, other people, and themselves by reaching a space where their full potential could be realized.

Termed a "flow" state by the psychologist Mihaly Csikszentmihalyi, self-actualization can occur in numerous ways and is often lampooned or dismissed by leaders, but effective levels of motivation are driven by individuals who can think about themselves and the team of which they are a part as one. Self-actualization is how people at an individual level think about themselves—this is often measured by the extent of successes and/or the types of challenges they seek to either overcome or avoid at work. At the group level, self-actualization is a difficult dynamic to define. For many groups or teams when they have reached "the top of the pyramid," the issue becomes two-fold: how to stay at the top without losing focus, drive, or ambition, and how to edge out other competitors on an ever-shrinking "fat" head. Loyalty, high levels of morale, teamwork, and strong communication all come together to create a fully-self-actualized team.

Don't Believe Your Lying Eyes

It is hard to see motivation. However, we can see the results of motivation in accomplishment, drive, ambition, curiosity, and so on. It is hard to see a lack of motivation. However, we can see the results of a lack of motivation in failure, defeat, lack of accountability, lack of results, and more. Many leaders view the results of a lack of motivation, or the results of a certain level of motivation in an individual, and then seek to reverse engineer the solution to the problem of motivation from individual results rather than investigating the root causes, facing the problems at the root of motivations, and then solving for those problems.

Leaders then scale such fallacious thinking across the team in a process that eventually results in lowered productivity, demoralized individuals, and a team that cannot perform at the lowest level, much less the highest level. If a leader is unwilling to believe they have little to no external control over an individual's internal motivation, then why would a leader be willing to believe they have more external control than they really do over the environment of a collection of individuals? Leaders want to control some factors of motivation, but often fail to recognize that morale is probably the place where they have the most control over the results they want on the team.

When leaders believe what they see in individuals and then vaingloriously plan for the hiring, developing, or training of more of those types of individuals, they can fall into a subtle victimization trap. It is important for leaders to be cognizant of this possibility, and to instead, build processes, systems, and procedures that will encourage and support alignment with culture and environment that will allow followers to grow. At a practical level, this may mean expending political capital on championing policies, processes, and procedures that may create short-term pain, but may bring about long-term gain. At a practical level, this may mean moving toward doing acts of leadership that may not make "sense" in an immediate context but are strategically beneficial to the development of the overall environment of the team. Finally, at a practical level, this may mean doing the hard work of moving against the typical grain of business and seeking to resolve the persistent mismatch between what science knows and what business does.

A Human O.S. for the 21st Century—Getting Alignment

Dan Pink addresses the dynamic of how to think about developing a human operating system of motivation for the 21st century in his book *Drive: The Surprising Truth About What Motivates Us*. In his book, Pink addresses ways for leaders to develop a new, more human-focused operating system for motivation. He cites research and analysis to support the building out of this operating system focused on getting the most out of people in three critical areas:

- Autonomy
- Mastery
- Purpose

Pink states that autonomy is the desire to do work without being micro-managed. Autonomy develops within a state of trust that develops between leaders and followers. Leaders can create an environment that supports autonomy by doing small things like delegating tasks, but they can also support the growth of autonomy in individuals by leaving people alone to do work and tasks, and by surrendering the impulse to "check-in" constantly. Autonomy also grows when followers' compensation for their work production is negotiated fairly and they are provided with a clear path for how advancement will occur in the organization, or the team.[7]

Many leaders struggle with the implications of full, or even partial, autonomy in their followers and this is because the message of the Industrial Revolution to leaders was that people were as interchangeable as widgets. Unfortunately, the overwhelming prosperity the "people as widgets" idea brought to the world of leadership has influenced so many people it's almost not even talked about anymore. And, to make matters worse, the post-Industrial Revolution has created deep fragmentation in how and why people do tasks—either for pay or for free—and leaders are often behind the curve on the implications of such fragmentation, focused as they often are, on merely getting through the daily grind.

Pink goes on to discuss mastery as the second pillar of motivation in the 21st century. Mastery is the state of becoming better and better at something a person cares deeply about. Mastery cannot come from repetitive drudgery, although that will develop a species of mastery. Mastery is about enjoying the process of getting better at accomplishing a task, while within the task itself. This is a redefining of the "flow" state described by psychologist Mihaly Csikszentmihalyi. Mastery is about engaging with failure through the application of the lessons learned from failing and then trying again. Grit, perseverance, self-control all contribute to the development of mastery within individuals. Discipline is also key to mastery because all the elements of the process aren't always available. There must be work put forth first to bring forth mastery later. Malcolm Gladwell talks about mastery in his book *Outliers*, and of course, references the 10,000-hour rule.

Leaders must be aware of a couple of hidden pieces inside of this mastery idea. If followers do not care about mastering the task you are asking them to master, they will resist all attempts to shoehorn them into mastery. This is where recruiting, selection, patience and risk-taking on the part of leaders matter more than whatever work needs to be done. The second thing leaders may want to consider is that talent is not a substitute for mastery. Yes, talents and skills are great and many times necessary for followers to have success, but leaders must understand the intrinsic drive toward teamwork, open communication, the willingness to engage in conflict, and the strength to negotiate with other people, matter more than raw talent for mastery. Finally, mastery of one task does not translate to mastery—or even competence—when faced with another task. Leaders must balance general competency with domain-specific expertise.

The final building block of a new operating system for motivation in the 21st century is purpose. Purpose is often given short shrift or little consideration by leaders because they tend to view the world in terms of work they want to do that matches their talents and skills and gives them enjoyment, versus work they do not want to do and cannot imagine anyone else would want to do either. Purpose as a motivator is used to explain why people work in non-profit organizations or have "passion" projects or hobbies that make "no money." The lack of purpose is also leveraged by leaders as a polite way of labeling a follower as "lazy" or "uncommitted." The idea of purpose matches none of these frames. It is instead, an indictment of the work, or task, itself. Leaders struggle with this because to them, all work matters equally in the pursuit of an ennobling vision of the future. But if they haven't sold that vision, created the environment for the vision to develop, or bothered to follow-up with the vision, then all the work does not matter equally. In the eyes of followers, the message is clear: the only work that has purpose is the work the leader deems important.

Followers, whether leaders like it or not, want their work to matter. The failure of leadership to explain sufficiently, clearly, and in a compelling and inspiring manner, how the work a person is doing fits into the overall scheme of a team, and then from the team to the overall organizational culture, is one of the greatest failures of leadership during the Industrial Revolution. And with the rise of automation, the exporting of more and more labor to low-cost providers in other countries, and the coming robotics and artificial intelligences explosion, more and more human beings are going to push back on leaders demanding to know the answer to this question: What's the point of this task?

When leaders focus on building environments that support the development of followers and the development of other future leaders, they begin to loosen the Gordian Knot of motivation and morale and start creating incubators where autonomy, mastery, and purpose can exist within a supportive framework. The risks inherent in developing morale and encouraging motivation within the structure of autonomy, mastery, and purpose are many, but the biggest risk is not that followers will "take advantage" of the environment or "become lazy and entitled." Those outcomes can occur at any time, in any environment. The biggest risk is that leaders will become lazy and entitled, take advantage of the environment in which they operate, fail to set meaningful goals, do the hard work of following up with followers, and fail to ever engage with their people. However, there are practical actions leaders can take that will neutralize some of the worst tendencies and encourage the best ones to rise to the surface.

Practical Actions to Build Morale and Encourage the Growth of Motivation

Leaders must walk a line on motivation that is blurry and hard to sometimes see. On the one hand, leaders must engage with their people, know their people, and ensure their people are getting the best resources for support and for accomplishing goals set before them. On the other hand, leaders must ensure their own fire does not go out inside and they are prepared for every contingency that could arise mentally, emotionally, and psychologically. The reason this line blurs in the minds of leaders is because they failed to establish parameters for actions that can create an environment where followers can develop while also being led to accomplish greater goals.

What follows are a few practical steps for leaders to engage in so they can create environments where morale is high, motivation can manifest itself, and where followers can grow.

Tip #1—Create clear, SMART goals. Leaders know what SMART goals are. SMART is an acronym that stands for Specific, Measurable, Attainable, Results-Oriented, and Time Sensitive. If leaders fail to create goals that match all these terms, then all their attempts at motivation will fail because their followers will not know what to accomplish, much less why. Setting goals involves figuring out what is the highest goal to be achieved and then creating smaller, more manageable goals, and then accomplishing them one by one. Leaders must clearly define the SMART goal and repeat it to followers as a compelling vision. They must align followers with those goals and provide them the resources, the rewards, and the recognition that followers desire. Finally, leaders must realign followers with the goal, not with the leader, when they get out of alignment. This process (Define-Align-Realign) can only happen in the context of clear and unambiguous communication.

Tip #2—Do not attempt to motivate people before they have achieved goals at one level of need. Returning to Maslow's Hierarchy idea for a moment, leaders must recognize that attempting to move people up their level of needs through appeal, coercion, or manipulation will have little to no effect on individuals' overall motivation. Such attempts to dislodge people psychologically from one level of need to another level of need can result in resentment, bitterness, and jealousy and lead to de-motivating and dysfunctional behaviors that can spread throughout the team like an emotional contagion. Leaders must communicate with followers at the level they are at in the hierarchy of their individual needs. This means creating and communicating a compelling vision of the goal accomplished, but it also means being curious and caring about the motivations of the people being led. Leaders who understand deeply the level of need their followers are at can work to set goals for followers so they feel supported in taking on as the risks inherent in moving up the hierarchy of needs increases.

Tip #3—Ask clear questions of individuals and the team and take the answers seriously. Many leaders fail the curiosity test. They do not want to ask their followers challenging questions about their motivations because they are afraid; afraid of the answers. Afraid of the questions. Afraid of the implications of responsibility. Afraid of being unable to "fix" a motivational problem. However, when leaders fail to ask the questions that would reveal the followers' motivations, they compound problems by eventually asking the wrong questions, or by asking the right questions and then failing to take the answers seriously. What follows is a template for asking questions that will probe and explore the individual's level of motivation. The questions should be asked out of a spirit of genuine curiosity, to understand the answers, while also not leaning too much into "problem-solving."

1. Why do you do the work you are doing here (e.g., the team, the workplace, the culture, etc.)?
2. What value do you believe your work provides to [ORGANIZATION NAME HERE]?
3. What do you believe is the hardest part of your work?
4. What do you do when you are confronted with conflict?
5. How do you respond when you hear people complain?
6. What do you think of the workload your team is dealing with?
7. How do you motivate people who aren't motivated?
8. What are you the most anxious about?
9. How do you know when you have done a great job?
10. What are your expectations of me?

Once answers have been gleaned from the above questions, then leaders can move on to questioning the team about morale. Now, if the morale is lousy, leaders should already be aware of it and should be engaged in taking steps to ameliorate the issue. However, if the state of the team's morale is unknown, then leaders should be performing regular "check-ins" and have established times for meetings where they can talk with individuals and establish trust to find out what the temperature of the team is. If leaders are struggling with how to make this happen, the following questions can help maintain an environment where morale stays relatively high and forward momentum on goals is easier to establish.

1. How can we help you attain proficiency in what you are doing?
2. What needs to change in your work for there to be more purpose?
3. What are the specific areas that need to change in the culture of the team for us to be better?

4. What do I need to advocate for as a leader to grow your focus on the tasks at hand?
5. How can the team assist you in reaching your goals?
6. What are the areas where we have negotiated poorly as a team?
7. What are we blind to as a team?
8. What ideas, innovations, and projects are hidden from us?
9. What do we already know about our work?
10. Do we trust each other as team members?

Leaders need not take any action with the answers to the above questions immediately unless there is a crisis going on, a cultural emergency, or another type of catastrophic team morale collapse. Many times, leaders need to listen with their ears and their hearts rather than seeking to solve the problem immediately. Once the questions have been answered and the answers have been digested, leaders need to have a bias toward action and take steps to ensure any issues of morale raised are solved quickly and decisively.

This may mean firing a high performing, yet toxic individual, and planning for how to replace that productivity. This may mean engaging the team in training around a difficult area. This may mean the leader might have to publicly acknowledge historical or cultural failures as a leader and engage humility in front of the team. This may mean the team may have to engage in publicly acknowledging historical or cultural failures as part of a larger organization. However, without some type of meaningful, significant action, morale will not improve and indeed, may worsen because of asking these types of questions with no follow-up.

Tip #4—Increase your own level of "buy-in," or "skin in the game" by following your own standards and meeting expectations you set for others. Leaders at the top of a hierarchy with little to lose emotionally, psychologically, or materially fail last. They know this and so does the system (or culture) they may happen to be leading in.

Tip #5—Follow-through on standards with clear consequences, applied consistently. Leaders who follow up when they are engaged in the work of ensuring the development of an environment that supports strong morale, ruthlessly and consistently follow up with the people they are leading. Such follow-up can be casual and informal, or more documented and formalized, but either way, follow-up indicates the leader cares and is invested not only in the growth of the overall culture but also in the continued development of followers as people.

CHAPTER EIGHT

Rule 8
Leaders Know Why Most Diversity Training Fails
Leadership and Diversity

"Leadership is often about embracing doing, saying, or executing the hard thing. Leaders very rarely tell this truth to other leaders. Leaders typically must extract this truth through experiencing the hard things."

Jesan Sorrells

This chapter focuses on developing leaders' understanding that diversity comes in many forms beyond the EEOC approved definitions. This chapter cautions leaders on how to approach problems that can arise from diversity-based disagreements and disputes between followers (the key is personalization and individualization). It stresses the point that much of this work does not scale quickly—or effortlessly—without intention and purpose and a focus on intercultural competency, trust building, and collaboration—on the small problems and conflicts on a team first. The chapter lays out the case that diversity of mindset is more in danger than ever before for leaders and that the temptations to Non-Obvious Sycophancy should be avoided at all costs.

Introduction: Why Most Diversity Training Efforts Fail

Diversity and inclusion are challenging topics to tackle for leaders. The modern definition of diversity has moved inexorably from the idea of *E Pluribus Unum*—from many to one—to the idea that not only should leaders see differences, they should also be compassionate, caring, empathetic, and above all else, act when diverse identities, perspectives, or opinions are not honored on the team, in the organization, and the workplace.[1]

Furthermore, while leaders are wrapping their arms around this conundrum, they are also being asked to integrate all the various forms of diversity and representation on their teams and in their organizations. They must create a coherent whole while also navigating competition and threats that can come from political, social, technological, legal, and environmental factors they have no direct control over, but will affect their teams' performance in the world of work—and beyond.

Leaders understand that diversity is a function of the biological and environmental differences that separate and distinguish people as individuals and groups. From an impartial (objective) point of view, it is the large number of physical and cultural differences that make up the range of human differences. These dynamics become even more heightened when economic, social, and cultural disruptions change and other circumstances affect not only how leaders communicate, but even begin to affect what type of communication is allowed and what type of communication is now *verboten* in the workplace. As a researcher in the future of the workplace once told us in discussing the overwhelming complexity of these issues for leaders of small business teams as well as scaled corporate teams, "the fact is, now *everyone has to care* [emphasis ours]."

That may be true; however, the question is not "Do leaders care?" They do. Instead, the question is "How can we competently communicate that caring in a way that scales across the team?"

Before we begin the process of caring and communicating in a manner that honors diversity, encourages inclusion, and promotes psychological safety, we must look at the list of EEOC (Equal Opportunity Employment Commission) approved categories by which an employee can be protected from discrimination in their ability to attain employment from any employer in the United States:

- Race
- Color
- Religion or creed
- National origin or ancestry
- Sex (including gender, pregnancy, sexual orientation, and gender identity)
- Age
- Physical or mental disability
- Veteran status
- Genetic information
- Citizenship.

These are just the protected classes at the time of this writing. Many states have their own definitions and classes of anti-discrimination categories that expand on—or cover in more depth and detail—the types of classes of protected people.

In addition, there are the secondary dimensions of diversity the EEOC is (currently) agnostic about in hiring, but increasingly is moving toward defining for employers—and leaders—actions they can and cannot take:

- Educational background
- Geographic location
- Income
- Marital status
- Military experience
- Parental status
- Religious beliefs
- Work experience
- ...and others[2]

However, leaders know hiring is just the first part of solving the diversity problem. Once you have recruited, hired, and onboarded people to your team, the real culture-building work begins.

Culture and Leadership in the Workplace—The Iceberg You Can Crash Your Leadership Boat Against

Leaders understand that tackling communication problems and concerns around diversity and inclusion begins with acknowledging and understanding the effect of workplace culture. Most workplace culture occurs without intention and springs up unintentionally as people begin working on a task together and begin to make decisions (See Leadership and Team Building Chapter) about their behaviors based on pre-programmed responses and reactions they have sharpened since they were children playing games in groups. Understanding culture, and appreciating and respecting diversity, begins with leaders recognizing culture is a pattern of values and beliefs reflected in lived behavior. "Culture constitutes learned and shared values. Values are enduring beliefs that one way of acting or being is better than another." (Carr-Ruffino, 1996).[3] Culture defines social situations; it creates the parameters for acceptable and unacceptable behavior and it molds leaders just as much as it does followers.

Leaders know inclusion is about creating environments intentionally that focus on psychological safety through effective collaboration and attaining deep intercultural competence. However, many business organizations, teams, and groups fail to acknowledge the power of culture as a driver for diversity and inclusion (much less psychological safety). Many leaders are compensated to be task focused, performance driven, and to maximize either owner value or shareholder values. Moreover, how can culture be measured, observed, and assigned a dollar value? Leaders know that to communicate well around diversity and inclusion, they must recognize and act on the fact culture creates communication patterns.

Culture matters when understanding the effect of diversity and the practical need to engage with and encourage inclusion. Leaders know culture happens at work and is built intentionally rather than just springing up accidentally as if it were a Pavlovian response to some invisible external stimuli. Furthermore, during times of political, social, financial, or personal crisis and disruption, workplace culture becomes more than just "in the air." It needs to be maintained and grown collaboratively.

Otherwise, just as an iceberg grows below the water deeper than whatever its height might be above the ground and presents an existential challenge to ocean-going vessels and distracted sea pilots, the iceberg of diversity can wreck the ship of an organization if leaders are not paying attention.

Intercultural Competence + Inclusion + Psychological Safety

Intercultural competence—the ability to listen, recognize, and communicate comfortably and competently with diverse people from different cultures—began as a pursuit in the 1970s with legal and social movements around affirmative action. It continued in the 1980s with social changes around multiculturalism, grew in the 1990s with diversity and inclusion efforts in the workplace and has exploded into public consciousness in the 2000s with social justice and intersectionality movements.

However, no matter where the academics and national culture may want to lead the overall population, leaders recognize that, on a day-to-day basis, intercultural competency grows in power through the development of specific knowledge, skills and attitudes that lead to visible behavioral and communication changes in people and teams in the face of diversity and inclusion. Successful communication with people from different cultures leverages a combination of many factors including mood, temperament, focus, experience, knowledge, wisdom, negotiation skills, active listening, and so on. Leaders access all these factors to successfully communicate candidly and with courage.

Leaders seek to design systems to overcome intercultural competency challenges. They seek to embed these systems deeply inside the bone marrow of the team culture. The challenges are different for a start-up or small business organization. The small business is built specifically around a leader's own internalized cultural understanding and competencies (or lack thereof). A large, corporate organization may be generations past where its founders desired it to be with attitudes, competencies and understandings of culture that may be non-verbalized, and yet extremely powerful.

Intercultural competency and its effects can be seen in how inclusive organizations seek to be, or in fact, may be. Inclusion is the measure of engagement to which individuals and groups can bring their various identities, perspectives, opinions, and experiences as a measure of contribution to the organization. The desire for inclusion as a measure of engagement ties directly into the rise of theories and ideas focused on psychological safety. From the researcher Amy Edmondson and her book *The Fearless Organization: Creating Psychological Safety in the Workplace for Learning, Innovation, and Growth*: "Psychological safety—an environment in which people believe that they can speak up candidly with ideas, questions, concerns, and even mistakes—is vital to leveraging the benefits of diversity, because it can help make inclusion a reality. In brief, psychological safety is about enabling candor. Inclusion is necessary for mutual learning—and mutual learning is necessary to progress in a volatile, uncertain, complex, and ambiguous (VUCA) world. Extensive academic literature on psychological safety has demonstrated its powerful association with learning and performance in teams and organizations."[Source: https://www.psychologytoday.com/us/blog/the-fearless-organization/202006/the-role-psychological-safety-in-diversity-and-inclusion].[4]

Below are a few ways to build intercultural competence into a leadership approach:

- Establish a baseline of expectations around attaining intercultural competency—this process can include assigning readings, paying for employees to attend workshops, and building in the expectation of competency into the actual tasks of work throughout the day by maintaining an open, continuous feedback loop (See Chapter Two, Leadership and Emotional Intelligence for more of this).
- Walk the talk on diversity and inclusion—this can be demonstrated by establishing and following through on consequences for behavior that does not match the values espoused by the organization, even if the team has high status/high-value players. In ensuring cultural competence around diversity, we recommend a three-step process:
  - The first time an expectation, value, or standard is violated, refer to education, conversation, and investigation.
  - The second time an expectation, value, or standard is violated, refer to written, formalized policies, and issue warnings.
  - The third time an expectation, value, or standard is violated, move to terminate the employment in the organization rather than moving the "valuable team player" to another department to become some other leaders' headache.
- Be prepared for questions as a leader—challenges really—by those below you in the hierarchy who may view objectionable language, behavior, or attitudes as evidence of a lack of competence in other areas, and move quickly to separate people's actions, language, and behavior from their actual competency at accomplishing a task.
- Document, document, document—High-status per-

formers with large egos who are unwilling to bend and change to conform to a culture (the "Reality-Warping-Field'-Steve-Jobs-types")[5] need to understand there is a higher value than merely attaining task-based competence at the highest levels. There is value in attaining intercultural based competence that can lead to much greater outcomes and rewards. However, if, or when, those high performers do not buy that argument, then processes and systems need to be in place to terminate those individuals and remove their presence from the team.

Leaders know the ultimate struggle is not to create diverse work environments driven by intercultural competence. The real struggle is to make judgments about who is part of the diversity and who is on the outside, looking in, both from within organizations and from without. In essence, the balance is between establishing a hierarchy that can be honored and respected as being a place of competency, while also managing the environment a dictionary definition of inclusion demands. And the challenge is to do that balancing act intentionally while also focusing on psychological safety through effective, productive, and meaningful collaboration to produce work that matters in the world and that makes a difference.

Otherwise, all the diversity training, inclusion efforts, appeals to psychological safety, and desire for intercultural competence become just window dressing. And at the worst, can lead to the creation of environments where the spark of rebellion can light a forest fire of recrimination and revenge that even the best leader will not be able to put out.

Leaders and the Challenge of Multiple Mental Models

Leaders recognize the effect of emotional intelligence, sensitivity, hard-headed empathy. They also understand these skill sets, knowledge bases, and attitudes matter to their teams when addressing the cultural issues that negative or poorly handled diversity and inclusion interactions can ignite.

One of the things leaders are real about is the presence of "blind spots," in their personal, mental models: biases, and assumptions about the power and depth of what they do not know. And although there is little compelling, replicable, social science evidence that points to the power of implicit (or explicit) judgments and biases unequivocally, there must be the acknowledgment that every follower of a leader carries biases and blind spots—things they aren't aware of—in their mental models. Follower's lack of awareness of their own blind spots, lack of curiosity about what they do not know, combined with a lack of compelling interest in pursuing such unknown knowledge because of the chaos in identity that such a pursuit usually brings, is a challenge that can flummox even the best leaders. This is particularly frustrating for leaders when a disruption—or new idea—pops out of the ether of a previously unquestioned, psychologically safe assumption, as a vicious Jack-in-the-Box, intending to destroy a business model, market, or strategy.

Culturally competent, emotionally intelligent, and mentally resilient leaders are aware that mental models are the source of much of the power in creating psychologically safe workplace environments. From the writer of the *Farnam Street* blog, and researcher, Shane Parrish, "Mental models are how we understand the world. Not only do they shape what we think and how we understand but they shape the connections and opportunities that we see. Mental models are how we simplify complexity, why we consider some things more relevant than others, and how we reason." [Source: https://fs.blog/mental-models/].[6] Additionally, all our mental models, which lead to the creation of beliefs, which then lead to the creation of values, which then lead inexorably to the creation of culture, come in multiple, different forms and descriptions:

- The Map is Not the Territory
- Second-Order Thinking
- Bayesian Updating
- Hanlon's Razor
- The Red Queen Effect
- The Matthew Principle
- Margin of Safety
- Bottlenecks
- Scale
- Churn
- Algorithms
- The Law of Diminishing Returns
- Regression to Mean
- Opportunity Costs
- Arbitrage
- Scarcity (see Chapter Four, Leadership Communication and Persuasion)
- Mutually Assured Destruction
- Counterinsurgency
- Denial
- The Pavlovian Association
- Language Instinct
- Hindsight Bias (see Chapter Eleven, Leadership and Adapting to Change)
- Survivorship Bias
- ...and a multitude more.

Mental models structure how people think about their work culture, team collaboration, biases, and organizations. What each of these mental models reveals for leaders is the presence of four, rock-ribbed truisms that prove out across mental models, and no matter what situation, or set of circumstances, the mental model is overlaid upon:

- Each person has blind spots, areas in their mental models where they are unaware of their communication patterns and behaviors on other people and situations.
- Each person wrestles with how to integrate personal blind spots and how they intersect with the team and the organization's blind spots.
- Each person knows and understands precisely the width, depth, and breadth of the territory of their own experience and struggles to "cross the chasm" from their own experiences to others.
- Each person makes judgments and descends into biases in their thinking, behaving, and speaking because the shorthand of preference and discrimination is hard-wired into human brains to navigate successfully a chaotic, confusing, and fast world of ever-changing information.

Leaders know blind spots are natural because there are many areas individuals are unaware of their own communication patterns and behaviors toward other people and situations. "Your blind spots cause you to fail to recognize that emotions, such as fear and distrust, change how you and others interpret and talk about reality. You think you understand and remember what others say when you really only remember what you think about what they say." [Source: https://www.psychologytoday.com/us/blog/conversational-intelligence/201705/blind-spots].[7]

Leaders are also aware most people respond to feedback about their blind spots with varying levels of defensiveness. Combating this emotional defensiveness—the space where the amygdala of the brain begins to short circuit the cortex of the brain to return to a safe and secure posture—is a tricky process that requires tact, deft, and empathy. When leaders deliver feedback appropriately, with sensitivity, emotional intelligence, and without their own defensiveness coming into play, that feedback to their followers about their blind spots around diversity and inclusion can sometimes help people become aware and open to changing their perceptions. However, leaders must be aware that trust is a key component of this feedback process and to role model for the team and help the team face their blind spots around diversity and inclusion, leaders must be willing—and in many cases, eager—to face and overcome their own blind spots.

Applying the insights from understanding and researching mental models can help leaders design inclusive systems and execute intercultural communication and collaboration efforts while also understanding some team members may have high resistance and low trust.

The Trust and Resistance Problem

Leaders know employees who work together learn information about each other that enhances the work experience. This information can be professional, personal, or cultural and helps the employees work better together. They begin to understand how to interact more respectfully.

However, when workplaces are high resolution in the representation of the visual—or non-visual—markers of diverse identity groups, but are low resolution in the representation of actual trust between those groups based on developing vulnerability attained through connecting with others' lives, personal experiences, then all the diversity, social justice, bias, and systemic oppression training, workshops, and internal memos in the world from management are going to fail.

In his book *The Five Dysfunctions of a Team: A Leadership Fable*, author Patrick Lencioni makes a point about the absence of trust in teams:

"The first dysfunction is an absence of trust among team members. Essentially, this stems from their unwillingness to be vulnerable in the group. Team members who are not genuinely open with one another about their mistakes and weaknesses make it impossible to build a foundation for trust."[8]

And as work environments have shifted inexorably toward the flattening of white collar, knowledge-based work that does not require the hard task of physical labor to accomplish, the demands for vulnerability, trust, humane understanding, and empathy have concurrently increased, even among leaders in blue-collar environments, to develop systems that allow such trust as Lencioni is describing, to grow.

And yet, we still have positional leaders with years of practical experience in leading people and teams through accomplishing hard tasks, and in watching those teams have low resolution diversity and identity mandates thrust upon them, respond to such appeals to trust with a shrug of disinterest. Or even worse.

We once worked with a client in the retail biotechnology market space who, after we had facilitated a mandatory training not about diversity but about conflict (which can raise its ugly head as a precursor to other issues), say to us in the form of one female manager in the room: "Why cannot people just suck it up? I do not want to give you a hug at work. I want you to show up, shut up, do the work, and take your identity home with you."

Thus, we pinpoint the second problem of building a system for diverse teams to operate in—the problem of resistance. Resistance is the psychological representation of the work of the amygdala at the biological level in the brain. The resistance is deceptive, tricky, persuasive, groveling, and primarily focused on three areas: surviving, safety, and reproducing. And not necessarily in that order.

One of the larger issues in organizations built based on deeply ingrained Industrial Revolution assumptions about work, people, motivations, and identity, is the failure to directly address workplace dysfunctions at a systems level, and just allowing individuals to "work it out" between themselves, invariably creates more of the problem the leader is seeking to resolve. However, the leaders' amygdala is just as short-term focused as anyone else's (the cortex cares about status) and leaders must check, not only their own mental models, but also examine and dissect their own resistance.

This is the space where leaders work on themselves to gain self-awareness about their blind spots around areas of diversity—both low and high resolution—and they work with their teams to ensure awareness of communication patterns and behaviors improves through effectively, empathetically, and firmly delivered feedback in an environment of genuine trust and vulnerability.

Here are the practical steps to building a trustworthy environment where psychological safety, vulnerability, empathy, and inclusion can adapt to the various identities workplaces currently espouse—and may begin to celebrate in the future:

- Lead with the heart by avoiding shaming, building trust through small acts, managing people's emotions, and separating people (who they are in their identity) from positions (the things they say about that identity).
- Develop intercultural, emotional, and leadership competency by knowing and caring about other people's "why," and developing a positive approach to anger and negative emotions.
- Employ the principles of Stop-Think, Listen, Communicate, where before acting, responding, or engaging, a leader stops their thinking cold, actively listens to the other party—which means listening attentively without the presence of "white noise" in the leader's head, and then communicate with clarity, candor, and courage to the other party (See Chapter One, Leadership Roles and Responsibilities).
- Lead yourself by avoiding confirmation bias, tunnel vision, a loss of ethics and a lack of vulnerability and sensitivity (See Chapter Two, Leadership and Emotional Intelligence).
- Monitor non-verbal communication, body language cues, and the power of signs and symbols, from which human beings attain deep, contextual clues about a leader's true heart, focus, and motivations and then seek to combine what

the leader is verbally communicating with what is non-verbally being signaled in an interaction.

Leaders are aware inclusion does not work without trust, and they are aware in work environments where trust is low, receiving feedback about a lack of inclusive behaviors can cause team members to behave or react defensively in the face of diversity problems and thus, further exacerbate problems. However, establishing, maintaining, and growing trust is only the second step in building a leadership environment that welcomes diversity and lives inclusion out practically. The third step is throwing teams into collaborative workspaces and not leaving until the collaboration is done.

In his book *The Five Dysfunctions of a Team: A Leadership Fable*, author Patrick Lencioni makes a point about the absence of trust in teams:

"The first dysfunction is an absence of trust among team members. Essentially, this stems from their unwillingness to be vulnerable in the group. Team members who are not genuinely open with one another about their mistakes and weaknesses make it impossible to build a foundation for trust."[9]

And as work environments have shifted inexorably toward the flattening of white collar, knowledge-based work that does not require the hardtack of physical labor to accomplish, the demands for vulnerability, trust, humane understanding, and empathy have concurrently increased, even on leaders in blue-collar environments, to develop systems that will allow such trust as Lencioni is describing, to grow.

And yet, we still have positional leaders with years of practical experience in leading people and teams through accomplishing hard tasks, and in watching those teams have low-resolution diversity and identity mandates thrust upon them, respond to such appeals to trust with a shrug of disinterest.

Or even worse.

Collaboration and Inclusion: The Final Frontier

One of the more interesting critiques of a pop culture property from the world of science fiction is the common critique of the leadership style of the fictional Captain Jean-Luc Picard of the starship Enterprise on *Star Trek: The Next Generation*. If you are not a fan of science fiction (or just chalk it up to being the overwrought fantasies of geeky man-children), this critique will be meaningless, outside of its application to the concept of leadership through collaboration. And, if you are a fan of science fiction, and at least have a passing familiarity with the show, this critique will anchor the remaining part of this chapter for you.

Captain Picard, leading a diverse team of human beings, aliens, and even an android, through space in the 24th century often encounters problems with other aliens, other civilizations, and even problems with the presence of space itself. His method of solving these problems—unlike his better known and more virile predecessor, the original Star Trek's Captain James T. Kirk—was to solicit, involve and fundamentally seek out the opinions of the professional crew around him and *then to do what they recommended*, while taking responsibility for the failure of an idea, and giving credit for successes away as fast as he could.

Among fans of the original *Star Trek* from the 1960s, this method of leadership was considered weak and heretical. And their critique focused on the fact Picard never left the ship because his crew was so adept at collaboration, vulnerability, and technology; they never faced an existential crisis that truly challenged their collaborative tendencies.

And then the alien species known as the Borg came along, and that, as they say, put paid to that.

In the unscripted, imperfect real-world leaders and followers inhabit, the critiques against collaboration on teams from both leaders and teams are the same:

- "It [collaboration] does not work."

- "When everyone has a right to their opinion, nothing gets done."
- "People are idiots."
- "If we solicit information from everyone, there will be too much information and then we will be paralyzed."
- "Failure is not tolerated here, so it is best if the person whose title says "boss" just tells us what to do."
- "No one wants to be accountable." And so on.

Leaders know if an organizational culture has previously unresolved problems in any areas of collaboration, vulnerability, bias, or other blind spots, the culture will struggle to shift no matter what the external factors. Team cultures built around the concepts of flatness (Zappos), self-government (August), or that strongly favor autonomy, mastery, and purpose as motivational drivers for collaboration (Atlassian), still struggle with maintaining meaningful collaboration at the ground level within the team. And when unresolved issues around trust, inclusion, and intercultural competency are thrown into the mix, appeals to collaboration can ring somewhat hollow.

This is because collaboration is not a buzzword. It is a practical set of actions leaders must take to ensure their team's culture is growing toward increasingly greater levels of collaboration. At a practical level, leaders must engage with collaboration at the cultural level by taking the following steps:

- Ensure a baseline level of understanding of tasks by everyone on the team.
- Create unambiguous consequences for failures of accountability.
- Move away from the process of blame after a failure (See Chapter Nine, Leadership and Accountability) and move toward a culture of doing better the next time.
- Be prepared to know every struggle and to stop a project

or work to actively address it.
• Create systems of communication (digital and in-person, remote and on-site) that provide team members with space to engage proactively rather than reactively.

Practical Actions for Creating Diverse Teams.

Leaders work to develop their teams to ensure diversity and inclusion efforts will "stick." Here are the practical steps to building a trustworthy environment where psychological safety, vulnerability, empathy, and inclusion can adapt to the various identities workplaces currently espouse – and may begin to celebrate in the future.

Tip #1 - Engage in intentional team building. Build teams around self-awareness and move toward higher levels of trust and collaboration. Lead with heart by avoiding shaming, building trust through small acts, managing people's emotions, and separating people (who they are in their identity) from positions (the things they say about identity).

Tip #2 - Establish and follow team expectations. Create expectations that match reality rather than objectives that may look great on paper but may not work in the real world. Develop intercultural, emotional, and leadership competency by knowing and caring about other people's "why," and developing a positive approach to anger and negative emotions.

Tip #3 - Establish an environment that encourages psychological safety. Grow environments where people can feel included rather than excluded. Employ the principles of Stop-Think, Listen, Communicate, where before acting, responding, or engaging, a leader stops their thinking cold, actively listens to the other party—which means listening attentively without the presence of "white noise" in the leader's head, and then communicate with clarity, candor and courage to the other party (see Chapter One, Leadership Roles and Responsibilities).

Tip #4 - Navigate conflict at work. Realize that confronting behaviors that do not match the culture we want is not conflict; however, it may make us uncomfortable. Lead yourself by avoiding confirmation bias, tunnel vision, a loss of ethics, and a lack of vulnerability and sensitivity (see Chapter Two, Leadership and Emotional Intelligence and Chapter Four, Leadership and Conflict Management).

Tip #5 - Become allies to others at work. Becoming allies to others at work requires active listening, objective assessment, and cultural sensitivity. Monitor non-verbal communication, body language cues, and the power of signs and symbols, from which human beings attain deep, contextual clues about a leader's true heart, focus, and motivations and then seek to combine what the leader is verbally communicating with what is non-verbally being signaled in an interaction.

In times of crisis, leaders step up to ensure diversity and inclusion efforts work for individuals and teams. Leaders do the hard work of building collaborative cultures around diversity and inclusion because this kind of work is the only work that allows trust to flourish, communication to be open, and feedback to be delivered and received, openly rather than defensively. Leaders are aware that inclusion does not work without trust, and they are aware that in work environments where trust is low, receiving feedback about a lack of inclusive behaviors can cause team members to behave or react defensively in the face of diversity problems and thus, further exacerbate problems. But establishing, maintaining, and growing trust is only the second step in building a leadership environment that welcomes diversity and lives inclusion out practically. The third step is throwing teams into collaborative workspaces and not leaving until the collaboration is done.

CHAPTER NINE

Rule 9
Leaders Avoid the Blame/Credit Trap
Leadership and Accountability

Leaders know that leadership means deciding to act with the information you have, not the information you wish you had, you could have had, or that you would have had. Leaders know that leadership after-action, "Monday morning" quarterbacking, is not actually helpful."
Jesan Sorrells

This chapter focuses on the "Holy Grail" of leadership: motivating followers to self-start and take on accountability, while counterbalancing with remaining interdependent and collaborative. It lays out the structural and philosophical difference between accountability and responsibility and shows how those are not both the same things. The rule makes the case for leaders to consider around being careful what they ask their followers for to reduce the surprise level when they get an outcome they were not expecting around accountability.

Introduction: Indiana Jones was Looking for It as Well

Responsibility, accountability, ownership, autonomy, mastery, and purpose, all link together on a high-performing team, where team members know what the goal is, understand the expectations of them, are highly trained and internally motivated by doing the work required of them, and know they can get better and better at the work they are performing and see the results of that growth every day. And yet, many leaders feel as though their teams are performing around accountability in a mediocre manner, falling into the traps of the victim cycle, blaming games, shaming others, and avoiding opportunities to own outcomes and consequences regularly. Many leaders feel the pursuit of accountability is the same journey the adventure hero Indiana Jones was on when he was searching for the Holy Grail, and indeed, accountability for many leaders is the Holy Grail of leadership. However, as with many leadership concepts, leaders have accountability conceptualized in the wrong way. And then, from that misconception, leaders move forward making mistake after mistake in their pursuit of accountability in others.

There are three main problems leaders have when they pursue accountability work with their teams. The first problem is the lack of a clear definition of what they want their followers to be accountable for. The second problem is failing to make clear the difference between responsibility and accountability so the follower can successfully navigate what is required of them. The author Seth Godin writes about the difference between accountability and responsibility in this way:

> "Accountability *is done to you*. It's done by the industrial system, by those that want to create blame. Responsibility *is done by you*. It's voluntary. You can take as much of it as you want." [Source: https://seths.blog/2019/05/accountability-vs-responsibility/].[1]

Leaders may disagree with Godin's conceptualization, but it makes clear the difference between responsibility and accountability for leaders. The third problem lies in leaders failing to be clear with themselves about what emotional fuel is driving their pursuit of accountability in others, whether that is avoiding blame, or taking credit.

Thus, problems of ownership spring from problems of

accountability. Followers aren't going to engage in the radical risk of ownership if they do not have clear coaching and guidance on what is to be owned and why. Because leadership in and of itself is a risk, leaders are usually blind to the fact for many followers, ownership is just as big a risk. When leaders dismiss or underestimate the risk appetite among their followers, or do nothing concrete to increase such an appetite, they inevitably create team environments where it is easier for followers to allow leaders to take on the risk of ownership.

Indiana Jones was not just interested in the Holy Grail as an object. He was interested in the journey toward the object as well. When leaders enroll followers on the journey to accomplish a mission or to achieve a goal, they ensure the people they are leading are going to be responsible, accountable, and will engage with ownership with autonomy, mastery, and with a focus on a much larger purpose. The leaders who stoke interest in the journey, leveraging skills of persuasion and communication, while dealing with the difficult people who may be following them, will have an infinitely higher level of success along the path. Accountable leaders pursue the creation of more accountable leaders.

The Blame Game

Back in the 1960s, there was a popular song titled "The Name Game," sung by Shirley Ellis. The premise of the song was that you could put any letter at the start of any name and then combine it with a nonsense pronunciation to create a "new" name. The song provides the singer (and listener) no clue as to what to do with the "new" name after it has been created and, like other nonsense doggerel, the "new" name provides little context, identity, or solutions for the newly named individual.[2] When a team engages in finger-pointing, avoidance, covering their tail, and other victim cycle behaviors, they are engaging in a similar pursuit of nonsensical doggerel of little practical value.

So why is the blame game so popular?

Leaders who are paying close attention to human behavior recognize people are driven either by avoidance of pain or loss or by the opportunity for success and pleasure. Although this is not a new idea, the fact of being able to blame others for personal failures becomes more of a problem as we move from doing the kind of work and tasks that require physical labor, such as digging ditches or mining coal, to labor that requires emotional and psychological investment. The fact of such labor is it requires people to engage fully in ways they may not be comfortable with around failure, loss, or missing the mark. There has always been a struggle with the psychological manifestations of failure in followers; however, leaders in the past could make appeals to physical prowess, physical heroism, or physical effort to distract, blunt, or mute the voices of failure and the tendency to externalize personal failures to others. This is no longer the case.

Leaders must understand the psychological underpinnings of individuals' tendencies to move in the direction of blame or failure to neutralize the effects of such tendencies at their source. Authors Roger Connors, Tim Smith and Craig Hickman in their seminal book on accountability, *The Oz Principle: Getting Results Through Individual and Organizational Accountability*, address the perils of the victim cycle in this manner:

> "A thin line separates success from failure, the great companies from the ordinary ones. Below that line lies excuse making, blaming others, confusion, and an attitude of helplessness, while above that line, we find a sense of reality, ownership, commitment, solutions to problems and determined action. While losers languish Below The Line® preparing stories that explain why past efforts went awry, winners reside Above The Line powered by commitment and hard work. People and organizations find themselves thinking and behaving Below The Line whenever they consciously or unconsciously avoid account-

ability for individual or collective results. Stuck in the victim cycle or the blame game, they begin to lose their spirit and resolve until, eventually, they feel completely powerless. Only by moving Above The Line and climbing the Steps To Accountability® can they become powerful again" (pg.10).[3]

It is a "thin line" and the line continually becomes thinner if leaders cannot create environments where empowerment and engagement with the overall goals and mission of the organization will not be lost in a sea of blame. In many cases, the past is the thing leaders fail to properly address or contextualize for followers and thus, the journey to the result (or the goal) falls victim to the easy tendency to focus on past failures and to allow those failures to poison the path forward to the future. Leaders must address the past but do it in a way that avoids shame as well as blame.

Shame is blame's sibling and walks alongside blame, but is often rarely addressed or acknowledged, because of the cultural and psychological constraints people have around even talking aloud about what they may be ashamed of. Instead, shame leaks out in social interactions in the form of language, behaviors, and attitudes that either push people to battle against shame or push people into silence about shame. Leaders can see this in times of stress and crisis most acutely when people fail to talk about the fact of a crisis or internalize the effects of external stressors in their psychological or emotional environment. When confronted directly, shame can be diffused but the fact is, much like the mole in the game Whack-A-Mole, a leader can never be too sure shame will not rear its ugly head again. The researcher and author, Brené Brown had this to say about shame:

> "Based on my research and the research of other shame researchers, I believe that there is a profound difference between shame and guilt. I believe that guilt is

adaptive and helpful—it's holding something we've done or failed to do up against our values and feeling psychological discomfort.

I define shame as the intensely painful feeling or experience of believing that we are flawed and therefore unworthy of love and belonging—something we've experienced, done, or failed to do makes us unworthy of connection.

I do not believe shame is helpful or productive. In fact, I think shame is much more likely to be the source of destructive, hurtful behavior than the solution or cure. I think the fear of disconnection can make us dangerous."[-Source: https://brenebrown.com/articles/2013/01/15/shame-v-guilt/][4]

To be sure, shame has a biological component as well as a psychological one, and leaders would be remiss to believe they can ever eliminate shame and blame from people individually. However, collectively, leaders can create environments where the power of blaming is reduced as much as possible. The first thing leaders should do is be aware of the steps of the Victim Cycle, described in *The Oz Principle*. Second, leaders need to engage in intentionally understanding and leveraging the emotional connection power of coaching as an act of radical change in people. The third thing leaders need to engage with is creating environments where their energy is spent appropriately, not on chasing blame or shame, but instead on working with the followers who are on board with responsibility, who are seeking accountability, and who thirst for radical—some would say extreme—ownership. Finally, leaders must be practical about the effects of critical, post-failure analysis processes that, when facilitated correctly, lead to understanding and future commitment, rather than finger-pointing or avoidance of blame.

The Land of Oz

Feelings of being "put upon."

Feelings of resentment.

Feelings of hurt from past disappointments.

Feelings of jealousy and envy.

These are drivers of the mentality that produces followers who are less concerned about shouldering responsibility, and who are more concerned with the question of Cain. In the Biblical story of Cain and Abel, Cain is driven by resentment, feelings of being "put-upon," and feelings of being hurt by past disappointments. He kills his brother Abel—in the world's first accurately reported murder—and then, when questioned by God about the killing, responds with the question many human leaders hear, in one form or another, from followers who are trapped in a cycle of victimization: "Am I my brother's keeper?" [Source Genesis 4:9. *KJV*].[5] When followers are looking to avoid, they ask the question of Cain and inevitably respond, either internally or vocally, with the word "no."

This feeling of victimization is at the heart of the avoidance of accountability and the inability of individuals to take responsibility. Ownership does not even make it into the mix, and the further people are away from the leader relationally—Cain lived in a world where God no longer walked with human beings and communicated with them face to face as He had just a generation prior with Cain's parents, Adam and Eve—or the further away people feel from the leader relationally, the harder it becomes to break the victim cycle.

The Oz Principle: Getting Results Through Individual and Organizational Accountability, addresses the steps in the Victim Cycle and describes their manifestations clearly and concisely. Below, we quote at length from this book:

> "While the victim cycle can be bafflingly complex, there are six basic stages common to most people and organizations:

- Ignore/Deny. A typical beginning point for those who become ensnared in the victim cycle is the ignore and deny stage where people pretend not to know that there is a problem, remain unaware that the problem affects them or choose to deny the problem altogether.
- It's Not My Job. This stage reflects an awareness that something needs to be done to get the result, coupled with an acute avoidance of getting involved.
- Finger-Pointing. In this stage of the victim cycle people deny their own responsibility for poor results and seek to shift the blame to others.
- Confusion/Tell Me What to Do. At this stage of the victim cycle, people cite confusion as a way of alleviating themselves of their accountability. If they do not understand the problem or the situation, surely, they cannot be expected to do anything about it.
- Cover Your Tail. The penultimate stage of the victim cycle is cover your tail, where people continue to seek imagined protection Below The Line by crafting elaborate and precise stories as to why they couldn't possibly be blamed for something that might go wrong.
- Wait and See. Initially, people remain mired in the victim cycle when they choose to "wait and see" if things will get better. In such a climate, however, problems can only get worse.

Every situation is different, every person is unique, but everyone reaches a critical moment when he or she recognizes having been stuck in the victim cycle" (p.24-33).[6]

Indeed.

Leaders must be aware of the stages of the victim cycle, but moreover, they must be aware that steps in the cycle can be layered upon one another, their effects compounded by the context of the situation, and that leaders themselves can fall into the trap of victim thinking when they are tired, stressed, disappointed or under other types of emotional and psychological pressure. Team morale can be undermined by the effects of the victim cycle, and leaders must know their people, encourage their people, and coach their people when the pressures that accompany both success and failure manifest.

Coaching as A Tool to Get Accountability

Coaching, supervision, and mentoring are all different acts that require different mindsets and attitudes from leaders to be effective. Unfortunately, many leaders default to a combined approach to coaching that seeks to blend elements of supervision and mentoring into the pot as well. On the surface, this seems reasonable. However, in the long-run, such blending creates confusion in followers and adds to a sense of leadership miscommunication or even leadership dysfunction. The subtle distinctions between the three lay in both how communication is delivered by a leader leveraging the skills, and how that communication is interpreted by the person receiving it.

Supervision is the relational act of closely monitoring a task and the person doing it. Supervision indicates a low level of trust, minimal relational communication, and the enforcement of punishment and/or discipline if tasks are not completed in a timely fashion. Acts of supervision do not encourage the growth of accountability in followers because followers know without being told directly and verbally, that if they make a mistake, make an error, or make an omission, the penalty for that error will not become their responsibility to correct. Because supervision is fundamentally an evaluative act, it is highly reactive (rather than proactive) and requires a high level of emotional commitment from leaders to engage effectively. Therefore, many managers in the middle of organizational cultures are very good at supervision and bad at leading. They enjoy the ego boost supervision provides, all the while complaining about the level of emotional commitment to followers at a micro-level that successful supervision requires. Supervision is fine at the beginning stages of a task or project, but leaders must overcome the need to boost their egos by confusing acts of supervision with genuine growth on the part of followers. And followers need to be hardened in the fires of failures.

Coaching is the primary act leaders must engage with to create a healthy environment that supports and encourages the growth of accountability and that encourages the development of skills that lead to ownership. Coaching is misunderstood—even by many coaches—and leaders often mistake acts of coaching for acts of supervision, or its older brother, mentoring. Coaching is the facilitative act of guiding another individual through an action you understand better than they do in a critical way they miss. This definition is why coaches who have never played a moment of a sport in a championship game are often the best coaches of other players seeking to win a championship game. It is also why coaches who have never won an award for acting are often the best coaches of acting talent, and why many successful coaches do not personally like the people they have coached to greatness. The effectiveness of acts of coaching do not lie in the success or failure of the skill set of the person doing the coaching. It lies in that person's ability to communicate the success or failure, and to tell a story about how the person being coached can do better. Coaching, as a form of active feedback, goes past the passive acts of role modeling and moves communication to a higher level where more trust is necessary.

Mentoring is the relational act of engaging with a person at a deeper level than either coaching or supervision. Mentoring requires high levels of trust on both sides of the relationship to be effective. Mentoring is not about getting followers to accomplish tasks; however, encouraging and externally motivating followers to accomplish specific, measurable, attainable, realistic, and time-sensitive goals is the core function of mentoring. Successful mentoring requires that leaders engage in intentional listening and hearing along with the building of two-way relationships. Leaders must care deeply about the people they are mentoring, and the person being mentored must care about their mentor. The follower also must care about themselves and their goals and be able to either accept, ignore or balance those two differentials to act with effectiveness in their lives. The reason many mentoring programs and algorithmic manipulations of people based on data points do not work with mentorship is that people must choose each other and already have demonstrated the strengths of character to be accountable before a mentoring relationship takes place. Organizations do not measure for such strengths. Algorithms do not pick it up. And leaders are often so blinded by a combination of ego, stress, and their own hunger for mentors, even they overlook this metric.

To be effective coaches and to coach individuals and teams to higher levels of accountability, leaders must abandon a mindset of supervision. This requires not only letting go of their own ego but also requires selecting people to lead and forming teams built on equitable principles, rather than corporate politics. To be effective coaches, and to coach individuals and teams to higher levels of accountability, leaders must be clear about their own principles while also being able to negotiate effectively with an organizational structure that may have other goals in mind. Leaders must also be clear about where the focus of their energy and drive is in moving team members inexorably toward accepting increased levels of accountability.

Reversing the Pareto Principle

The idea of the Pareto Principle is a simple one: for many outcomes, across almost all fields of endeavors from book publishing to winning a chess championship, roughly 80 percent of the consequences come from twenty percent of the causes. The Pareto Principle is also known as the power-law distribution, which is a way of measuring the functional relationship between two quantities: inputs and outputs. The Pareto Principle is evident in economics, computing, sports (where fifteen percent of all the players of a particular game in a year produce 85 percent of all the wins of all the players combined) and in occupational safety, engineering, quality control, health, and social outcomes, etc. The law also applies to leaders and acts of leadership, particularly in the space of supervising followers in their attempts to ensure accountability: leaders spend 80 percent of their available time, emotional, and psychological energy on attempting to change, transform, and move the twenty percent of followers who are "problems." In doing this, leaders neglect to supervise, mentor, or serve the 80 percent of followers who are ready to take on more accountability, are already shouldering responsibility, and innately understand the difference between accountability and responsibility.

By unthinkingly following the Pareto Principle (or being led by it), leaders often fail themselves by burning leadership "fuel" on followers who they would be better off firing or removing from the team. This principle becomes even more apparent when leaders are faced with the political repercussions of firing a talented follower who has trouble taking on full accountability, leading a team of individuals who have failed to "gel" and are still behaving as individuals, or when the leader has misread the team landscape and is pushing individuals to levels of accountability that they are not ready to take on emotionally, psychologically, or materially. Leaders then complain, burn out, or wind up becoming calloused to the people they are tasked with leading in that twenty percent category. The other team members may coast along, but more likely than not, they will leave the team to pursue other avenues of success with higher performers who are dedicated at the same level they are, or they will languish on the team and the leader will have an only marginally accountable team at best.

Leaders must do the hard thing and reverse how they engage with the team around accountability. Instead of spending 80 percent of their available time, emotional, and psychological energy on the twenty percent of followers who are "problems," leaders should focus their majority energy—their 80 percent—on the 80 percent of the followers who are moving in the direction of greater accountability. This is a hard truth that leaders with open hearts and higher levels of emotional intelligence will reject…at first. But over time, as leaders continually grow closer to emotional burnout around establishing and maintaining accountability, they are going to subconsciously decide to shift their leadership efforts anyway. Leaders should analyze themselves first and get clarity around their emotional boundaries, then get clear with their followers around the expectations about accountability and responsibility quickly, and finally, be ruthless in following up with consequences when a lack of accountability or responsibility is becoming evident. These actions will ensure leaders stay aligned with followers and the team stays engaged with the overall mission, vision, values, and goals (MVVG).

Ownership Begins with Actions Followers See

Ownership comes after responsibility and accountability and should be the highest goal for a leader to achieve with their team, outside of the more general focus on accomplishing immediate goals. When followers exhibit ownership, they perform acts of the process without needing supervisory level direction. When followers exhibit ownership, they are constantly on the lookout for new ways to improve the process and, if they cannot convince the leader the improvement is necessary, they dare to make the change and accept the consequences of failure personally, or to give away the credit for success to the team. When followers exhibit ownership, they do not focus on problems; instead, they are constantly searching their portion of the mission horizon for solutions. When followers exhibit ownership, they are driven by the need to accomplish whatever goals are placed in front of them and, once they do, they are ready, willing, and able to accept more responsibility, while articulating and defending clearly and rationally where their "breaking point" is.

The type of ownership we are describing does not take place in a vacuum. It can only grow and develop in an environment where the baseline of responsibility, accountability and ownership is role modeled by the leader. This means that if leaders want followers to take on 100 percent ownership of their sphere of influence, leaders need to be prepared to take on 100 percent ownership of problems and failures in their sphere of influence as well. The typical objection immediately provided to this idea is the one that asserts that followers do sometimes make mistakes and they do fail many times. This is, without a doubt, a thin excuse for leaders to avoid ownership for their inability to effectively communicate the MVVG of the organization to followers. It is, in essence, an example of the Victim Cycle working through leaders' mindsets. Leaders must be engaged with the idea that if there is failure, it is their fault. Not the fault of their followers, their leadership, or their instructions and directions around accomplishing goals.

This is a hard truth with significant consequences for leaders. When I was leading my team in the higher education industry, I was tasked with establishing a culture of ownership and accountability on teams across several different institutions. These teams had been led by people who failed to take accountability and ownership of 100 percent of the problems in their sphere of influence. The leaders had encouraged an environment on the teams of moving toward accomplishing goals by using collaboration without establishing the skill set of accountability on the team among the followers. Most higher education teams I led featured individuals who were around the 19- to 22-year-old age range. They were also populated by people who were in their first, or maybe second, professional position and they had few examples of effective, intentional leadership practices.

On one of these teams, where there was a history of failure at the accountability level, there was a team member my superior up the hierarchy tasked me with either "straightening out or firing" because the individual failed to live up to the promises they made to the organization to change their behaviors. It was a "three strikes and you're out" situation and the individual in question was on their third strike. What followed was an unmitigated disaster from day one of leadership for me: I spoke to the individual and attempted to realign them with the mission, vision, values and goals of the team and the organization. What I failed to realize was that in performing this alignment process, I did not receive, nor did I request, feedback on the issues and problems the individual was facing with ownership and accountability. Strike one to me. Next, I attempted to massage the other team members through persuasion tactics, failing to realize the individual in question was far more influential than I was in my position of formal authority. In failing to recognize this fact, I failed to acknowledge just how broken down and splintered into factions the team was. I believed, egotistically, I could bring everyone together if I talked to everyone individually and kept part of the status quo of the past rather than breaking from it completely. Strike two to me. Finally, when it came time to fire the individual because of a minor infraction that—when compared to previous infractions of policy was probably more of an offense that deserved sanction rather than firing—I failed to manage the firing process beyond managing paperwork and did not acknowledge or engage with other team members who were seeing this firing from a variety of angles. In failing to do so, I did not take full responsibility for the firing immediately and thus, begin the rebuilding process early. Strike three to me.

These three mistakes: failing to receive feedback from the individual follower, failing to recognize the power of informal authority and alliances, and failing to manage the emotional and psychological aspects of firing a problem team member who was popular among factions of the team, compounded to my detriment as a leader across time. Over a year, I gradually replaced people who quit with their fellow team member with followers who were more loyal to me. I also worked to establish a baseline of trust with the remaining team members and sought to keep them engaged as much as possible with the mission, vision, values, and overall goals of the organization. However, the pressure of not addressing the ownership issue built up to such a degree that I ended up having to write a *mea culpa* letter and make a public apology for my failure to take ownership and 100% accountability and responsibility for my role in the failure with the team member.

None of this was enjoyable, nor would I want to repeat it. Instead, in future leadership roles I internalized the lessons from this disaster and proceeded to move in the direction of establishing clear parameters and expectations around behavior, role modeling the expectations, over-communicating to ensure understanding, and following up. There is one element of this experience though that I would go back and revisit to ensure the trauma of the initial firing of the team member was not as damaging to the team.

Achieving Accountability 101

Once a leader is clear in their own minds about which communication act they are engaging in with their followers around responsibility, accountability, and ownership, then they can formulate a plan to execute successfully on the communication act, whether it be via coaching, supervising, or mentoring—or a combination thereof. The planning stage of the conversation is where many leaders, including many leaders of elite teams, fall. They do not plan conversations, make lists of questions, or prepare mentally and emotionally for the approach to an individual performer or team. Instead, many leaders just "wing it" and hope for the best in a communication scenario where the stakes are high, accountability is on the line, and where failure to engage properly has massive ramifications for successfully accomplishing goals and engaging in strategy.

There are four parts to embedding accountability to create a high-performing team from day one:

1. Be aware of the steps of the Victim Cycle, as described in *The Oz Principle*.
2. Engage in intentionally understanding and leveraging the emotional connection power of coaching as an act of radical change in people.
3. Create environments where their energy is spent appropriately, not on chasing blame or shame, but instead on working with the followers who are on board with responsibility, are seeking accountability, and who thirst for radical—some would say extreme—ownership.
4. Get practical about the effects of critical, post-failure analysis processes that, when facilitated correctly, lead to understanding and future commitment, rather than finger-pointing or avoidance of blame.

To be successful at having a conversation about a follower's accountability, leaders must start their planning with clear thinking, and follow that up by asking and answering the following questions of themselves in the planning stages before engaging in conversation or correction with a follower:

- What do I want out of this conversation?
- What can I reasonably expect to get from the other person out of this conversation?
- What do not I want out of this conversation?
- What am I comfortable with as an outcome of this conversation?
- What is an unacceptable outcome of this conversation for me?

Yes, these questions are incredibly self-focused. And that is because, while the conversation with a follower is other-focused, planning is always a self-focused act. It is comparable to the practice of beginning a workout program or going to the gym. Leaders do not lose weight or gain muscle mass by getting other people to attend the gym. It all starts with the leader. In asking these questions, leaders should document their answers on paper. Not on their phones or a computer. Putting pen to paper (or pencil) creates a stimulus between the brain and the finger that leads to deeper cognitive memory and emotional impact for adults. The answers to these questions provide the basis for clear thinking on the part of leaders. They represent a clear call to candor, for the questions, if truthfully and honestly answered, will reveal for leaders the depth of what they are asking their subordinates to take on. They represent a clear call to courage and can be leveraged successfully by leaders to demonstrate vulnerability, honesty, and truthfulness to followers.

The least addressed factor in practically developing accountability on teams and in organizational culture is the factor of alignment, which is the second point leaders must address practically to ensure accountability. Alignment is the leadership activity that begins practically with understanding the motives and critically examining the intent of followers, but then moves to selecting followers for the team who match the clearly stated MVVG of the team. That selection process is critical at the beginning of planning for having conversations about accountability, responsibility, and ownership, but it is also critical for understanding how to role model these principles and how to leverage alignment when leaders do not get to select team members.

Leaders begin the process by aligning their teams and followers with the MVVG of the organization. Then, they leverage coaching, persuasion, and penalties for failure to readjust followers' attitudes toward goals and outcomes. Finally, leaders realign their teams and followers with the MVVG to ensure followers recognize and act on responsibility for processes and outcomes and do so as a valid pursuit with benefits to them and the team. In creating an environment that supports successful alignment, there may be occasions when spending political capital to advocate for and stress changes to goals, missions, or visions is called for because people further up the hierarchy thrust them upon them. If leaders are unwilling, or unable, to do this advocacy work in the service of achieving alignment and executing on accomplishing an organizational vision, they should not be surprised when their calls to ownership and accountability fall on followers' deaf ears further down the hierarchy.

The three steps to building alignment are as follows:

- Align the team with the MVVG
- Readjust followers through leveraging coaching, persuasion, and penalties for failure
- Realign the team with the MVVG

Attempts to perform any of these alignment practices without first establishing clarity of thought, candor about past failures, or demonstrating the courage on the part of leaders to act as advocates and role models, will result in leaders continuing to engage with the power law of distribution. This will manifest as resistant team members, a lack of positive forward action toward goals, an increase in the stress level of leaders and a decrease in their overall effectiveness, and a mediocre to failing team barely—or never—reaching goals or accomplishing an aligned mission. There will also be an inevitable return to Victim Cycle inspired behaviors such as avoiding accountability, laying blame, ignoring solvable problems, making excuses, covering your tail, etc.

The most effective tool to ensure followers remain on the path to greater accountability beyond the fact of effective planning, role modeling, and an assertive posture toward alignment, is coaching. Coaching is the most effective tactical tool to engage with resistant and recalcitrant followers, to encourage followers who may be struggling with the implications of even a little bit of accountability, and to grow those followers who are already taking responsibility, stepping up to accountability, and are ready to move into the space of ownership more assertively. Leaders leverage coaching the least out of any tactic in their arsenal. Below is a list of questions to get a leader started on effective coaching:

- What are your strengths?
- What do you do best?
- What are the positive words people who know you would use to describe you?
- What do you enjoy most about your current role?
- What do you believe you are compensated in your position at work to do?
- What do you want to accomplish in the next month?
- What do you want to accomplish by the end of the year?
- What do you think I expect of you this year?
- What do you expect of me this year?
- What do you find the most satisfying about your work role?
- What about your work role motivates you the most?
- When you achieve goals, how would you like to be recognized?
- When you are successful, whom do you want to know about it?
- Is there a particular skill you would like to develop in the next year?

For leaders to be effective coaches, they must be self-aware of their limitations and be able to critique their failures and hold themselves accountable. They must have a measure of courage and resilience in the face of failure. Leaders must know the basic tasks the person they are coaching knows how to do, and if they have no experience in those areas, they must be willing and able to humble themselves to learn. Effective coaches also tell the truth—or at least they do not lie—even if those truths about accountability at an organizational, team, or individual level are unfair, inequitable, or unjust. Leaders are role models while they are coaching another person to greatness. Finally, at a practical level, leaders leverage the power of relationships within the coaching dynamic in a positive way and do not seek to weaponize coaching and make it a tool, or a vessel, for hazing, bullying, or other types of damaging or dysfunctional behaviors.

In summary, leaders construct environments that are conducive to leadership growth and behavioral change by intentionally creating team environments where their energy is spent appropriately, not on chasing blame or shame, but instead on working with the followers who are on board with responsibility, are seeking accountability, and who thirst for radical—some would say extreme—ownership. Leaders understand such environments are not built in a day. It takes many years of successes and failures to achieve such a growth-oriented team environment and then those practices that developed that environment must be codified and cemented into the foundation of team culture. Without doing that, intentionally, leaders wind up recreating the wheel with every new team, rather than merely reinforcing what was already there.

Speaking and Thinking Without Blame: Post Failure Reporting

No leader enjoys experiencing failure. No team wants failure to occur. However, the reality is that when leaders fail—or when the team fails—to accomplish a highly sought-after goal, the temptation to play the blame game and to descend into the Victim Cycle is so strong that many times, leaders feel helplessly sucked in. Intentional leaders avoid the maelstrom of blame, recognizing that accountability and ownership require acknowledging the risk of failure in taking up the pursuit of any task. However, they balance that risk at the back end of the process of accomplishing a goal by engaging in a post-action—or post success or post-failure—a process that is known as After-Action reporting.

Documenting what happen, why it happened, and most critically, how to avoid having it happen again, and doing so without blame but instead, with the team taking responsibility for their part of the problem is a critical step many leaders do not do. After-Action reporting and documentation allows leaders to figure out what went wrong and where to determine how best to prevent such scenarios from popping up again. However, such reporting and documentation also allows followers to safely experience the emotional catharsis necessary to purge the negative feelings a failure can imbue onto the team. That catharsis may not feel good in the moment, and the leader needs to be effective at balancing negative and positive feedback, breaking social proofing, and checking group think. However, during the act of reporting, followers need to feel as though they can talk about failure openly without rancor, and without shame.

Resentment, anger, mistrust, secretiveness, passive aggressive behavior—all of these are important variables to check in the pursuit of an accurate formulation about what happened and who performed what action to have successful After-Action reporting. Leaders must write down what they hear, document what they see, and integrate those lessons from the hearing and the seeing into their follow-up actions with their followers. Leaders who fail to call After-Action meetings, fail to listen to their people during the meetings, and who fail to implement the insights from such meetings, invariably fail at the leadership challenge around accountability and ownership, which leads to cascading failures in other more critical areas. Leaders must have an internal emotional system for engaging with feedback, which we will explore further in the chapter on feedback and discipline.

Practical Tips for Growing Accountability

Tip #1 - Avoid the "blame/credit" trap. Disconnect your leadership identity from avoiding blame or taking credit. Leaders must work emotionally to connect with the importance of ownership and be driven by the process of growing ownership, seeing team members and followers expand their abilities, and advocate for better team environments up the hierarchy rather than be driven to accomplish tasks or lead people out of fear of blame or greed for recognition and credit. This process represents a mindset shift of a radical nature that requires leaders to understand themselves and their limitations, and it requires leaders to have their identities firmly embodied in their self-conception. Clarity and self-awareness are required to avoid the Victim Cycle, or to recognize when there is the danger of falling into that trap because of pressure and stress, and then to avoid those traps. Intentional leaders are real with themselves about their responses to the "blame/credit" trap.

Tip #2 - Do not ignore history but also do not become encumbered by it. Leaders understand that team history and past experiences have weight, but that history and those experiences are not an anchor. Anchors weigh ships down and keep them from leaving the harbor or the dock. Weight can be discarded, thrown overboard once a ship is ready to proceed on its way or when the sea threatens to capsize the ship. Intentional leaders know when to throw history overboard and when to raise the anchor of history no matter where it may manifest in the teams' behavior or individual behavior. Not caring about the impact of history on a team is just as willfully blind a leadership position as is being held captive to that history. Intentional leaders open their eyes and are accountable to the past, present, and future of their team.

Tip #3 - Recognize that all humans fall into the Victim Cycle, but leaders get out of the cycle sooner with less damage. Leaders are human and the basic tendency of human beings is to revert to the mean, or average, of their baseline behaviors when stressors, external or internal, arise. Leaders who are unintentional or accidentally driven by the Victim Cycle mindlessly and subconsciously sabotage their leadership efforts, and many times succeed in sabotaging the whole team. Intentional leaders recognize the traps of the Victim Cycle and engage with pulling themselves out of the destructive behavioral cycle before it damages the team by impacting communication and relationships. There is no substitute for self-aware, clear, and intentional self-leadership when it comes to navigating and overcoming the Victim Cycle and then role modeling and coaching that behavior for others on the team.

Tip #4 - It all starts with you. Leaders understand that "the fish rots from the head down." However accidental leaders—or leaders who are leaders due to position, status, or political reasons—may struggle to accept the idea that everything in their sphere of influence is their responsibility. That includes people, processes, and systems. This idea means that ownership begins with accepting the idea that all the communication and relational dynamics around responsibility and accountability fall on the leader first before falling on anyone else. Intentional leaders know how to respond to such a call to ownership and make plans and have habits developed to engage in emotional and psychological self-care. Intentional leaders are not overwhelmed by ownership and accountability.

Tip #5 - Responsibility is about autonomy and agency. Accountability is (often) about coercion and force. Leaders understand that, when addressing ownership, accountability, and responsibility, the words they deploy matter. They pick their words carefully and judiciously to ensure the people and teams they are responsible for have a clear understanding of what is being discussed. Intentional leaders perform this picking and choosing of language at scale and work hard to ensure that opportunities to grow autonomy and agency are embedded in the team culture, from recruiting to hiring, onboarding, and even when a team member is removed. Intentional leaders understand that in team environments with a strong "command and control" atmosphere, enforcing accountability sometimes reverts to coercion, threat, or force. This is not optimal and the intentional leader leverages these tools as a last resort rather than a first option.

CHAPTER TEN

Rule 10
Leaders Remove Barriers to Trust, They Do Not Erect Them
Leadership and Discipline, Feedback, Strengths, and Well-Being

"Leadership requires a mix of both justice and mercy. The problem is people want all mercy—for themselves—and all justice—for others. Leaders must operate in the mode of wisdom, balancing both justice and mercy. Yes, that is hard. And that's leadership."
Jesan Sorrells

This chapter focuses on how to deliver feedback to followers as a leader and emphasizes the point that if you do not know your people, then any feedback you provide will be tone-deaf, unsupportive, and probably absorbed and engaged—if at all—in a passive or hostile aggressive manner. This is a chapter that also talks about the value of knowing what followers do well and being hyper-focused on providing feedback in a way that compounds followers' likelihood of doing more of those actions they do well, i.e., their strengths. The chapter makes a case for understanding that in collaborative environments, discipline must be nuanced, and feedback must speak to strengths rather than only to improving weaknesses.

Introduction: Making Hard Decisions
The mantra of Jocko Willink, former Navy SEAL and now leadership consultant, podcaster, entrepreneur, and published book author is: "Discipline equals freedom."[1] And for people

who are martially minded, willing to motivate themselves, and open to the suffering and physical, emotional, and psychological challenges such an appeal automatically generates in their psychology and emotions, he's correct. However, leaders lead teams of people who are motivated differently, have different attitudes toward accountability, and who exist in different psychological spaces emotionally about being a follower. The type of discipline leaders think of when they are faced with the act of sanctioning, documenting, and excising the people on the team who have broken the rules, is not the type of discipline a SEAL is thinking of. However, leaders are faced with the decision to punish, sanction, and document, or not, behaviors that are damaging to the team.

These types of decisions fall into the category of "hard" decisions. They are that way, not because of the decision itself—that usually has already been made in the mind of the leader—but because of the emotional and psychological results leaders face. The fallout from a hard decision can range from team members no longer trusting the leaders, all the way to the team fracturing into dissolute and disparate parts. No leader can predict the consequences of any decision. And past outcomes of decisions are rarely predictive of future outcomes of current decisions.

The element rarely talked about by leaders in the pursuit of sanctioning the rogue, undisciplined, or rebellious followers on teams, is the element of relationships. Leaders hate to admit it, and professional authors in the space of leadership development rarely, if ever, mention it, but even bad—or mediocre—actors on a team usually have the strong capability and talent at building relationships. They rely on the strength of those relationships to buoy them through being outed as bad actors, their behaviors no longer being accepted, and in the last stage, punishment and sanctioning happening to them. At every stage of this progression, leaders must make hard decisions, question their own motives and intention, avoid being manipulated by the bad actor, and walk the line between being a hero and a villain to followers on the team who the bad actor may exert a stronger influence over the behaviors of the team than the leader.

To make those hard decisions easier, leaders need to have an established system for communicating with followers. They must understand the power of persuasion. They must create expectations that are aligned with the MVVG of the overall team and organization. They must be emotionally capable of hearing feedback about their performance and be capable of delivering feedback when followers would rather not hear it. None of these elements work if the leader is a robotic person, incapable of connecting at a human level with their followers and developing a rapport. None of these elements work if the leader is emotionally or psychologically, or even spiritually weak or indecisive. And none of these elements work without trust being established up and down the team hierarchy.

The difficult aspect of hard decisions is other people and their reactions and responses. The more a leader is relationally tied to their followers' needs, wants, desires, and dreams, the more successful they are when discipline—which may equal freedom, but is a hard sell to the manipulative, the undisciplined, the unmotivated, and the disinterested—must be meted out by someone.

And, congratulations. If you are the leader, the delivery of the discipline is up to you.

Discipline and The Toxic Follower

Discipline, punishment, coercion, obedience, and compliance all merge when leaders consider correcting poor or substandard behavior. In specific organizations, there are usually policies and procedures, driven by paperwork and legal considerations, leaders must follow to formally put a stop to bad behavior. However, instances of formalized, documented, and paperwork-driven human resource processes usually lie at the end of a long road. That road is usually paved with missed clues, mixed messages, poor or non-existent communication practices, and bad judgment on the part of both leaders and followers. The specter of emotional contagion looms large over the path to a formalized sanctioning process and many leaders would prefer not to go down that road.

There are "soft" tools a leader is called to deploy before moving in the direction of larger interventions involving time, effort, and the leveraging of formalized, positional, authority. Some of these have already been discussed in previous chapters, including negotiation, persuasion, culture work, appeals to diversity, and leveraging a follower's level of motivation. However, many leaders ask, "what is the best principle to addressing the person who just will not bend, just will not go along, ever?" The reality is, every leader has had to face at minimum a disruptive or conflict driven individual, and at maximum has had to deal with individuals with more sinister motives who foment and leverage toxicity intentionally.

Leaders occasionally run across the intentional hard bargainer, the follower who is working their way across and up the Dark Triad of narcissism, psychopathy, and Machiavellian behavior, or the follower who is driven by conflict. This type of individual goes beyond merely being a naysayer and is an individual who is toxic and displays behavior incapable of being dealt with via other "soft" means. In this case, leaders must be intentional—dare we say disciplined—about dismantling the structure and system of enabling and support that lies behind the individual's (or the team's) bad behavior, while also maintaining their own humanity.

"In 2006 and 2007, Mitchell Kusy and Elizabeth Holloway, co-authors of *Toxic Workplace! Managing Toxic Personalities and Their Systems of Power* (Jossey-Bass, 2009), conducted a U.S.-based study of over 400 leaders to explore what they referred to as toxicity. "Ninety-four percent of the sample reported they had worked with a toxic individual in the last five years," Kusy said.

Kusy and Holloway, who are also professors at the Antioch University Ph.D. Program in Leadership and Change, said there are three primary types of toxic behavior:

- Shaming, such as verbal humiliation, pot-shots, and sarcasm.
- Passive hostility, such as passive-aggressiveness, manipulation and territoriality about physical space and information.
- Team sabotage, such as meddling in team performance and using one's authority to punish others.

Some believe toxic behavior is a solo act, but Kusy and Holloway said there is often a "toxic protector" who enables the individual to get away with things and a "toxic buffer" who shields the team from their antics. Toxic protectors may enable this kind of behavior because of their relationship with the toxic person (such as a subordinate) or because the individual has valuable knowledge or is highly productive. Toxic buffers, on the other hand, place themselves between the toxic individual and the rest of the team, as needed, and may try to rationalize the toxic behavior.

Although feedback does not generally work when it comes to the toxic individual, Kusy says "it can be an effective means of curbing the behavior of protectors and buffers."[2]

The reality is that intentional leaders must work to pull apart the cultural systems that support such toxic behavior and create unnecessary stressors on the organization and the culture. Then, effective, and intentional leaders scale that surgical process across the team, the organization, and the culture. This work is unpleasant, is accompanied by relational friction, and rarely results in a leader gaining approval or credit if it works, and if it fails, the enterprising leader is sure to get all the blame. However, if the work of removing toxic individuals and dismantling their enabling systems is left undone, the damage a dysfunctional or toxic team or individual can have on an organization or a team can be immeasurable.

The decision to remove or replace toxic individuals from the team becomes more difficult to make and implement as the individual in question ascends the hierarchical ladder of an organization. There is a rational, tactical, effective, and intentional way to remove a toxic leader from a team and reorient the culture. However, this requires leaders to tap into areas of their psychology they may not have previously explored. It also requires understanding all the elements at stake in taking action to remove a bad leader, while also simultaneously leveraging influence to ensure co-workers and other leaders at the same level are on the same page with the action. Leaders must be clear and candid with themselves and with others about the consequences of rebelling against bad leadership and the risks associated with such action. Finally, the adage from Omar Little (played by Michael K. Williams) in *The Wire*, written by David Simon and Ed Burns (2002-2008), applies to leaders who decide to remove toxic leadership above them in the hierarchy: "If you come at the king, you best not miss."[3] Leaders only get one chance to remove a toxic leader above them and change the hierarchical structure, so such actions cannot be accidental, ill-thought-out, or taken impulsively.

Feedback When You'd Rather Not Give It—Evaluations, Change Talk, and Advice

In the space of discipline—which can come about as formal sanctioning of bad behavior, subtle cultural coercion, or just outright removal from a system—leaders must be open to hearing and absorbing feedback at every stage of the process. Communications researchers Claude Shannon and Warren Weaver originally pioneered the concept of feedback. The Shannon–Weaver model of communication demonstrates how feedback works:

"According to the Shannon-Weaver model, communication includes the following concepts: sender, encoder, channel, decoder, receiver and feedback. Furthermore, there is also the concept of "noise," which affects the communication process going through the channel and makes the message more difficult to understand by the receiver. Each of those concepts is defined as follows:

Sender: the originator of the message.

Encoder: the transmitter, which converts the message into signals (the way message is changed into signals, for example sound waves).

Channel: the signal carrier or medium

Decoder: the reception place of the signal, which converts signals into message. Decoding is done by the receiver when he gets the message.

Receiver: the recipient of the message from the sender. He usually gives feedback to the sender in order to make sure that the message was properly received. Noise the message, transferred through a channel, can be interrupted by external noise (for instance, conversation may be interrupted by thunder or crowd noise).

Feedback: The receiver can get an inaccurate message. This is why feedback from the receiver is important in case the message is not properly received. Furthermore, the noise can also affect the decoding of the message by the receiver." [Sources: Weaver, Warren and Shannon, Claude Elwood (1963). *The Mathematical Theory of Communication*, University of Illinois Press; and Shannon, Claude (1948). "A Mathematical Theory of Communication." *Bell System Technical Journal*, 27 (3): 379-423, 623-656).[4]

There are several critical points for leaders to contemplate when considering the effect of feedback within this communication—or information decoding—model. Sheila Heen and Douglas Stone describe feedback in their book *Thanks for the Feedback: The Art and Science of Receiving Feedback Well* as,

> "Feedback includes any information you get about yourself. In the broadest sense, it's how we learn about ourselves from our own experiences and from other people—how we learn from life. Feedback is not just what gets ranked; it's what gets thanked, commented on, and invited back or dropped. In today's workplace, feedback plays an important role in developing talent, improving

morale. Aligning teams, solving problems, and boosting the bottom line. And yet, 55 percent of respondents in one recent study said their performance review was unfair or inaccurate, and one in four employees dreads their performance review more than anything else in their working lives. The news is no more encouraging on the manager's side: Only 28 percent of HR professional believe their managers focus on more than simply completing forms. Sixty-three percent of executives surveyed say that their biggest challenge to effective management is that their managers lack the courage and ability to have difficult feedback discussions." [Source: *Thanks for the Feedback: The Art and Science of Receiving Feedback Well*, introduction.][5]

Leaders are cowards when it comes to providing and receiving feedback because of two obvious areas of struggle: being challenged in their blind spots and challenging others in their blind spots. Because of a lack of intentionality, not in paperwork processes, policy understanding or procedural familiarity, but because of a lack of confidence and courage in their abilities; not to navigate the feedback conversation, but to address the emotional, psychological, and relational dynamics inherent in confronting and critiquing follower's misbehaviors. Leaders who are high in agreeableness and high in sensitivity to negative emotion may experience an inability to provide necessary feedback, and yet this is a skill leaders must attain. On the other hand, leaders who are low in agreeableness and low in sensitivity to other people's negative emotional responses may barrel through a feedback conversation and not realize—or be actively blind to—the damage they cause to a follower or a team because of poorly delivered feedback.

Leaders' cowardice, psychological profile, degree of self-awareness, acknowledgment of blind spots, and ability to compartmentalize to process information, all can be considered as noise in the channel of communication. In essence, leaders are stymied most often not by external noise—although because of the nature of digital communication in the workplace and other settings and the level of distractions that dopamine triggering media produces at a biological level in the brain, such external noise is significant and not to be casually dismissed—but instead are undone by the power of internal noise. Combine this with negative self-talk about performance, status, position, self-worth, and other areas and leaders are stymied at every level by noise in the channel of their own minds when attempting to provide feedback in complex leadership situations where decision making—most often right decision making—is valued and rewarded. And where wrong decision making is devalued and often sanctioned.

Leaders who have the highest success rate at providing feedback, receiving feedback, and changing from feedback leverage three separate skills, regardless of their strengths, to lead other people through the rocky shoals of feedback without wrecking the relationship. First, they develop an internal identity based on a growth mindset and are intentional about deploying that mindset across all their interactions. Second, they pay attention to their own internal triggers—relational, contextual, or other triggers—that may create dynamics in the conversation that may lead to future unnecessary confrontations. Third, they are clear with the person receiving the feedback about what is going to happen in the conversation: coaching, supervision, or evaluation.

Leaders who can do those three things have far greater success rates in feedback conversations, eliminate, or manage, much of the internal noise and self-talk in their heads before leaping into a conversation with an individual, and develop the psychological calluses that allow them to grow in toughness to face the difficult, dysfunctional, high conflict, narcissistic, and toxic individuals with whom they may be saddled. Of the three feedback conversations leaders have, evaluative conversations are typically driven by paperwork, procedure, and process. Supervision conversations are driven by a combination of acts of coaching and acts of micromanaging. Coaching conversations are driven by relationships and reciprocal trust, built up over time. Leaders tend to want to scale past the "boring" or hard conversations to get to the exciting ones. With the rate of competitive change in our organizations and pressure to compete and make decisions with confidence at an all-time high, leaders are often driven to make short shrift of coaching conversations to get followers "back to work." But leaders lead. And they push back actively and assertively against this paradigm and insist that the emotional labor of providing feedback well, taking time to get to know followers and build relationships with them, and creating work environments where psychological safety for psychological labor is protected, are bottom-line considerations that can no longer be safely ignored.

Leaders know change talk only lands when trust and safety are at the highest possible levels. They also know that knowing a follower's strengths, and tactically leveraging those strengths against weaknesses, is the hallmark of a true leader in complicated workforce environments. Leaders know their people, they know their teams, they know their cultures, and they leverage this knowledge through the application of feedback to ensure morale stays high and scales across the enterprise.

Know Your People and Know Their Strengths

Facing a tough, toxic, or just disruptive follower requires a strong dose of clarity, candor, and courage. The reality is, many leaders will not be faced with such a follower more than maybe once or twice throughout the growth of their team, or even their careers, if they choose to follow the maxim: know your people. Knowing your people is the precursor to demanding they take on accountability and ownership. However, it is also the precursor to providing them feedback, taking feedback from them, building the team, and maintaining morale. The team leader who fails to know their people fails in accomplishing the goals set before them, before pen is on paper, before team meeting number one is held, and before any directives are issued and expected to be obeyed.

Leaders fail to know their people for a variety of reasons, but at the end of the day it is mainly because they misplace the effort of leadership, thinking it lies anywhere other than in building relationships with the people you are working with to achieve goals. Leaders who fail to get to know their people—within appropriate and clear boundaries—fail to achieve even the basic standard of leadership. This reveals a lack of curiosity on the part of leaders about who they are leading, which can lead to rebellion, usurpations, unnecessary disputes, divisions, and toxicity in the team environment and overall work culture.

Leaders who know their people—their emotional quirks, their relational patterns, their verbal ticks, and non-verbal behaviors—are "dialed in" and can use this information to shape, mold, and channel courses of action that can have a profound effect on their teams outside of accomplishing the goal itself. Leaders who know their people—even if the mission is not accomplished, or fails—can demand even higher levels of commitment from their people and can channel that commitment into active, dynamic action. Leaders who know their people know their strengths.

Strengths are defined not by what people are "good" at just in the realm of learned skills and innate talents. Strengths are much more diffuse than that. In the late 90s and early 2000s, the concept of "strengths-based leading" was a popular notion coming from the space of positive psychology.

> "Positive psychology began as a new domain of psychology in 1998 when Martin Seligman chose it as the theme for his term as president of the American Psychological Association. It is a reaction against past practices, which have tended to focus on mental illness and emphasized maladaptive behavior and negative thinking. It builds on the humanistic movement by Abraham

Maslow, Rollo May, James Bugental and Carl Rogers, which encourages an emphasis on happiness, well-being, and positivity, thus creating the foundation for what is now known as positive psychology." [Source: https://en.wikipedia.org/w/index.php?title=Positive_psychology&oldid=1051550910].[6]

Positive psychology focuses on ideas of achieving happiness, well-being, positive self-regard, and categorizing negative emotions. It has been criticized over the last twenty years for not focusing enough on the power of negativity and the critique of viewing self with too much unconditional positive regard as a form of toxic positivity has also taken hold. And yet, there is no known psychological balance against the reams of negative emotions, high levels of anxiety sensitivity, and the consistent tendency of human beings to focus on negative aspects of life and the lived experience. Leaders would be remiss to dismiss positive psychological practices and ideas when it comes to delivering feedback meant to assist followers in growth. Leaders who know what their people are good at—or their strengths—fare better at delivering feedback required for continued development of those strengths.

Stemming from positive psychology, the concept of strengths comes from the work of industrial psychologist Donald O. Clifton and the extensive survey work of his organization, Gallup.

The origin of StrengthsQuest lies in a mixed-methods program of research directed by Donald Clifton, primarily in association with the Gallup Organization. Rath (2009) reports that the Gallup research began 40 years ago with semi-structured interviews, the original purpose of which was to support the development of tools for employee selection. Clifton proposed a large number (hundreds) of modular and stable ''raw talents that can serve as the foundation of strengths'' (Asplund et al., 2007, p. 6).[7] According to Clifton, Anderson, and Schreiner (2006), talents ''naturally exist within you'' (p. 4) but ''are refined with knowledge and skills" (p. 4).[8] In the common parlance of career assessment, this would make *talents the genetic predisposition toward particular aptitudes*, whereas *strengths would be developed abilities, arising from the combination of such aptitudes with experience (via the acquisition of skills and knowledge)*. At any rate, strengths would at least overlap with the domain of abilities.

During the 1990s, the focus of Clifton's research shifted to translating this list of candidate talents into self-report items, in turn yielding approximately 5,000 items that, after further research (based on over 100 predictive validity studies; Asplund et al., 2007, p. 8), supported a reduction of the number of themes to 35. By 1999, some additional research reduced this to 34 themes measured by 180 items. Since then, there have been only minor changes in theme names and no substantial changes in the description of the themes or their content (Asplund et al., 2007, p. 8). [Source: *Mapping StrengthsQuest Themes to Holland's Vocational Personality Types* by Andrew D. Carson, Karen Evans, Elena Gitin, and Jonathan Eads, *Journal of Career Assessment* 19(2) 197-21, 2011 SAGE Publications sagepub.com/journalsPermissions.nav DOI: 10.1177/1069072710385653 http://jca.sagepub.com].[9]

Strengths come about from a combination of talents, a non-teachable, naturally recurring pattern of thought, feeling, or behavior that can be productively applied, knowledge, all the experiences and lessons of which you are aware, skills, the teachable capacity to perform the fundamental steps of an activity, and the clustering of talents together in certain, identifiable patterns that can be carefully observed by others. When leaders provide feedback to followers that can help them grow based on how they are already oriented toward the world, toward a particular task, or toward a particular experience, followers grow significantly in those areas. Many leaders balk at providing followers with feedback based on what they do well. They would much rather continue to engage in leading and improving deficiencies in followers' behaviors and continue to remain frustrated when those deficiencies either get worse or fail to improve at all. Leaders who focus on determining, developing, and supporting followers' strengths wind up with elite teams that cover each other with support in weak areas, make appropriate demands on their teammates' time and talents, and advance toward accomplishing goals ruthlessly without getting bogged down in blame/credit games, or pursuits of personal ego.

Much of this reads like "pie-in-the-sky" to leaders who are immersed in the overwhelming natural tendency to move toward the negative, to "fix" broken people and teams, and who have adopted fully the dominant mindset of many organizations that human talent cannot be developed, but merely needs to be recruited, acquired, and then unleashed. These views all lead to environments where what is rewarded is the inability to confront bad behavior, the failure to provide performance feedback that leads to performance improvement, and an overall lack of relational curiosity about people and the depth of their human potential. It also leads to goals being barely accomplished, hierarchies that become compromised by ego-driven decision making, and produces leaders who blame teams for failures that should be placed at their own feet. Knowing your team means knowing their motives, as well as their strengths and weaknesses and is at the core of scaling emotional intelligence across organizations and cultures. Daniel Goleman, the author of *Emotional Intelligence*, had this to say about leading with heart and leaders knowing their people almost forty years ago now:

> "The cost effectiveness of emotional intelligence is a relatively new idea for business, one some managers find hard to accept. A study of 250 executives found that most felt their work demanded 'their heads but not their hearts.' Many said they feared that feeling empathy or compassion for those they worked with would put them in conflict with their organizational goals. One felt that

the idea of sensing the feelings of those who worked for him was absurd—it would, he said, "be impossible to deal with people." Others protested that if they were not emotionally aloof, they would be unable to make the "hard" decisions that business requires—although the likelihood is that they would deliver those decisions more humanely." [Source: *Emotional Intelligence: Why it Matters More than IQ* by Daniel Goleman, pg. 149.]

Forty years later, the tussle continues in many leaders between knowing their people at a depth that allows them to be productive and effective as a team, and accomplishing goals and making the "hard" decisions business requires. The cost effectiveness of knowing your followers' strengths and pursuing that knowledge relentlessly is the hallmark of an intentional leader. One who is focused on both sides of the coin—maintaining the hierarchy of the structure of leadership and responding to the transforming emotional landscape, driven by globalization and information technology and work that requires emotional labor and psychological safety to perform.

Practical Tips for Strengths Based Discipline

The rejection of the concepts of positive psychology, evaluating followers by their strengths rather than trying to reshape weaknesses, and the human desire in leaders to avoid emotionally hard confrontations has led many organizations into spaces where the team lacks accountability, individuals do not grow in their potential, and where leaders receive financial rewards if the shareholders (or customers) are "happy." For leaders to become intentional and practical—or even strategic—about delivering feedback to their followers, doling out discipline when they would rather not, and growing their organizations and teams, leaders need to start building out the feedback structure in five critical ways:

Tip #1 - Leverage insights from personality and psychological testing and move those insights out of the human resources department. When leaders reject the assumption that personality and psychological testing are either "happy sheets" exercises, or all-explaining tools, they place their value in the appropriate organizational context. This means they value the insights such testing reveals, but they also know such testing is not the sum of an individual's lived experience. Leaders also recognize the insights from such testing must expand beyond recruiting, hiring, and onboarding a recruit and must be made part and parcel of the entire leadership structure to design effective teams, assign productive work, and create efficient team structures that can adapt to both external and internal stressors. Leaders who grasp the insights from psychographic tools like StrengthsFinder©, (developed from Strengthsquest research), DiSC© and others, have another tool to leverage in their leadership toolbox.

Tip # 2 - Advocate up the hierarchy about the value involved in the time-consuming work of building relationships with your followers. When leaders engage in the hard work of advocating up the hierarchy for the value of building relationships, they are astute and strategic about placing their leadership capita on the line. This is not an easy feat and it requires leaders to develop the ability to hear ideas from people in authority over them in the hierarchy while also engaging with that same hierarchy at a social level. Many leaders, much like many followers, do not want to do this work because of the deep influence of team and hierarchical social norms, the power of social proofing, and the desire to be accepted and have their status acknowledged by the same hierarchy they may have to advocate against. However, building relationships up, down, and across the hierarchy is what humans do naturally. But not always intentionally. Leaders do not have the luxury of doing "what comes naturally" when they are advocating for the emotional space, psychological safety, and emotional investment to perform work that seems to have no immediate financial benefit to the organization. Leaders also must battle the historical cynicism embedded deeply in some cultures where the idea that "our people are our greatest strength," is proclaimed in words, and yet, in fact, those leaders are rewarded who ignore their people's needs, treat their people like dirt, and continue to contribute to the overall organizational dysfunction. Advocacy begins within the leader's sphere of influence and ends at the top of the hierarchy.

Tip #3 - Remove barriers to trust, collaboration, and accountability by honestly evaluating how you perform those acts as a leader. When leaders remove the barriers and obstacles to trust, collaboration increases. Removal of such barriers and obstacles—both in the material and emotional operations of a team—demands leaders consciously and practically align their behaviors and decision-making with what they say. Walking the talk is inspirational to team members in and of itself because so few leaders do walk their talk. However, such a commitment to clarity, accountability, ownership, and communication is no substitute for the hard work of listening to the followers a leader has, knowing when to lead, when to delegate, and when to get out of the way, and determining how much accountability followers can take on. Honest self-evaluation is tied to high levels of self-awareness, but also the willingness to change. The internal, emotional, and psychological resistance of leaders is sometimes a higher barrier to cross than the resistance of followers, and leaders must intentionally critically question their own objections and arguments, looking for cognitive biases and inaccurate mental models. This builds trust with team members.

Tip #4 - Plan your communication carefully and intentionally before providing feedback, by planning to listen more than you talk. When leaders listen with "unconditional regard" they are practicing a skill set that is not natural or comfortable. At least at first. Listening to hear and carefully responding to subtext as well as context is a basic negotiation and conflict management strategy. However, listening is emotionally exhausting and many times, leaders believe if they are listening—just as they believe the same thing when they are advocating—that they aren't "doing anything." From a feedback interaction to a performance review, leaders who listen more than they talk tend to move toward better outcomes in the conversation. The reality of impatience with other people, historical organizational cynicism, bureaucratic foot-dragging, attempts to "game" the hierarchy, and general resistance to hearing new information that may require a mental model update, all contribute to leaders failing to listen and hear when that skill set most critically needs to be deployed. A conscious effort to listen—without either waiting for the next turn to speak in the conversation, or without planning the next mode of argumentative attack on the other party—requires leaders to plan their communication carefully, think through the critical questions and answers they need to hear, and be able to sift through information quickly to reach the core of an issue. True feedback processes begin when leaders listen intentionally more than they speak.

Tip #5 - Document conversations and outcomes from hard conversations and commit to following up with followers as an intentional leadership habit. When leaders commit to following up with team members after a hard conversation, they begin—or continue—the process of creating relationships with team members. Relationships matter to engaging team members when feedback must be provided. Many times, leaders struggle with engaging around follow-up because of two beliefs. The first belief commits to the idea at its core, that if they have done their job as a leader in talking with a team member once, they should not have to repeat or reinforce that which they already stated. This is a mistake because people forget the content of interactions almost as soon as they are over, and because memory as a tool for ensuring compliance and obedience does not comply with a leader's intention. The second belief is one of proximity to the issues at hand: If team members are not emotionally invested in the problem being a problem, they aren't going to be invested in the solution or its follow-up.

Leaders can become stymied in a cycle of talk-sanction-repeat that can only be broken through the time and emotional investment in practical follow-up meetings, one-on-one interactions, and continued conversations about the same issue. Leaders document those conversations because memory is faulty and a distracted leader is seen by many as a competent leader. The drive to avoid documentation is embedded in cultural hierarchies at a broad scale and has moved down to teams and even individuals. Writing down the issue, and then using that write-up for follow-up, helps establish a paper trail but also helps establish a change trail, where the team member can see how they progressed or regressed over a some time. The feedback process transforms into a personal and professional change process when leaders document, track, and follow up on the feedback about performance they provide to team members.

CHAPTER ELEVEN

Rule 11
Leaders Find Their Team's "Zero"
Leadership and Adapting to Change

"Leaders must be linchpins. There's no other way." "
Jesan Sorrells

This chapter focuses on combining philosophy and approaches to theories (and the fact) of change and uncertainty from The Army War College (VUCA), Nicholas Nassim Taleb (*Black Swan* and *Antifragility*), and Peter Theil (*Zero to One*) into one package of thought leaders can employ to address not only their resistance to change, but also their follower's resistance to change. The chapter serves as a summary of the previous chapters' materials, because without being intentionally and consistently successful in all the other previous areas, when changes come, the team will fracture and break. The chapter makes the case for thinking differently about change as a leader, rather than just adopting a "one size fits all" tactical approach.

Introduction: Leaders of Antifragile Teams, With Skin in The Game, Face Black Swans Better

There is a compelling argument to make that human beings have always lived in times of change, and that those changes were believed to be swift, unyielding, unwelcome, and unexpected by the people of the era experiencing those changes. There is a compelling argument to be made that such conditions for change have always existed. Indeed, there is a growing body of biological evidence that indicates that human beings have evolved almost exclusively to adapt and re-adapt to conditions of chaos. People seeking to refute an alternative way of analyzing and critiquing the present environment of change put forth this line of argumentation. That is, the changes people, cultures, and societies are experiencing now are unprecedented, unusual, and will surely lead to either irrevocable change or destruction of humanity.

The fact is no one now alive lived in the past, and the voices of many were silenced in the past through illiteracy and the strength of traditions more inclined toward the oral recording of historical changes and events than the world of chattering voices we experience now. Thus, thinking, critiquing, and analyzing change through a historical lens often fails. Or descends to arguing unfalsifiable counterfactuals.

There is one aspect of change that is agreed upon no matter what angle of the change discussion is being put forth, and that is the fact change is inevitable. Leaders who struggle with this inevitability fail to lead their teams and become passive actors, waiting on the circumstances of the organization, the culture, or the moment they are in to dictate their actions. The fact is, the increased speed of change has caught many organizations, leaders, cultures, and individuals off guard, and off balance. Leaders of organizations used to have at least twenty years to adapt and respond to a change in the market, in the culture, or in government. In the present era, leaders have only the speed of an Internet search to react to a change in real-time. One that is sure to have long-term and unpredictable effects on the team, the organization, and the culture.

The harsh light of truth around the fact of skills attainment in the emotional, psychological, and intellectual realm exposes leaders and leadership when change rapidly appears on the horizon and engulfs an organization or team. When leaders are slow emotionally, psychologically, and intellectually to activate their skills, and the skills of their team, to respond to change, they and the team may yet survive; but, only long enough to observe even more reactive, and less skilled, leaders take the credit for decisions they made. Leaders must understand that adapting to change requires all the skills we have addressed so far in this book, from managing conflict and engaging in negotiation to being willing to remove bad actors from the team by leveraging the power of performance feedback. Leaders who have not sharpened their learning and who have failed to move these lessons from the realm of theory into practice will fail and be replaced when Black Swans[1] show up, flapping their wings.

The environment for leaders in the current era is volatile, uncertain, complex, and ambiguous, with unexpected events—that carry immense impact—occurring every single day all around them. The temptation to battle this constant chaos balances with a desire to hide or to rely on technology and predictive modeling as ways of ensuring stability and security. As one leader asked us many years ago at a training session, "What do you do when all the Black Swans come flapping in the room at the same time?"

The fact is, all models of "how the 'world' works" are just guesses. Informed and data backed guesses, but guesses nonetheless. Just as with psychic guessing, model-based guessing is based on shrewd analysis, emotional engagement, and a dollop of truth. Teasing out the biases inherent in leadership thinking around change and approaches to managing change requires leaders to deploy all the information in this book at a practical, tactical level before giving up and just reacting blindly.

Leaders understand that adapting to change is far from being "just one more damn thing" they must deal with, and instead, represents the highest actualization of leadership practices, leadership mindsets, and leadership focus.

The US Army War College Would Like a Word...

In analyzing the outcomes of military activities and decisions during the last two, major world wars (World War I: 1914-1918 and World War II: 1938 -1945) and the U.S. involvement in those conflicts—as well as the Cold War—the U.S. Army War College, drawing on the research of Warren Bennis and Burt Nanus—introduced the concept of change to the military. In the years following that analysis, business leaders began to adopt these ideas and theories to wrestle with the implications and speed of change in their organizations, in the cultures around them, and in the social climate locally and globally. [Source: Johansen, Bob (2007). *Get There Early: Sensing the Future to Compete in the Present*. San Francisco, CA: Berrett-Koehler Publishers] The method, entitled VUCA, is an acronym that stands for Volatility, Uncertainty, Complexity, and Ambiguity:

The deeper meaning of each element of VUCA serves to enhance the strategic significance of VUCA foresight and insight as well as the behavior of groups and individuals in organizations. It discusses systemic failures and behavioral failures, which are characteristic of organizational failure.

V = Volatility: the nature and dynamics of change, and the nature and speed of change forces and change catalysts.

U = Uncertainty: the lack of predictability, the prospects for surprise, and the sense of awareness and understanding of issues and events.

C = Complexity: the multiplex of forces, the confounding of issues, no cause-and-effect chain, and confusion that surrounds the organization.

A = Ambiguity: the haziness of reality, the potential for misreads, and the mixed meanings of conditions; cause-and-effect confusion.

These elements present the context in which organizations view their current and future state. They present boundaries for planning and policy management. They come together in ways that either confound decisions or sharpen the capacity to look ahead, plan, and move ahead. VUCA sets the stage for managing and leading.

The meaning and relevance of VUCA often relate to how people view the conditions under which they make decisions, plan forward, manage risks, foster change and solve problems. In general, the premises of VUCA tend to shape an organization's capacity to:

- Anticipate the Issues that Shape
- Understand the Consequences of Issues and Actions
- Appreciate the Interdependence of Variables
- Prepare for Alternative Realities and Challenges
- Interpret and Address Relevant Opportunities

For most contemporary organizations—business, the military, education, government, and others—VUCA is a practical code for awareness and readiness. Beyond the simple acronym is a body of knowledge that deals with learning models for VUCA preparedness, anticipation, evolution and intervention." [Source: Suhayl Abidi, and Manoj Joshi (2015). The VUCA COMPANY. Mumbai, India: Jaico Publishing House. ISBN 978-81-8495-662-7.][4]. [Source: Satish, Usha and Siegfried Streufert (June 2006). "Strategic Management Simulations to Prepare for VUCAD Terrorism." *Journal of Homeland Security*. Archived from the original on 2011-06-08].[5]

Leaders who leverage the concepts behind the VUCA concept understand that failure builds resilience and adapting to change will always bring about the risk of failure. Leaders who perform the best in rapidly changing environments do so only after examining and assessing their appetite for failure and their risk profile and that of their teams. Leaders who have success in times defined by VUCA also work to establish trust with their followers through relationships before change shows up. Leaders who have success in driving their teams toward adaption to change seek to determine the level of complexity evident in ambiguity and the level of volatility in uncertainty while also working to calm their followers' fears about the path forward through disruption. In essence, leaders work to manage both their own biological and psychological reactions to change, and those reactions of their followers without engaging in the exhaustive carnival of blame gaming or shaming.

During times of uncertainty—when Black Swans are prevalent—leaders work to maintain an open-minded approach to problem solving. They are also methodical and intentional. Often followers will become impatient with the pace of progress toward an anticipated conclusion and leaders who manage change effectively seek to manage expectations regarding the speed to resolution. They are also clear and candid in their communication that change is a constant and they psychologically, spiritually, and intellectually prepare their followers to live with that reality. During times of uncertainty, leaders seek out opportunities and do not fall for the trap inherent in the idea that every threat is indeed a threat. During times of change, threats cannot easily be pigeonholed as such and demand clear-eyed analysis and leadership to navigate and succeed against.

When leaders understand the deeper strategic implications of a VUCA contemplation of the fact of change, they return to first principles thinking. In essence, they return psychologically and practically to the root of the team's reactions and responses to change and seek to re-adjudicate those reactions and responses. When handled badly, this re-adjudication can result in team tension, mistrust, the rise of fake conflict, and a breakdown of the relational threads that bind the mosaic of the team together. When handled well, this re-adjudication can result in a strengthening of team confidence, deeper levels of team trust, a reduction in negative conflict and an increase in positive conflict, and the rebinding of people together.

Finding Your Team's "Zero"

The venture capitalist, Stanford lecturer, investor, and

writer, Peter Thiel, wrote in his book *Zero to One: Notes on Startups, or How to Build for the Future*:

> "You can expect the future to take a definite form or you can treat it as hazily uncertain. If you treat the future as something definite, it makes sense to understand it in advance and to work to shape it. But if you expect an indefinite future ruled by randomness, you'll give up on trying to master it.
>
> Indefinite attitudes to the future explain what's most dysfunctional about our world today. Process trumps substance: when people lack concrete plans to carry out, they use formal rules to assemble a portfolio of various options. This describes Americans today. In middle school, we are encouraged to start hoarding "extracurricular activities." In high school, ambitious students compete even harder to appear omnicompetent. By the time a student gets to college, he has spent a decade curating a bewilderingly diverse resume of to prepare for a completely unknowable future. Come what may, he is ready—for nothing in particular.
>
> A definite view, by contrast, favors firm convictions. Instead of pursuing many-sided mediocrity and calling it "well roundedness," a definite person determines the one best thing to do and then just does it. Instead of working tirelessly to make herself indistinguishable, she strives to be great at something substantive—to be a monopoly of one. This is not what young people do today, because everyone around them has long since lost faith in a definite world. No one gets into Stanford by excelling at just one thing unless that thing happens to involve throwing or catching a leather ball.
>
> You can also expect the world to be either bet-

ter or worse than the present. Optimists welcome the future; pessimists fear it" (p. 61-69).[6]

The idea of indefinite optimism that has ruled in the United States for the last 80 years or so has caught the imagination of team leaders. In extraordinarily large ways (leading in developing next generation commercial infrastructure) and in infinitesimally small ways (personal retirement planning), leaders have failed to lead their teams, their families, and their communities. Thus, forces of uncertainty, randomness, and the challenges of operating in a VUCA environment changes drive planning and leaders fail to leverage the one tool they have that will allow their teams, whether at home or at the office, to thrive and survive.

Leaders are intimately aware of what their team's "zero" is. This concept is the idea that a team innovates, adapts to change, or creates a new idea, product, or service by performing in a way that no other team can. This concept goes beyond merely performing at a higher level, spending more money, acquiring better skilled people, or leading and coaching at a higher level. This concept revolves around the idea that leaders should be so sensitive to the team environment that they can sense, describe, leverage, and lead the team to have the courage, optimism, and will to engage with their own "secret sauce."

Leaders understand this knowledge does not emanate from leveraging a "hack" or a shortcut on the hard road to accomplishing goals. Instead, this knowledge comes from understanding and knowing all the team members as individuals, and then challenging them to go beyond the banality of familiarity, which even the most elite teams can fall into. Leaders also must know themselves and their own shortcomings to determine their own, personal "zero," in the face of change.

Much of this is psychological, emotional, and spiritual knowledge that flies in the face of rational approaches to managing change, many of which focus on whittling away at the edges of a problem until the leader establishes a sense of security and return to the status quo or the "normal" course of business. Or, the rational approach manifests as leaders sitting around a table, dissecting their responses and reactions to the last change, and attempting to project forward plans to address the next problem when it arises. The leadership failures that result from both approaches have, at their root, a lack of curiosity, a lack of broad enough and narrow enough thinking about the team environment and culture, and a species of leadership arrogance that begins with a presupposition of the right of the team, the organization, or the culture to survive in the face of whatever change is next on the horizon.

To adapt to change, leaders must go beyond contingency planning and have the courage to make definite plans out of either a fear of the future, or a hope in the future. To execute these plans, leaders must examine at a deep level, the ways their team acts when times are seemingly "good" and calm, and the ways the team behaves in a crisis. They must also examine how the change equation of dissatisfaction with the current status quo times an established vision times first steps toward a solution being great than resistance, can serve to guide and define the team's "zero." If change were a steady process, predictable, punctuated, and driven by courageous leaders, teams, and cultures, where the differences between people, cultures, teams, and environments were greater than the chaos that change creates, there would be no need to find a team's "zero." However, the fact is, change is inherently chaotic, people (leaders and teams alike) fear the disruption change brings, and contingency plans and whittling at the edges do not work anymore—if they ever really did in the first place. Leaders must have the courage to question the team, determine the culture, the team, and the organization's "zero" and then have the will to ruthlessly pursue making that "zero" the central differentiator from every other team, organization, and culture in the face of never-ending, random, and chaotic disruption. All that discovery begins with defining and facing the resistance.

Resistance to Change

We have addressed resistance quite a bit in the previous chapters and when it comes to engaging intentionally with the reality of change, leaders and teams have no greater foe than resistance. Remember that resistance lives in both the biological and psychological workings of the human brain and mind and burrows itself insidiously and deeply at the intersection of could have, would have, should have--but did not. Fear drives resistance in the face of change resistance. Fear of the unknown primarily, but also fear of failure, fear of trying a new strategy or tactic, and fear of losing status or appearing foolish to peers or the group. Ego drives the fear of learning a new approach. The fact is, many adults do not want to expose themselves to new learning, because their egos—the self-image they possess that controls their deepest perceptions and identity—are so strongly developed that they fear the loss of that identity more than they fear the disruption that change will bring to their way of behaving in the world.

Leaders must be aware of their resistance to change, recognize it, and defeat it. This is not an easy fight, because a leaders' ego wraps around the same identity matrix as many of their followers. The influence of a leaders' peers is also undeniable, particularly in an industry vertical or in a small group. Resistance to change among leaders can be damaging to the team and the culture. So can acceptance of too much change and being open to too much disruption and chaos. Leaders must establish and preserve the delicate balance between their desire to destroy or manipulate resistance in followers to achieve ends, the fact of change, disruption, and chaos, and the need to have stability to ensure that projects get completed and work gets out the door.

Intention and planning are the two antidotes to resistance. The intention is that leaders need to recognize in themselves and their teams when resistance driven by fear and ego is apparent and call it out. Leaders need to be prepared with backup plans to face change and disruption when it arrives. The third antidote to the resistance is trust and transparency. Trust in that leaders need to have established solid relationships with followers built around habitual behaviors of keeping commitments and performing open communication before chaos and disruption arrive. And the transparency in that leaders need to have behaved and communicated, both verbally and nonverbally, in a committed and consistent way their thoughts and feelings to the team about a myriad of issues and problems historically.

In general, people tend to prefer safety, conformity, predictable patterns of behavior, and pleasure. During times of change, the Bystander Effect manifests, and followers psychologically, and in some cases biologically, freeze into inaction. The discipline, persistence, and perseverance--or grit--to break that desire to freeze in place must be role modeled by the leader consistently and a bias toward action, rather than paralysis by over analysis, should be at the core of every leader's approach to the fact of change. The shadow of resistance can also make its appearance in the most subtle way through what leaders remember about the past and choose to forget (historical amnesia), the impact of unaddressed trauma on the team (PTSD), or through the tendency of leaders and teams to exhibit both Hindsight Bias and Survivor Bias at the same time. The only way to intentionally address these areas is for leaders to publicly and openly address them head-on when they surface, through commitment to telling the truth rather than molding a narrative (historical amnesia), counseling and therapeutic interventions for followers who need them (PTSD), and through a humble acknowledgment that spheres of influence and options are often limited (Hindsight Bias) and that the mere existence of the team or the organization is not always proof of correct decision-making (Survivor Bias).

John Kotter With the Last Word on Adapting Change

One of the ironies of engaging in leadership development is that the fact of people's responses to change is often viewed as a behavioral challenge that can be solved through the diligent application of leadership content, delivered by a book, a live facilitator, a webinar, or a podcast. Once this behavioral challenge is presented with content, the thinking goes, individuals and teams will transform into agile beasts able to address any change no matter how large, how small, or how traumatic or stressful. And they will do it with savvy, aplomb, and grace.

And then the global pandemic of 2020 began and in the real world, people and teams did not adapt to the changes the pandemic created.

When intentional leaders think about leading their teams through the process of change, they would do well to consider the practical tips for addressing change from the researcher and Harvard Business School professor, John P. Kotter:

> "American John P Kotter (b 1947) is a Harvard Business School professor and leading thinker and author on organizational change management. Kotter's highly regarded books *Leading Change* (1995) and his follow-up *The Heart of Change* (2002) describe a helpful model for understanding and managing change. Each stage acknowledges a key principle identified by Kotter relating to people's response and approach to change, in which people see, feel, and then change.
>
> Kotter's eight-step change model can be summarized as:
>
> 1. Increase urgency—inspire people to move, make objectives real and relevant.

2. Build the guiding team—get the right people in place with the right emotional commitment, and the right mix of skills and levels.

3. Get the vision right—get the team to establish a simple vision and strategy, focus on emotional and creative aspects necessary to drive service and efficiency.

4. Communicate for buy-in—Involve as many people as possible, communicate the essentials, simply, and appeal and respond to people's needs. De-clutter communications—make technology work for you rather than against.

5. Empower action—Remove obstacles, enable constructive feedback and lots of support from leaders—reward and recognize progress and achievements.

6. Create short-term wins—Set aims that are easy to achieve—in bite-size chunks. Manageable numbers of initiatives. Finish current stages before starting new ones.

7. Do not let up—Foster and encourage determination and persistence—ongoing change—encourage ongoing progress reporting—highlight achieved and future milestones.

8. Make change stick—Reinforce the value of successful change via recruitment, promotion, new change leaders. Weave change into culture."[7]

When leaders weave change into culture from how they build teams to how they even talk about changes that are right on their doorstep, they move the communication window away from panic and disorder on the team and toward the place of engagement and planning. Here is the point to consider: The leader who walks around while the Titanic is sinking, and calmly begins rearranging the deck chairs, organizing the evacuation, and gets everyone off the ship before it sinks becomes, by default, the future captain of the rescue vessel in the North Atlantic.

That person also becomes a new Noah, building an Ark to rescue the team.

Below is a list—compiled in a pre-COVID environment so leaders can add that one to the list—of 26 icebergs (non-exhaustive). As a leader, your list (and mileage) may vary. These areas represent places where an intentional leader can contribute to the ability of a team to survive major changes that are on the horizon globally. And as the Titanic ship of state known as global society collides with them and begins to sink, calm, intentional, and adaptive leaders become the default captains of the rescue ships:

1. Climate change
2. Fear of change
3. Growing use of A.I. based technology
4. Biodiversity disappearance
5. Lack of sufficient explanations that people can understand for necessary changes
6. Financial systems collapse (global and local)
7. Refusal by leaders to be held accountable for their actions
8. Developing world debt
9. Connection economy of the Internet
10. Rethinking of Labor Value
11. The electrical grid in the postmodern world
12. Lack of access to creation on the Internet
13. Lack of courage in individuals to take risks
14. First world educational system
15. Scarcity of emotional labor
16. Child abuse and victimization
17. Lack of true, courageous statesmanship
18. Human trafficking

19. Increased spiritual hopelessness among the old
20. Increased spiritual hopelessness among the young
21. Lack of self-efficacy among everyone
22. Growing ability to hide from doing what matters
23. Thinking harder about the answers to binary questions
24. Lack of interest in self-awareness
25. Lack of ability to emotionally care
26. The increasingly intractable nature of conflicts (interpersonal all the way to the nation-state level)[8]

There are other icebergs out there as well.

There are no lack of icebergs.

There are, however a lack of leaders who are calmly and intentionally prepared to be captains of rescue boats as changes rock the Titanic ships of teams relentlessly in the future.

Practical Tips for Adapting for Change

Tip #1 - Expect change, the disruption that comes with it, and the conflict it engenders. Act on dissatisfaction quickly and be ready for change. Accidental leaders may want to create disruption as a means of encouraging creativity. But intentional leaders know that change and disruption are constant companions and that there exists a fine line between stirring up change and managing change when it comes. The leaders who avoid even thinking about how they are going to adapt to change will not be leaders for long.

Tip #2 - Learn how to manage the people who are in the change from any source you can. This includes other industries as well as the varied resources the Internet provides. There is no excuse for leaders with an intentional approach to leadership to not grab resources, ideas, and approaches to change and managing the people involved in change from other areas. This is exemplified most notably in the "Burning Platform" memo, written by Nokia CEO Stephen Elop in 2011. The memo serves as a great example of how a concept from one area (oil rigs) can help a leader think differently about their approach to business and organizational change in another unrelated industry vertical (mobile phone technology).

Tip #3 - Build antifragile mindsets, teams, and cultures. Companies, organizations, and teams that know their zero plan for an uncertain tomorrow put resources toward such planning, rather than giving lip service to such preparation. Building an antifragile team, one that can withstand the many knocks and disruptions change inevitably produces takes time, effort, and care. Leaders must lay the foundation for an antifragile culture by working with people who have an adaptive mindset, or who are able to adopt one. The fact is, smallness, creativity, and speed to action are all important aspects of an antifragile team and they contribute to building that type of culture.

Tip #4 - Know how to be courageous, not mindless. Make courage a part of their DNA rather than just a "side" (or skunk works) project. Courage is a core component of managing change when it arrives in the form of an unpredictable Black Swan, or when it arrives as a tsunami. Too many teams and organizations do not encourage the development of courage through delegating assignments, encouraging accountability and ownership, and engaging in positive conflict behaviors. And then they wonder why their teams fail when the pressure of change becomes too weighty to bear emotionally or psychologically. However, there is a difference between encouraging courage and encouraging mindless behavior. Leaders need to be clear what they are advocating for.

Tip #5 - Understand that just because you survived a change today, does not mean you will survive a different one tomorrow. Intentional leaders are unafraid of the circumstances black swans could create and they do not fall victim to Survivorship Bias. They are constantly aware that the next change could be the one that either they or their teams fail to adapt to. They avoid hubris, manage their ego, and give credit where it is due. Leaders know that the call will come to navigate unforeseen changes on their teams in an endless array and that these changes—if adapted to successfully—can allow their teams to innovate truly and deeply, in the future without fear.

CHAPTER TWELVE

Rule 12
Leaders Take Time Away to Avoid Becoming Pagliacci
Self-Care and Compassion Fatigue for Leaders

"Leadership can be a real nail-biter sometimes."
Jesan Sorrells

This chapter focuses on the idea that leaders need to intentionally find places to hide, retreat to, and engage in daily practices (such as journaling) to have success as leaders in the first place. It acts as a caution to leaders who believe charisma, the process, or "the system" will protect them and cushion them psychologically. The chapter lays out the idea that without a robust self-reflection system and process, leaders will fail at the core thing they need to do—lead—and then burn out and become exhausted.

Introduction - The Great Clown Pagliacci

Many years ago, we sat with a young man during a workshop session on compassion fatigue. Our leadership sessions include information about how to recognize the signs of compassion fatigue, as well as its more often talked about cousin, burnout. This young man was overweight, bearded, downtrodden looking, and had less than a glimmer of interest behind his eyes during the time we were talking about this topic. Compassion fatigue is one of those areas that leadership consultants, trainers, advisers, and authors seldom talk about because it does not resonate well with a leadership information-consuming public that tends to buy stories of heroes and villains that are didactic and unambiguous.

However, we created a workshop series focused on compassion fatigue because while its cousin burnout is often recognized and addressed, outside of social work literature, there is little good advice about how to recognize or combat compassion fatigue for leaders.

When we sat with this young man, he asked us if we could help him overcome the apathy that he felt was bordering on compassion fatigue. He had the order reversed, but the idea was correct, and while we do not "do" therapy, it costs us nothing to ask and answer some questions, particularly during a ten-minute break between sessions of a workshop. He expressed that he was no longer excited about his position, and he had not been excited significantly since about six months into the position. We asked him how long he had been working at the organization and he stated that he had been working there for about four years. He said that he no longer experienced happiness in his role and he was declining to take on new projects and avoiding co-workers and peers because he felt as though he had nothing to offer them. Finally, he stated "and to make matters worse, I just took the test for the supervisor's position and got a promotion. So now I must lead these people."

This story suggests the plot of the Italian opera, *Pagliacci*. Written by Ruggero Leoncavallo in the late 19th century the opera tells the tale of Canio, actor and leader of a commedia dell'arte theatrical company, who murders his wife Nedda and her lover Silvio on stage during a performance. The opera itself focuses on murder, betrayal, and death and led to, may years later, the character Rorschach, remembering a morbid joke about the opera in the graphic novel, *Watchmen*, written by Alan Moore and illustrated by Dave Gibbons.

> "Heard joke once: Man goes to doctor. Says he's depressed. Says life seems harsh and cruel. Says he feels all alone in a threatening world where what lies ahead

is vague and uncertain. Doctor says, "Treatment is simple. Great clown Pagliacci is in town tonight. Go and see him. That should pick you up." Man bursts into tears. Says, "But doctor...I am Pagliacci." [Source: *Watchmen*, pg. 27][1]

This is an old joke (at least 100 years old by the time it appeared in *Watchmen*) and it reflects the point that leaders are often those who weep on the inside with exhaustion and fatigue, while ensuring that others get the work done in an organization and a culture.

Compassion fatigue is defined as "…a condition characterized by emotional and physical exhaustion leading to a diminished ability to empathize or feel compassion for others, often described as the negative cost of caring. It is sometimes referred to as secondary traumatic stress (STS). According to the Professional Quality of Life Scale, burnout and STS are interwoven elements of compassion fatigue. [Source: https://en.wikipedia.org/wiki/Compassion_fatigue].[2] Leaders in healthcare, emergency services, teaching, and other "people interaction intensive" occupations suffer burnout and compassion fatigue and struggle to explain to their families, their teams, or even themselves why they are exhausted emotionally by the work they have chosen to do. A news story a few years ago addressed this dynamic by investigating the experiences of nurses working at Northwestern Memorial Hospital's trauma unit. This hospital in Chicago deals with the results of gun violence in the city and its staff is overwhelmed regularly with compassion fatigue, burnout, secondary trauma, and apathy:

> "Nurses and physicians in Chicago's trauma units say they feel these shootings in their souls. Day after day, they work 12-hour shifts without enough resources to handle the shooting victims. When their shifts end, it is not the body disfigurement or the gore that haunts them

when they get home. It's witnessing despair. A child who suffers a life-altering head injury. A mother who loses her first-born son.

Over time, some caretakers become numb. Researchers call the condition compassion fatigue: a mixture of burnout and traumatic stress. Local physicians and nurses say they haven't lost their compassion, but some say they've been in situations where they try to isolate their emotions in an attempt to distance themselves from the grief they witness each day.

Perhaps that's because caretakers fear they cannot do enough to save their patients, researchers say, or because the patients they do help are sent right back into the violent neighborhoods they came from.

"It's devastating to see that over and over. You lose hope. You ask, 'When is it going to stop?' And no matter how hard you work and how good you do your job, (the shooting victims) just keep rolling through the door," said Kate Sheppard, a clinical associate professor at the University of Arizona College of Nursing who studies compassion fatigue.

Several Chicago trauma physicians and nurses interviewed by the Tribune say burnout and traumatic stress are tough to talk about, not only in the workplace but at home with family members. When caretakers go home at the end of their shifts, instead of telling their partners about their experiences, they keep it in. Their stories might be offensive to loved ones, they say, or they might be asked detailed questions they do not want to answer." [Source: https://www.chicagotribune.com/news/breaking/ct-hospitals-compassion-fatigue-gun-violence-met-20170421-story.html][3]

Leaders know this type of trauma is the hardest to address on teams when the culture of the organization, the historical attitude of executive leadership, and the lack of monetary and personnel resources are given as reasons to ignore the issue. Leaders also know that the experience of individual team members in this area can be detrimental to the team overall, resulting in a decline in morale, reduced effectiveness, and an increase in the opportunity for negative and toxic interpersonal communication behaviors to arise. And yet, when team members fail to push themselves to perform higher levels of emotional labor with competency, the team stagnates and fails to grow. Finally, who helps the leaders when they are burned out, secondarily traumatized, or just ready to quit? Who takes care of them when their ceiling of emotional labor has been reached? Yes, we want to watch out for Pagliacci, and we want to watch out for Pagliacci's boss who might not get the time off from the theater company to get therapy in the first place.

The Fatigue Brought on by Carrying a Cross

Leadership as a concept exists in many different contexts, but the two most important to consider when looking at leadership compassion fatigue, burnout, and apathy are the contexts of how the followers on the team feel about leadership and what the leader knows about leadership that followers will never realize, care enough about to explore or dismiss as being unimportant to the overall accomplishing of the task or goal. Leaders know that followers many times fail to understand—or appreciate—the work of leadership until leadership is absent, or fails. Followers know that leadership is easy and if they just had the authority—not the responsibility that goes with managing the results of consequences, just the authority to dish them out—then they would "make better decisions." Both views are incorrect; however, one is more incorrect than the other: leadership and authority create emotional and psychological burdens rather than tactical and practical. The leaders who understand this fact deeply know that leadership is a cross and bearing the burden of it carries consequences.

The fact of the burden does not lessen the weight of the burden, which is the reason many astute people who have at least a modicum of self-awareness avoid leadership opportunities, or when tasked with leading, do so competently, yet reluctantly. The burden of authority can transform leaders from competent and reluctant to competent and cautiously confident in their leadership prowess. But the burden of authority can also transform leaders from competent and reluctant to competent and burned out and frustrated. The fatigue they experience comes from agreeing to pick up the cross of leadership and climb an organizational Golgotha to the top.

Intentional leaders—and by extension, intentional leadership—requires that leaders know how to take time to preserve the most important asset they know they have: themselves. This is not selfish or self-centered. This type of preservation of self requires courage, tenacity, honesty, and vulnerability. It also requires a large dose of humility and self-awareness. Ego, ambition, pride, arrogance, and willful blindness to the human need to take a break and get away can cripple even the greatest leader and severely limit their capacity to lead effectively.

The Symptoms of Compassion Fatigue

Leaders must be self-aware and recognize the signs of compassion fatigue. At a lower level, leaders may experience the cycles of disconnection, distrust, and dysfunction in their communication style. They may experience the results of anger and the effects of anger on their performance as leaders. If left unaddressed, anger issues and lack of self-control contribute to leaders being ineffective at affecting the development of negative communication traits and toxic behavior on their teams. The fish always rots from the head down.

When leaders are aware of the nature of apathy and burnout—as well as the initial presence of anger and negative communication—they can recognize the signs of compassion fatigue, not only within their teams but also in themselves. According to the writing and research of Charles R. Figely (1995), there are multiple symptoms of compassion fatigue, some of which include:

- Affects many dimensions of your well-being
- Nervous system arousal (Sleep disturbance)
- Emotional intensity increases
- Cognitive ability decreases
- Behavior and judgment impaired
- Isolation and loss of morale
- Depression and PTSD (potentiality)
- Loss of self-worth and emotional modulation
- Identity, worldview, and spirituality impacted
- Loss of hope and meaning = existential despair
- Anger toward perpetrators or causal events[4]

When addressing the symptoms of compassion fatigue, leaders must recognize that very often, the effects of compassion fatigue are often minimized and can be hidden for many years and then can manifest all at once. There is also the team dynamic of leaders being unable to reveal their need for help and their feet of clay. This is a tendency supported by an overall team and organizational attitude or approach to positions and roles where the intersection with the public is "high touch." Outside of areas of psychological research, there is a growing body of evidence, particularly coming out of the field of positive psychology, strengths, and emotional intelligence, that resiliency--a process whereby the ability of an individual, a team, or an organization to withstand and rebound from stress grows overtime—is on the wane in many organizations and teams and cultures. This represents a shift in thinking and research from a focus on deficiency (weaknesses) to a focus on strengths. Resiliency research is the study of how some people, despite the stressors in their lives, manage to adapt, and in some cases, thrive despite traumas. Leaders cannot confuse developing resiliency in themselves and among their team members with papering over bad behavior on a team with false positivity.

Then there is the silencing response. From *The Heart of Learning and Teaching: Compassion, Resiliency, and Academic Success* by Ray Wolpow, and Mona M. Johnson:

> "One sign of compassion fatigue is when we find ways to silence those who are manifesting trauma symptoms. We are not talking about setting boundaries or redirecting inappropriate behavior. Silencing involves shutting down our empathy and demanding that the trauma survivor keep their problems to themselves. Unfortunately, this form of compassion fatigue is not frequently discussed. It is rarely mentioned.
>
> Some signposts may help us determine if the silencing response is operating in our leadership, our organization, or our team culture. These include:
> - Wishing the employee would just "get over it."
> - Not believing employees, or blaming them for the problem.
> - Using anger or sarcasm towards an employee when he manifests trauma symptoms.
> - Using humor to change or minimize when an employee starts to talk about his problems.
> - Fearing what the employee with start to talk about, or fearing that you will not be able to help.
> - Seeing clear signs of employee trauma and choosing to ignore them, or the situation, altogether" (p. 44).[5]

The presence of the silencing response to addressing compassion fatigue is a place where leaders must lead by role modeling effective responses to individuals and the team overall, manifesting trauma symptoms. To lead effectively, leaders must have and execute a self-care plan for themselves and reinforce the importance of team members to do the same.

Growing Well-Being on Your Teams as a Leader

Leaders who pursue well-being on their teams and encourage the development of an environment focused on team members attaining well-being lead better. This should not be a revolutionary observation; however, there is a lot of mental infrastructure about the assumptions and expectations of leadership and leaders still standing in the rubble of the end of the Industrial Revolution, so the observation still reads likes "molly-coddling" or "supporting bad behavior." This is not what the assertion is about.

As authors and positive psychology advocates, Tom Rath and Jim Harter noted, "We [leaders, organizations, society, culture, etc.] do not actually care about well-being. We do not really believe that the workplace needs to change."[6] And we would add that the larger the enterprise, the more likely it is that leaders will conform to being politicians in pursuit of gaining leadership points and accolades for appearing to create environments where team well-being is encouraged. However, just as in the pursuit of diversity and inclusion, managing conflict and difficult people, or ensuring accountability, leaders are less likely to expend the political and leadership capital to ensure that well-being is a lived commitment versus a stated goal in a PowerPoint presentation.

For leaders, as well as followers, well-being is a state of happiness and contentment, with low levels of distress, overall good physical and mental health and outlook, or good quality of life [Source: https://dictionary.apa.org/well-being].[7] Well-being, according to authors Tom Rath and Jim Harter occur in five circles of people's lives: career, social, financial, physical, and community.[8] Creating work environments where well-being is given more than lip service is critical to developing leadership and supervisory styles that are based on leading people based on their strengths rather than bossing people to success based on managing their deficiencies. One of the important dichotomies of leadership is knowing how far to emotionally and psychologically pressure team members to perform before they break and are no longer able to perform because of burnout, secondary (or vicarious) trauma, or compassion fatigue. Leaders know their people and know how far to push them, and they also know how much impact environmental factors have on team members' performance. High-performance teams may not have happy and contented people working on them 100% of the time, but all high-performance teams have leaders who are committed to creating and maintaining an environment where stress and resilience are balanced with psychological safety and well-being.

Practical Tips for Re-Engaging: A Leader's Self-Care Plan

Leaders need to engage in self-care at a deeply practical level. Below is an example of a journaling and self-reflection tool leaders can use to better engage in self-care. Just as with any other tool, if it is not used it will not work. Leaders must stop the lip service to self-care and begin the hard work of reorganizing their mental, emotional, and even spiritual lives to remain effective as leaders. The tool below can help leaders accomplish that goal. Leaders should read the prompts and consider carefully the questions. Fill out the form in ink and then pairing it with their calendar and task list, start with a commitment to managing themselves away from burnout, compassion fatigue, and other types of stress. The work of intentional leadership takes time as does the work of self-care.

♥ Physical Self-Care:

The things I do to take care of my body in healthy ways. Examples include: sleep, nutrition, exercise; and regular health care visits. How well do you take care of yourself physically? Identify three activities that you currently do/plan to engage in from this point forward to take care of yourself physically.

A.

B.

C.

♥ Emotional Self-Care:

The things I do to take care of my feelings in healthy ways. Examples include: maintaining personal and professional support systems; counseling and therapy as needed, journaling; and talking about feelings in healthy ways. How well do you take care of yourself emotionally? Identify three activities that you currently do and/or plan to engage in from this point forward to take care of yourself emotionally.

A.

B.

C.

♥ Cognitive Self-Care:

The things I do to improve my mind and understand myself better. Examples include: reading for pleasure or work; writing; engaging in continued education for additional knowledge/skill. How well do you take care of yourself psychologically? Identify three activities that you currently do/plan to engage in from this point forward to take care of yourself psychologically.

A.

B.

C.

♥ Social Self-Care:

The things I do in relation to others and the world around me. Examples include: spending time with friends, family, and colleagues you enjoy; having fun and playing; belonging to groups, communities, and activities that encourage positive social connections. How well do you take care of yourself socially? Identify three activities that you currently do and/or plan to engage in from this point forward to take care of yourself socially.

A.

B.

C.

♥ Financial Self-Care:

The things I do to spend and save responsibly. Examples include: balancing a checking account; planning for the future; and spending money in thoughtful and productive ways. How well do you take care of yourself financially? Identify three activities that you currently do/plan to engage in from this point forward to take care of yourself financially.

A.

B.

C.

♥ Spiritual Self-Care:

The things I do to gain perspective on my life. Examples include: prayer, meditation; contact with nature; connection with God or a Higher Power; participating in worship with a community; and 12-step recovery. How well do you take care of yourself spiritually? Identify three activities that you currently do and/or plan to engage in from this point forward to take care of yourself spiritually.

A.

B.

C.

CONCLUSION AND FINAL THOUGHTS

The book concludes by wrapping every topic together into a package and presents it to the reader to move forward into the world of leadership. The conclusion focuses on the future of work, teams, and leadership considering the work on artificial intelligence and its adoption at scale. We have also included a summary overview of the key points from each rule we have covered in the book.

Welcome to Revolutionary Times

The fact of the matter is, that leaders right now, in small and medium-sized businesses, are the most important leaders of our times.

The leaders who lead right now in their businesses and communities, who make what they believe are innocuous decisions, and who believe their decisions and actions do not—or cannot—possibly matter in the long term nearly as much as the leadership actions of a mayor, a president, a prime minister, or even the CEO of a large corporation are the most important and consequential leaders of our times. Our lives at the smallest level have been blown up to the highest resolution possible not only because of the vagaries of technology, but also because of the second, third, and fourth-order impacts of the actions of people who have leveraged these technologies to change the world. There is a lot of talk and writing about "privilege," but little talk and less writing about responsibility. And leaders in innocuous places, making seemingly innocuous decisions on how to lead their teams, develop their people, and change their enterprises for the better, have a greater responsibility than they ever were told about before they signed up to lead.

As we go forward in the next decade and beyond in the West, leaders have a responsibility to be more focused, more definitive, and more willing and able to battle the dragons of chaos in the world at their lowest possible resolution—at the family, community, and workplace levels. And to do so without self-deception and ego, and with clarity, candor, and courage. This is not a task for the faint of heart, but genuine, intentional leadership has never been a task for the faint of heart. Thus, being an excellent, clear-eyed, and resolute follower becomes a location of meaning for leaders as well. There are very few good, clear guides on how to follow, and this is a cultural and technological struggle, as well as a psychological and emotional one.

When leaders lead in times of change, they can lead in the most critical areas possible, over the longest period possible, and begin to separate the wheat of leadership and followership from the chafe of everything else. Leaders leverage the times they are in to change the times that are to come, and those times are more volatile and demanding of clear-eyed leadership than ever before.

The Future of Work

Writing and research is being done right now in the organizational psychology, industrial psychology, and organizational behavior spaces about the "future of work." Much of that writing and research focuses on the effect of technologies such as artificial intelligence, machine learning, data manipulation and management, and even the design of workspaces and teams. All of this is good research and we need more voices speaking and fingers writing about these important topics that will change the environment's leaders lead-in. However, in all the talk and writing about the "future of work," there is very little talk, and less writing, about the future of leadership. And when thinking about the future of work, there are a few questions that bear considering:

- Will leaders change their behaviors markedly in the future in response to technology, or will the technology change in response to them?
- Will leaders work with technology or against it?
- Will leaders work in smaller and smaller teams to perform more and more specialized cognitive work (solving Karl Duncker's Candle Problems)[1] or will leaders work to merely manage processes that occur so smoothly they are not even noticed by people at all?
- Will leaders become constant advocates for change or remain in a constant state of reactive stress?
- Will leaders redefine what "work" means for their followers or will they retain and defend whatever the status quo happens to be at the time?

These are just some unexplored questions that cannot be papered over by appeals to the "future of work," because the answers require human beings to engage and act in the world to provide the answers in real-time. This is unpredictable, messy, prone to failure, and inherently risky. And it is the only way forward with some of the "gee-whiz" technologies that are on the horizon—and here right now.

The Future of Teams

The future of people in groups, performing work of some kind, and getting paid money to do that work, remains bright and unquestionable. Humans have devised no better way to address the problems in our world than to get people together to make a team to solve the problem. That will not change in the near—or far—future. The human need for structure, order, the pursuit of a goal, and the need to belong in a hierarchy of value are not going away. Those God-given yearnings are buried so deeply in our biology, our history, our psychology, and our spirituality, that no technology will be successful at uprooting them.

This is good for leaders to recognize because it means teams will always need a leader and leaders will always want people to lead. The future of work may be a little bit cloudy, but the fact is, there will be work. Which means there will be teams. Which means there will be leaders. And thus, there will be opportunities for leaders—and everyone cannot be a leader—that will be interesting, engaging, frustrating, stressful, and challenging, as well as deeply fulfilling.

How to Lead in a World of Artificial Intelligence

We are concerned about the development of computational tools that appear to be "intelligent" and that appear to behave in ways humans would behave. And while mimicry is not the genuine article, we are not frightened of computational tools and their power to "eat the world" in the way that an Elon Musk, the Tesla and Space X founder is frightened. The challenge leaders face with the rise of artificial intelligence is two-fold: one, teams and organizations will outsource left-brain skill sets more and more to these programs that appear human but cannot make decisions about real people beyond a sophisticated analysis of ones and zeros; and two, leaders will be handcuffed to these systems and processes and, just as the political leaders in Europe did just before World War I, they will "follow the protocols" without thinking and lead actual real people into destruction.

We saw the beginning of such a leadership challenge in the way in which leaders of all stripes handled the COVID-19 pandemic, from politics to culture. The business environment was not immune either to the immediate effects of this two-fold challenge or to the long-term "knock-on" effects. Small and medium-sized business leaders were hampered by the consequences of decisions arrived at from computational modeling driven by artificial intelligence, machine learning, and data manipulation. This type of challenge—and the failure to lead in the face of it—was one of the many lessons for leaders to absorb in the wake of the COVID-19 pandemic.

Leaders must think holistically about how people, systems, and processes come together and how the decisions they make based on what is in their leadership toolbox, can make a difference for their teams no matter what the "ones and zeros" may demand.

Summary of What Has Come Before

In this book we addressed what leaders should do, the rules they should follow in addressing conflict, defining their roles and responsibilities, engaging with emotional intelligence, leveraging persuasion to communicate, dealing with difficult people and situations, building morale, and engaging with motivation, leaning into accountability, responsibility, and ownership, and delivering feedback. These rules, these principles are not just "on-offs" or practices for when it is convenient or when it works for leadership. Books, podcasts, videos, and training as stand-alone workshops explore each of these practices. This is complicated and may not necessarily support any of the other topics. These topics collapse into adapting to change and how leaders respond while knowing their teams are "zero," combating resistance, engaging in a volatile, uncertain, complex, and ambiguous environment, and preparing antifragile teams for the effects of Black Swans.

Conflict is the baseline behavior for many individuals and teams. Leaders develop sophisticated emotional, psychological, and even structural processes aimed at dulling the knifepoint of conflict or avoiding it entirely. When changes arrive, conflict overwhelms the sophisticated systems designed to deal with it because those systems were designed with the assumption of a non-conflict laden environment being the primary operating environment. Leaders must internalize the fact of conflict is part of the process of change and must neither attempt to squash it nor stir it up. The best leaders develop calm equanimity in the face of conflict and "act as if" when conflict arrives.

Persuasion in communication drives acceptance of the fact

of change; along with relational trust, telling the truth, and being as authentically transparent with the team as possible. When leaders face a changing landscape--whether it be social, political, or cultural--they do not avoid persuasive communication practices. Leaders leverage all the tools at their disposal to persuasively calm fears, manage anxieties, and keep the team on track. The seduction of change for leaders--its dark side, if you will—is the belief that defaulting to command-and-control language and behavior during the stressful times that change brings, will somehow be more relevant and task-oriented than taking the time to engage in persuasive communication. This is an incorrect assumption.

The lessons—the rules—in this book if read, absorbed, and followed can help any individual lead any team to accomplish any goal. The reason is that these lessons—these rules—represent the distillation of knowledge gleaned from human interactions and human behaviors. Leaders can lead their teams to greater and greater success if they think about all these areas individually and collectively. Leaders must be intentional and thoughtful in their planning, strategy, and tactics, before they lead anyone, anywhere, and before adopting a "style" or "approach" to leadership that will, in the end, only work for a specific situation and context. And to lead intentionally—even in an uncertain future—leaders must engage in the following activities to be effective:

- Be intentional with mindsets, thoughts, and behaviors to role model leadership effectively.
- Be engaged with the world—internally and externally—to be effective as a leader.
- Be able and willing to confront dysfunctional and destructive communication behaviors quickly and unequivocally in the team.
- Be empathetic with both the left and right brain by listening before speaking.
- Be ready to fail—sometimes spectacularly—when leading.

Practical Conclusions

If you would like resources that are practical, scalable, and reflect the uniqueness of what I have attempted to do in this book, head over to HSCT Publishing (https://hsconsultingandtraining.com/)[2], Leadership Toolbox (https://leadershiptoolbox.us/)[3], and LeadingKeys (https://leadingkeys.com/).[4] For long-form conversations with interesting people about the future direction of leadership by visiting the great writings of the past, check out the *Leadership Lessons From The Great Books* podcast[5] on all the platforms you listen to podcasts.

Finally, at the end of the day, no matter what actions or behaviors you choose to take on as a leader (and we believe that being an intentional leader is YOUR choice) we ask that you make the choice to do something with the information contained in this book.

It will represent the best choice you can ever make as a leader.

INDEX

Author's Note: While we have gone to great lengths to document and to provide appropriate attribution of the materials and resources (books, podcasts, articles, YouTube videos, etc.) used to build the concepts and arguments around intentional leadership in this book, we cannot guarantee the presence (or absence) of the resources on the Internet when a reader attempts to search them out independently. Nor can we guarantee any updating of third-party websites that we do not own.

As usual, "Internet searcher beware."

Chapter One – Leadership Roles and Responsibilities

1. I Thought It Was Just Me (but it isn't): Making the Journey from "What Will People Think?" to "I Am Enough" by Brene Brown (2007).
2. Linchpin, Are You Indispensable? By Seth Godin.
3. The Leadership Challenge: How to Make Extraordinary Things Happen in Organizations by James Kouzes and Barry Posner.
4. IveyBusinessJournal.com - https://iveybusinessjournal.com/publication/followership-the-other-side-of-leadership/ Retrieved 04-02-2022.

Chapter Two – Leadership and Emotional Intelligence

1. Mayer, J.D., Caruso, D. R., & Salovey, P. (2016). "The ability model of emotional intelligence: Principles and updates." Emotion Review, 8, 1-11. DOI: 10.1177/1754073916639663. Retrieved 12-12-2018.

2. Emotional Intelligence Course - https://www.emotionalintelligencecourse.com/ history-of-eq/. Retrieved 12.7.2018.
3. Emotional Intelligence: Why it Matters More Than IQ by Daniel Goleman.
4. Wikipedia "Stanford Marshmallow Experiment" - https://en.wikipedia.org/wiki/ Stanford_marshmallow_experiment. Retrieved 12.5.2018.
5. Ibid.
6. Dan Pink, TED Talk: "The Puzzle of Motivation" - https://www.youtube.com/watch?v=rrkrvAUbU9Y. Viewed 10-25-2010.
7. Von Hippel, William and Trivers, Robert. (2011) "The evolution and psychology of self-deception." Behavioral And Brain Sciences (2011) 34,1–56 doi:10.1017/S0140525X10001354. Retrieved 4-15-2017.
8. Leadership and Self-Deception: Getting Out of the Box by The Arbinger Institute (2009).
9. Principles: Life and Work by Ray Dalio (2018).
10. LinkedIn Post, "Learning is the Product of Continuous Real Time Activity" by Ray Dalio - https://www.linkedin.com/posts/raydalio_learning-is-the-product-of-a-continuous-real-time-activity-6415592291729186816-6XMe. Retrieved 10-2-2022.

Chapter Three – Leadership Communication and Persuasion

1. Influence: The Psychology of Persuasion by Robert Cialdini (1984).
2. The Crossroads of Conflict by Kenneth Cloke (2006).
3. The End of Power: From Boardrooms to Battlefields and Churches to States, Why Being in Charge Is not What It Used to Be by Moise Naim (2014)
4. Alice Walker, poet and author of The Color Purple - https://www.lofficielusa.com/pop-culture/alice-walker-best-quotes-the-color-purple. Retrieved 4-15-2022.
5. Raven, B. H. (1959). "Social influence on opinion and the communication of related content." Journal of Abnormal and Social

Psychology, 58, 119–128. Retrieved 8-2-2011.
6. Peter Drucker. Consultant and Management Guru. https://www.managementcentre.co.uk/management-consultancy/culture-eats-strategy-for-breakfast/. Retrieved 4.15.2022.
7. Influence: The Psychology of Persuasion by Robert Cialdini (1984).
8. Wikipedia "Attribution (psychology)" - https://en.wikipedia.org/wiki/Attribution_(psychology). Retrieved 5.6.2019.
9. The Black Swan: The Impact of the Highly Improbable by Nassim Nicholas Taleb (2007).

Chapter Four – Leadership and Conflict Management
1. The Five Dysfunctions of a Team: A Leadership Fable by Patrick Lencioni (2002).
2. PsycheStudy.com "Ebbinghaus Forgetting Curve" - https://www.psychestudy.com/cognitive/memory/ ebbinghaus-forgetting-curve. Retrieved 2.11.2021.
3. The Crossroads of Conflict: A Journey into the Heart of Dispute Resolution by Kenneth Cloke (2006).
4. Mindtools.com – "Managing in a VUCA World" - https://www.mindtools.com/pages/article/managing-vuca-world.htm. Retrieved 6.30.2021.
5. Conflict Management Survey: A Survey of One's Characteristic Reaction to and Handling of Conflict Between Himself and Others by Jay Hall (1969)
6. Image Copyright The Leadership Center© at Washington State University.
7. Zero to One, Or Notes for Start-Ups and How to Build the Future by Peter Thiel (2014).
8. The Five Dysfunctions of a Team: A Leadership Fable by Patrick Lencioni (2002).

Chapter Five – Leadership and Teambuilding
1. Crestcom Blog "Soft Skills Development" - https://crestcom.

com/blog/2020/07/07/soft-skills-development/. Retrieved 7.20.2021.

2. University of Minnesota – Housing and residential Life (Qualities of a Team Player) – (2002-2010).

3. The Five Dysfunctions of a Team: A Leadership Fable by Patrick Lencioni (2002).

4. Leadership the Outward Bound Way: Becoming a Better Leader in the Workplace by Outward Bound USA, edited by Rob Chatfield, Christine Ummel Hosler, and Kris Fulsaas (2007).

5. The Five Dysfunctions of a Team: A Leadership Fable by Patrick Lencioni (2002).

6. Psychology Today "The Fearless Organization" by Amy Edmondson - https://www.psychologytoday.com/ us/blog/the-fearless-organization/202006/the-role-psychological-safety-in-diversity-and-inclusion. Retrieved 9.20.2021.

7. The Five Dysfunctions of a Team: A Leadership Fable by Patrick Lencioni (2002).

8. Donald Rumsfeld, Secretary of Defense, 2000-2008. - https://carryingthegun.com/2014/12/09/you-go-to-war-with-the-army-you-have/. Retrieved 4.1.2022.

9. Wikipedia "Failure is not an Option" - https://en.wikipedia.org/wiki/Failure_Is_Not_an_Option. Retrieved 4.5.2022.

Chapter Six – Leadership and Dealing with Difficult Teams and Individuals

1. The Book of Matthew, Chapter 23, verse 24. KJV.

2. Gary Gam, Gam at Camp Services, Inc. Used with permission.

3. True Grit by Charles Portis and Marguerite Roberts (1969) - https://www.imdb.com/title/tt0065126/quotes/. Retrieved 4.15.2022.

4. Qz.com "Angela Duckworth Explains Grit is the Key to Success and Self-Confidence" - https://qz.com/work/1233940/angela-duckworth-explains-grit-is-the-key-to-success-and-self-confidence/. Retrieved 11.2.2019.

5. Goodtherapy.org "Trigger" - https://www.goodtherapy.org/

blog/psychpedia/trigger. Retrieved 5.3.2019.

6. Harvard Program on Negotiation Dealing with Difficult People Report, "What Type of Hard Bargainer are you Facing?," by Katherine Shonk (2013).

7. Ibid.

8. Ibid.

9. Bill Eddy - https://www.highconflictinstitute.com/. Retrieved 8.5.2019.

10. Bill Eddy "Who Are High Conflict People" - https://www.highconflictinstitute.com/hci-articles/who-are-high-conflict-people. Retrieved 7.8.2021.

11. Leadership BS: Fixing Workplaces and Careers One Truth at a Time by Jeffrey Pfeffer (2015).

12. The Five Dysfunctions of a Team: A Leadership Fable by Patrick Lencioni (2002).

13. Never Split the Difference: Negotiating as if Your Life Depended On It by Chriss Voss and Tahl Raz (2016).

Chapter Seven – Leadership and Building Morale and Encouraging Motivation

1. "Maslow's Hierarchy of Needs" - https://www.verywellmind.com/what-is-maslows-hierarchy-of-needs-4136760. Retrieved 2.14.2022.

2. Liminal Thinking.com "Six Principles" by Dave Gray - https://liminalthinking.com/six-principles/. Retrieved 6.20.2020.

3. IndiaFreeNotes.com "Motivation and Morale" by Edwin Flippo - https://indiafreenotes.com/motivation-and-morale/. Retrieved 3.6.2013.

4. General Dwight D. Eisenhower, President and World War II General - https://www.eisenhowerlibrary.gov/eisenhowers/quotes. Retrieved 4.15.2022.

5. Dan Pink, TED Talk: "The Puzzle of Motivation" - https://www.youtube.com/watch?v=rrkrvAUbU9Y. Viewed 10-25-2010.

6. Maslow, A. H. (1943). A theory of human motivation. Psy-

chological Review, 50(4), 370–396. https://doi.apa.org/doi/10.1037/h0054346. Retrieved 3.15.2011.

7. Drive: The Surprising Truth About What Motivates Us by Dan Pink (2009)

Chapter Eight – Leadership and Diversity

1. Wikipedia "E Pluribus Unum" - https://en.wikipedia.org/wiki/E_pluribus_unum. Retrieved 4.15.2022.
2. EEOC List of Discriminated Groups - https://www.eeoc.gov/. Retrieved 5.15.2014.
3. Gilbert, Carr-Ruffino, Ivancevich, & Konopaske (2012) "Toxic Versus Cooperative Behaviors at Work: The Role of Organizational Culture and Leadership in Creating Community Centered Organizations." International Journal of Leadership Studies, Vol. 7 Issue 1, 2012, 29-47. Retrieved 10.16.2015.
4. PsychologyToday.com "The Fearless Organization: The Role Psychological Safety in Diversity and Inclusion" by Amy Edmondson https://www.psychologytoday.com/us/blog/the-fearless-organization/202006/the-role-psychological-safety-in-diversity-and-inclusion. Retrieved 2.19.2021.
5. Steve Jobs: A Biography by Walter Isaacson (2011).
6. FarnamStreet.com "Mental Models" by Shane Parrish - https://fs.blog/mental-models/. Retrieved 7.25.2021.
7. PsychologyToday.com "Conversational Intelligence: Blind Spots" - https://www.psychologytoday.com/us/blog/ conversational-intelligence/201705/blind-spots. Retrieved 7.15.2017.
8. The Five Dysfunctions of a Team: A Leadership Fable by Patrick Lencioni p. (2002).
9. Ibid.

Chapter Nine – Leadership and Accountability

1. Sethsblog.com "Accountability and Responsibility" by Seth Godin - https://seths.blog/2019/05/accountability-vs-responsibility/. Retrieved 5.5.2019.

2.	The Name Game by Shirley Ellis - https://www.youtube.com/watch?v=NeF7jqf0GU4. Viewed 4.16.2018.
3.	The Oz Principle: Getting Results Through Individual and Organizational Accountability by Roger Connors, Tim Smith and Craig Hickman (1994).
4.	BreneBrown.com "Shame v. Guilt" by Brene Brown - https://brenebrown.com/articles/2013/01/15/shame-v-guilt/. Retrieved 03.18.2022.
5.	The Book of Genesis, Chapter 4, verse 9. KJV.
6.	The Oz Principle: Getting Results Through Individual and Organizational Accountability by Roger Connors, Tim Smith and Craig Hickman (1994).

Chapter Ten – Leadership and Discipline, Feedback, Strengths, and Well-Being

1.	Discipline Equals Freedom: Field Manual by Jocko Willink (2017).
2.	Toxic Workplace!: Managing Toxic Personalities and Their Systems of Power by Mitchell Kusy and Elizabeth Holloway (2009).
3.	The Wire (2002 – 2008).
4.	The Mathematical Theory of Communication, University of Illinois Press; and Shannon, Claude (1948). "A Mathematical Theory of Communication." Bell System Technical Journal, 27 (3): 379-423, 623-656 by Weaver, Warren and Shannon, Claude Elwood (1963).
5.	Thanks for the Feedback: The Art and Science of Receiving Feedback Well by Sheila Heen and Douglas Stone (2014).
6.	Wikipedia Article – "Positive Psychology" - https://en.wikipedia.org/w/index.php?title=Positive_psychology&oldid=1051550910. Retrieved 12.14.2020.
7.	Carson AD, Evans K, Gitin E, Eads J. Mapping StrengthsQuest Themes to Holland's Vocational Personality Types. Journal of Career Assessment. 2011;19(2):197-211. doi:10.1177/1069072710385653. Retrieved 4.15.2022.
8.	Ibid.

9. Mapping StrengthsQuest Themes to Holland's Vocational Personality Types by Andrew D. Carson, Karen Evans, Elena Gitin, and Jonathan Eads, Journal of Career Assessment 19(2) 197-21, 2011 SAGE Publications sagepub.com/journals Permissions.nav DOI: 10.1177/1069072710385653 http://jca.sagepub.com. Retrieved 9.15.2012.

10. Emotional Intelligence: Why it Matters More than IQ by Daniel Goleman (1995).

Chapter Eleven – Leadership and Adapting to Change

1. The Black Swan: The Impact of the Highly Improbable by Nassim Nicholas Taleb (2007).

2. Wikipedia Article "Volatility, Uncertainty, Complexity and Ambiguity" - https://en.wikipedia.org/wiki/Volatility,_uncertainty,_complexity_and_ambiguity. Retrieved 11.15.2021.

3. Johansen, Bob (2007). Get There Early: Sensing the Future to Compete in the Present. San Francisco, CA: Berrett-Koehler Publishers.

4. Suhayl Abidi, and Manoj Joshi (2015). The VUCA Company. Mumbai, India: Jaico Publishing House. ISBN 978-81-8495-662-7.

5. Satish, Usha and Siegfried Streufert (June 2006). "Strategic Management Simulations to Prepare for VUCAD Terrorism." Journal of Homeland Security. Archived from the original on 2011-06-08.

6. Zero to One: Notes on Startups, or How to Build for the Future by Peter Thiel (2014).

7. HBR's 10 Must Reads on Change Management (including featured article "Leading Change," by John P. Kotter by Harvard Business Review, W. Chan Kim, Renée A. Mauborgne, et.al. (2011).

8. HSCTPublishing.com "Captain of the Rescue Boats" by Jesan Sorrells - https://hsconsultingandtraining.com/captain-rescue-boats/. Retrieved 3.12.2022.

Chapter Twelve – Self-Care and Compassion Fatigue for Leaders

1. Watchmen by Alan Moore and Dave Gibbons. - https://share.transistor.fm/s/737fe663
2. Wikipedia Article "Compassion Fatigue" - https://en.wikipedia.org/wiki/Compassion_fatigue. Retrieved 4.12.2022.
3. The Chicago Tribune "Chicago Hospitals Compassion Fatigue and Gun Violence" - https://www.chicagotribune.com/news/breaking/ct-hospitals-compassion-fatigue-gun-violence-met-20170421-story.html. Retrieved 8.5.2018.
4. Figley CR. Compassion fatigue as secondary traumatic stress disorder: An overview. In: Figley CR, editor. Compassion fatigue: Coping with secondary traumatic stress disorder in those who treat the traumatized. Brunner-Routledge; New York: 1995. pp. 1–20.
5. The Heart of Learning and Teaching: Compassion, Resiliency, and Academic Success by Ray Wolpow and Mona M. Johnson. (2009).
6. Wellbeing: The Five Essential Elements by James K. Harter, Jim Harter, and Tom Rath (2010).
7. APA.org "Well-Being" https://dictionary.apa.org/well-being. Retrieved 3.16.2022.
8. Wellbeing: The Five Essential Elements by James K. Harter, Jim Harter, and Tom Rath (2010).

Conclusion – The Future of Leadership

1. APA PsycNet "On Problem Solving" Duncker, K. (1945). On problem-solving (L. S. Lees, Trans.). Psychological Monographs, 58(5), i–113. https://doi.org/10.1037/h0093599. Retrieved 4.15.2022.
2. HSCT Publishing website – https://hsconsultingandtraining.com/. Retrieved 4.15.2022.
3. Leadership Toolbox website – https://leadershiptoolbox.us/. Retrieved 4.15.2022.
4. LeadingKeys website – https://leadingkeys.com/. Retrieved 4.15.2022.

5. Leadership Lessons From The Great Books Podcast - https://leadershiptoolbox.us/lessons/. Retrieved 4.15.2022.

If Your Boss Doesn't Care About Your Workplace, What Are *YOU* Going To *DO* About It?

You can continue to work at work, or you can change your workplace. Leadership begins at the end of your bosses' control. In My Boss Doesn't Care: 100 Essays on Disrupting Your Work By Disrupting Your Boss, Jesan Sorrells provides a philosophical blueprint for practical disruption in the workplace. Read this little red book and check out the little red podcast of the same name!

Listen to the podcast that links great literature to the leadership work you're doing now!

Listen and Subscribe to the Leadership Lessons From The Great Books on the HSCT Publishing YouTube Channel!

LEADERSHIP TOOLBOX

If you manage a small or medium sized business, you probably don't think that your leadership decisions matter that much. Leadership Toolbox helps you become a better leader and make better decisions. And encourages you that your decisions DO matter.

Become the leader you always were meant to be, and for only around $300 per participant, per session.

**Find out more today at
https://www.leadershiptoolbox.us/**

www.ingramcontent.com/pod-product-compliance
Lightning Source LLC
Chambersburg PA
CBHW070420010526
44118CB00014B/1836